EVERGREEN DREAMING

EVERGREEN DREAMING

TRAIL TALES OF AN AGING HIKER

Peter Kurtz

Published by *Longitudes Press*, Cincinnati, Ohio

Library of Congress Control Number: 2018908860
First American Paperback Edition, 2018

ISBN-13: 978-1-7324789-0-9 (paperback)
ISBN-13: 978-1-7324789-1-6 (ebook)

Cover concept by Peter Kurtz
Artwork by Ana Grigoriu

Back cover photograph: *The author near Winding Stair Gap, North Carolina* (photo by Scott Fontaine)

Words and Music for composition "Night Rider's Lament" copyright by Michael Burton

Words and Music for composition "This Here Mandolin" written and composed by Michael Peter Smith, Bird Avenue Publishing—ASCAP. Copyrighted material used with permission

"Radio Montana" by Casey Neill from the album *Goodbye to the Rank and File*, all rights reserved, reprinted with permission

This title issued as print-on-demand for reduced waste.

For Lynn, Holly, and Nicholas with love

"Take a course in good water and air;
and in the eternal youth of Nature you
may renew your own. Go quietly, alone;
no harm will befall you."

—John Muir

CONTENTS

ACKNOWLEDGEMENTS

I thank the following people for their consistent support of my writing: Dave Schulz, Tad Imbrie, Mary Kaye Welch, Rock Lucas, Marylou Ryan, Neil Scheinin, Dean Wray, Music Enthusiast, hotfox63, Rob Mullen, Phil Brown, Leah Alford, Diana Peterson, Virginia Salvia, and my mom, Nancie Kurtz.

I'm also indebted to Paul Groueff and JoAnne Duncan for graciously sharing their memories; Dave Schulz and Rick Taubold for proofreading and editing; and David Kettlehake for publicity advice.

I'm grateful to Chris McCandless and Christopher Knight for their unique resolve.

And for their inspiration, special thanks to Walkin' Jim Stoltz and Biff Schlossman.

AUTHOR'S NOTE

This book is a memoir and work of creative nonfiction. All the characters are based on real people, and the narrative is inspired by true events. Memory being imperfect, however, I embellished certain passages, including dialogue, to compensate for limitations, and also for literary effect. Also, to protect their privacy, I used fictitious names for some of the people. If any person remembers anything in this book differently, I apologize in advance.

Introduction

When I was fifteen, my family went on a camping trip to the Blue Ridge Mountains in Virginia. Our campsite was near where the Appalachian Trail twisted up a mountain called The Priest. One day, my brothers Rich, Steve, and I attempted to climb it. They were younger, became tired, and stopped about halfway up. But I pushed myself to the top, where I was rewarded with a spectacular view of a broad, green valley. On the other side of the valley were smaller, neighboring mountains; smooth, undulating, avocado dreamscapes cloaked in wispy white clouds. A light breeze rustled the evergreen boughs. Tiny, moving dots far below indicated vehicles.

The valley and mountains were nice. A canvas of green, ranging from cheerful lime, where the sun shone, to darker, spinach green where the shadows lay. But this canvas, as picturesque as it was, was just the outline. It was the huge void that affected me the most. I'd never seen so much empty air. The space encompassed the azure sky. It was majestic but frightening.

While sitting in quiet in my private perch off the trail, I glimpsed some movement behind me. I turned and saw a tall figure moving slowly along the path. I had thought I was the only one here. But there was a shape that dipped behind the trees, then briefly emerged into a leafy opening, then dipped behind again. Eventually it entered a long stretch of clearing, and I got a good look. It was a lanky man with a bushy beard, ponytail, and a huge pack on his back. An Appalachian Trail distance hiker. I watched him for about fifteen seconds. Then he disappeared as he made his descent from the mountain.

I didn't know how long this man had been hiking nor his destination. He looked like he was in his twenties, but I couldn't be sure. I didn't know where he was from, if he had a girlfriend or wife, whether he'd attended college. Maybe he had no family or friends. Perhaps he'd fallen on hard times and been forced to haul his home on his back. Then again, maybe he was from a loving family with the security of monetary wealth, and he'd merely decided to take a break from college…or he'd recently returned from Vietnam…and stepped into the woods, alone, to "get his head together," as so many young adults seemed to be doing in the early 1970s.

He was a total enigma. But his solitary stroll through the mountains fascinated me.

By age fifteen I'd read several books about nature, the wilds, and living off the land—a schoolchild version of Henry David Thoreau's *Walden*, Jack London's *Call of the Wild*, Jean Craighead George's *My Side of the Mountain*, among others. I liked to camp with my family. While living in the Detroit suburbs in the late 1960s, I captured raccoons, opossums, feral cats, and an occasional skunk in my Havahart box trap. When I was eleven, my friends and I talked about traveling to northern Michigan to "live off the land." We discussed gathering roots and berries, hunting small game for our food, and living hermit-fashion in homemade wooden huts. We fantasized about sitting around a large campfire and watching the stars dot the heavens. I fantasized about bringing my pet raccoon with me, a furry chatterbox to play with and keep me and my friends entertained. I remember lying in bed at night and planning this dream trip. Deep down I doubted we could ever pull it off. But thinking about it gave me a good feeling.

When I saw that lanky man on the Appalachian Trail a few years later, it reignited that feeling. I saw an older version of me. Someone who was experiencing adventure and getting close to nature. I wanted to believe that he'd *chosen* to hike and not been forced into it by bad circumstances. He'd realized his dream. He was living something that I'd only read about or planned while lying in bed at night.

After graduating from college in 1981, I came close to the lanky hiker. I went West, looking for adventure and evading the responsibilities of career and family. While there, I visited the Cascade Mountains of west-central Washington. Within those lofty peaks that towered above deep, blue Lake Chelan—a gigantic crevasse gouged millions of years ago by ancient glaciers—I managed a four-day hike. Part of my route took me up a trail that meandered along Prince Creek, on the eastern shore of the lake. I got as far as Middle Fork, where I discovered that the June snowmelts of Sawtooth Ridge had turned Middle Fork into a raging whitewater river. It had washed away the wooden footbridge that I needed to cross the river. A rude interruption.

I'd planned to cross Middle Fork because there was a little oval tarn tucked away in the forest to the north. It had a slightly comical name: Surprise Lake. I wanted to go there because I liked the name, and I wondered what the "surprise" could be. But without a bridge, it was impossible to cross the rushing whitewater. So, I had to sabotage my plans. I backtracked to Lake Chelan, eventually reached my car, and ended up dousing my disappointment with mugs of bitter beer in the bars of Seattle.

But I learned two things: first, I discovered that as much as I wanted to play mountain man, I missed my family and friends. Also, I learned to expect the unexpected.

Not long after, while living in Colorado, I did a few overnight hikes in the Rockies. I saw my first bear while backpacking in the mountains just outside of Boulder. I was hiking with a friend on a ridge near Bear Peak. We'd summited the peak, had just finished a lunch of cheese and crackers, and were traversing a ridgeline when my friend tapped me on the arm and pointed to the forest valley below. Being nearsighted, it took me a few seconds, but eventually I made out a burly, black form rummaging in the brush. We watched the bear for a few moments. Then he vanished. We waited a while, then carefully moved down the hill to see if there was a cave, or some remnant of his presence. Nothing.

This bear experience was a thrill. It didn't amount to much, but it was fun to tell others about the "mysterious, disappearing bear," and others seemed to have fun hearing about it.

But it wasn't until the summer of 2013, when I was age fifty-five and spent a week on the Appalachian Trail, that I felt I came close to the lanky hiker on The Priest. I didn't know at the time that a late-in-life, eight-day wilderness experience would usher in a new stage for me, climaxed by a trek into the clouds along the Continental Divide, following the trail of a friend from long ago.

I'm not a globe hopper or adventure junkie. Maybe because I'm from the American Midwest, where life tends to move a little slower, but I'm used to mundane, simple things: burgers on the grill, a cold beer after work, a late-night film noir. I've read Ernest Hemingway, but I'm not interested in emulating him. And I don't think I'd call my middle-age urge to ramble a "crisis."

But like most people, I started losing some family members and friends when I reached a certain age. I wanted to see the wild places before the curtain falls and while I'm still healthy, and hike into green before it turns to brown. I'm still the little boy who dreams of living off the land in northern Michigan. I still dream of the enigmatic, lanky hiker with a bulging backpack, hiking over a misty mountain peak into the unknown.

The Appalachian Trail—Georgia and North Carolina

"Whatever landscape a child is exposed to early on, that will be the sort of gauze through which he or she will see all the world afterwards."

—Wallace Stegner

Companions

The Appalachian Trail (AT) is a 2,200-mile footpath
through the rugged Appalachian Mountains of the
eastern United States, stretching from Georgia to
Maine. It was conceived in the 1920s by a bookish
forest official named Benton MacKaye, who envisioned a
series of hostels and wilderness workshops connected by a
path. A young Washington lawyer named Myron H. Avery,
more pragmatic than MacKaye, advanced MacKaye's idea
without the hostels and workshops. The trail was completed
in 1937 and covers fourteen states.

Today the trail is a monument to public activism and
wilderness protection. All but a few miles of the trail are
under the domain of the National Park Service (NPS), but it
is maintained by the NPS along with the USDA Forest
Service, various state agencies, the Appalachian Trail
Conservancy, and over thirty local clubs. Though the route
is continually changing, the terminus points now remain
fixed at Mount Katahdin in northern Maine, and Springer
Mountain in northern Georgia.

Those who walk this trail come in different shapes and sizes: day hikers, overnighters, section hikers and thru-hikers. Thru-hikers are an interesting breed and have become noticeably prevalent in recent years. They attempt to do the full 2,200 miles in one stretch. This, obviously, requires extensive planning and preparation, and from four to six months actual hiking. Supposedly, less than one-fourth of thru-hikers who start ever finishes. To do a thru-hike, it helps if you don't have educational or job responsibilities, a mortgage, loans to be repaid, or dependents to support. You also must be physically healthy. An idiosyncratic sense of adventure also helps.

Not many people meet these criteria.

I would have liked to, at minimum, attempt such an adventure. I can easily see myself part of this exclusive club: skinny and wild-eyed, crawling hands and knees up Mount Katahdin with a bottle of champagne tied to my pack straps and a faraway look in my eyes. But as much as I'd like to quit my job, forget about mortgages and college loan payments, and transform myself into a 21st-century, Eastern mountain man, I was afraid of the long-term consequences of such rashness.

So, in August 2013 I decided to use some vacation time for a weeklong section hike. I chose to tramp along a 75-mile section in Georgia, the unofficial trail beginning. *Hey, maybe I can string together enough of these "gentle" hikes to eventually complete the entire AT!*

This dream evaporated even before I stepped on the trail. I've never been good at math, but I finally did the math—after cementing my travel plans—and determined that I would be hiking the exceedingly difficult "100-Mile Wilderness" section of eastern Maine, the last segment of the trail, at age eighty. And this is only assuming I was still healthy and had already achieved my earlier goals of running a marathon in all fifty states and visiting all fifty-nine national parks.

I didn't like the odds.

But a one-off section hike would at least pull me out of the Midwest and away from grilled burgers, so I forked over thirty bucks for a guidebook that I later discovered was fifteen years out of date. I also did one overnight, practice hike in Kentucky's Red River Gorge to test my long-neglected equipment. (Everything seemed to be in working order except my body.) I then contacted a man to shuttle me from the Dalton, Georgia bus station to the trailhead at Georgia's Springer Mountain.

I told myself I was as ready as I'd ever be. I had Georgia on my mind.

The car turns into a cramped parking lot outside the Greyhound bus station in downtown Cincinnati, Ohio. I glance into the backseat at my brown, bulging backpack. Then I look over at the driver…my wife, Lynn. She's smiling, but it's not her typical joyful smile. It's more like her nervous "Why does he do this to me" smile.

Lynn was opposed to my hiking alone on the Appalachian Trail. I'm used to her concern, though. When I proposed marriage to her thirty-one years earlier, I told her I didn't want to give up my freedom (whatever that word means these days), and I still wanted to occasionally go off by myself…even at age fifty-five. She was fine with that. But there's always been a little pushback from her. I guess it's normal. Loyal to a fault, ever-protective and loving, she inevitably worries whenever my health or safety might be in the slightest jeopardy. This time, it was the possibility of bears attacking me, or my stepping on a poisonous snake, contracting hypothermia, or falling off a cliff.

"Honey, just pull around the corner of the building" I mutter weakly. "You'll probably see signs to get back on the interstate." This evening, on the cusp of riding the bus to Georgia, where I will be transported to mountain forests for a week, she isn't the only one who's nervous.

Her anxiety, and my trepidation, make for a hasty goodbye kiss. I shut the car door, clean-and-jerk my bulging, 35-pound backpack, and stumble into the grimy-looking bus station. The linoleum floor is stained with dirt, most of the people look grief-stricken, and the place reeks of cigarette smoke.

My biggest fear, now, is that my pack will be broken or misplaced during the bus trip. I hardly ever use public transportation, and I only venture into cities when I absolutely must. (When you hail from the Midwestern suburbs, and you travel, you always feel like you've done something wrong). I have nightmarish visions of the bus driver rummaging through the luggage compartment, searching for my lost pack, while I hold my breath in the bus depot in Dalton, Georgia.

But despite my fears, and an uncomfortable, sleepless night sitting in an aisle seat next to a guy who stank of tobacco and cologne, I am reunited with my pack—my combination kitchen, bedroom, and man-cave—in Dalton. After a five-minute wait outside a McDonald's that doubled as the bus depot, I see a brown Toyota Rav4 spin into the parking lot.

A grey-haired man wearing a brown t-shirt gets out of the car. *Must be my shuttle-driver, Rance.* I lift my pack, cradle it in front of me and walk over.

"Rance?"

"Yessir…Pete?"

"Yeah, nice to meet you" I exclaim. "You're right on time." Rance opens the trunk door of his Toyota, grabs my pack out of my hands like it's a bag of toilet paper, and stuffs it violently into already crowded trunk space. I'm amazed at his strength. It's a heavy pack, and while wearing it, it towers over my head. *Careful, Rance, that pack is my lifeline for the next week.*

I slide into the passenger seat, and we drive off in early-morning darkness.

During the drive, I learn that Rance is an ex-park ranger and native of New Hampshire. He now lives in Ellijay, Georgia, near the Springer Mountain trailhead, and he makes his living shuttling people like me to and from various points on the trail. He lost his ranger job during the 2008 recession. But he isn't bitter.

"I've got less money now, but I'm a helluva lot happier. You don't choose a life, life chooses you."

Rance tells me about some of the more interesting people he's shuttled. "I shuttled one guy who insisted on carrying his heavy, cast iron skillet. I tried to talk him out of it. Told him it added unnecessary weight to his load. But this crusty skillet was really important to him." Rance said the man was related to the actor who played the cook in the old television Western *Wagon Train*, and he hauled around this heavy hunk of metal in honor of his relative.

He also tells me of the obese man who managed only one or two miles per day at the start, but nailed all 2,000-plus miles to Mount Katahdin.

"I know he finished because he sent me a photo. I barely recognized him, he'd lost so much weight. But it was him. He was holding up the pants he had when he started, and you could've fit three of him inside."

I look around Rance's car. There's a red and yellow "Semper Fi" sticker on the glove box. A messy stack of road atlases and topographic maps are on top of the dashboard. He also has a GPS device that occasionally groans "Things are getting very strange" as we become immersed in the forest. A few other gadgets are scattered here and there. Several wires dangle from the dash to the floor, including one to charge cellphones.

One of the reasons for my hiking was to divorce myself from digital technology for a week. I don't own a smartphone, only an old-fashioned flip phone, but I planned to remove the battery from even this after calling Lynn from Dalton. (She was, reluctantly, privy to my anti-technology scheme.) I was going to leave the battery with

7

Rance. I wanted a purist experience. But Rance talks me out of it.

"The reception is spotty up there, but you may need that thing for emergency, you never know. Just turn your phone off the whole trip." He convinces me, and I do just that.

Rance is energetic. He keeps glancing into his rear and side-view mirrors and messing with his GPS. He tells me he had several shuttle trips scheduled for today, and I'm the first.

"Is this your first AT hike?" he asks.

"Sort of. This is my first *serious* hike. I did a few minor backpacking trips out West after college, and when I was fifteen I did a day hike in Virginia on a mountain called The Priest."

"Forgive me, Father, for I have sinned!" Rance blurts out, without missing a beat. "So, you're a greenhorn, then, huh?"

"Yeah, I guess."

I'll bet I look like a greenhorn, too. He's probably laughing to himself about my ugly backpack. At least I didn't bring an iron skillet.

Since I figure I have nothing to lose, I pepper Rance with questions about the trail. He patiently answers each one, even the ones that I think sound naïve, like how much weight I should be carrying.

"These days, everyone's into lightweight. Not like the old days when packs towered over a person's head and carried everything imaginable."

Sheesh. Wait'll he sees me wearing my own monstrosity.

He continues. "I shuttled one guy who actually transferred his toothpaste into a plastic baggie because he didn't want the extra weight of the toothpaste tube."

He asks me what my pack weighs, and I hesitantly tell him "about thirty pounds."

"Hey, that's pretty good! I'd say that's just about right!"

Rance has learned a little psychology in his shuttle work.

Rance drops me off at a forest service road parking lot just north of the trailhead. From here I need to hike 0.9 miles southward to reach the Springer Mountain terminus, sign the hiker register, then turn around and begin my northward trek, re-crossing the parking lot. Then another hundred miles or so to Franklin, North Carolina, where I will meet Lynn and our daughter Holly.

I remove my pack from his car, he fills my canister with complimentary campstove fuel, and we shake hands goodbye. As I walk across the parking lot, I feel his eyes on me. When I get about fifty yards away, I hear him yell out the now-familiar "I shuttled one guy who…" But I can't make out the rest of it.

The parking area is empty but for one vehicle. Outside the car, two college-age guys look like they are preparing for a hike, too. We exchange furtive glances. Other than the occasional murmur of their conversation, it is hushed silence. I hoist my pack onto my back and look to the left at a narrow opening in the woods. The trail. This will be my home and my lifeline for the next eight days. I take a deep breath and walk slowly toward the opening.

Looking at the open pathway in front of me, I think of Armstrong and Aldrin stepping off the ladder onto the moon, or Alice on the verge of tumbling down the rabbit hole. Instead of the moon or a hole in the earth, though, I am entering a different wonderland. I shuffle quietly through the mighty oaks, the eerie half-light of morning, and the smoke-like fog. I listen for wildlife sounds, but only hear a slight creaking of my pack frame and some jostling of plastic and foil in my pack's food pouch. After a few minutes, my breathing becomes heavier, and I suck in the tangy odor of wet leaves, bark, and moss—a thick porridge of primordial smells, smells of the wild. There are deep, dark forest tales waiting to be unraveled. Forms of things unknown. What will I discover these forthcoming days and nights? What mountain mysteries await me?

I am surprised at how rugged the AT is. There are lots of rocks, some of which classify as boulders. There are also a lot of gnarled, twisted roots that protrude from the dirt path, telltale signs of innumerable hiking boots tamping the soil for many, many years. Here had walked Benton MacKaye, Myron Avery, distance hiking champion Earl Shaffer, the eccentric, sneaker-clad Grandma Gatewood, as well as several authors whose books I'd read and whose adventures I'd reveled in. I've always shunned fraternities and clubs. But I liked being part of this club.

On the hike south, I find a slightly bowed, chest-high tree branch. Sturdy, not a lot of knobs, and the bowed look gives it distinction. I adopt it as my walking stick. I christen it "Kip" after a boy from my youth with whom I attended summer camp. (Kip occupies a special place, and I talk about him later in the book.) I also pass a few hikers, the first being a blonde woman who says she is doing a short section to Neels Gap.

I arrive shortly at a large rocky clearing shrouded in fog: the top of Springer Mountain.

This is it. I'd dreamed about this place. Sure enough, to the right is the 1933 bronze plaque showing a hiker with a hat and backpack. On the left is a large boulder with a more recent plaque. At the bottom of the boulder is a shiny metal door with a handle. It is a cabinet drawer that is tucked into a drilled cavity of the boulder. I grasp the handle and pull the drawer open. Inside I find a notebook that is damp from rain and humidity. Within this notebook are short essays penned by dozens of recent hikers who'd also reached this spot.

I write a few sentences about my motivations for being here and sign with a made-up nickname, a "trail alias." Trail aliases are colorful names that distance hikers either adopt themselves, or which are bestowed upon them. I like the name that follows the entry directly above mine: "Rainbow Slug."

I'd like to take a photo from Springer Mountain, but it's so foggy that I can only see about fifty feet in front of me. The damp air and smoky haze adds to the phantasmagoric feeling I already have. The dirt path under my feet, leading into the haze, is pregnant with possibilities this coming week.

It is so good to be hiking, to be moving. Some people think distance hiking, even a short weeklong trip like mine, is difficult. It is, and it isn't. Yes, muscles hurt at the end of the day. Sores and blisters are irritating. Thirst and hunger are frequent companions. But it's all temporal. Hikers know there's an endpoint. The pain on the way will soon be supplanted by a feeling of achievement, of having surmounted hurdles, and of surfacing alive. The endpoint drives the hiker, which enables him or her to get up in the morning and begin the ritual anew.

Most hikers and backpackers I know are attracted by simplicity. Hiking is contemplative and Zen-like. Buddhism in the out-of-doors. I feel that way about running, which is why I run marathons. Like distance hiking, marathons are physically challenging, but they're very doable if you put in the training time and prepare well. Like backpacking, running equipment is minimal, and other than tying shoelaces, there's little technical knowhow, very appealing to people attracted to the purest forms of things.

This marathon courses through the forest. North Carolina is the finish line. I estimate I need to do about thirteen miles per day to reach Franklin. *Easy. Heck, my marathon training runs are longer and only last a few hours.* As I soon find out, hiking on rocks and roots for ten hours, up and down mountains, with a small hippopotamus straddled on your back, is much different from running a couple hours on a flat, paved bicycle path with nothing at your back except breeze.

11

I arrive again at the gravel parking lot where Rance had dropped me off, but I am pushing northward this time. I see a few other hikers unloading their gear. After a couple hours of heart-pumping, muscle-churning exertion, I start humming an old Bob Dylan tune. I only do a few verses when I detect someone close behind me.

Whoops. Did he hear me humming? Should I let him catch up, or keep walking? What the heck, might as well be sociable. I walk a little slower, then turn around. It is a young guy with sandy, shoulder-length hair.

"Thought I heard someone behind me," I remark, then wait for him to catch up. Up close he looks even younger. His backpack looks brand new. Like me, he's using a wooden walking stick. It's shiny, and straight, compared to my recently acquired stick, Kip, which is bowed.

"My name's Pete," I say.

"I'm Dylan."

His name, after my singing, is the first of several strange coincidences.

I learn that Dylan is a 24-year-old from Augusta, Georgia. Like me, hiking the AT is a longtime dream. His parents had dropped him off at Amicalola Falls State Park, 8.8 miles south of Springer. Dylan enjoys hunting, flounder fishing, and winemaking. He has a girl back home who is pressuring him to get married. He tells me he loves her, but needs a little distance, a little breathing room. He took time off from work and hopes a short AT hike will provide this.

Dylan's singular features are his southern Georgia accent, long hair, narrow eyes, and high cheekbones. *I wonder if he's part Native American—maybe Creek, Seminole, or Cherokee?* Dylan seems easygoing. He has a strong gait but doesn't rush his walking.

There isn't much conversation, at first. It's a little awkward, being thrust together with someone at the beginning of a long journey, especially one young enough to be my son. I intended to hike alone, since I'm a loner by nature, and I wanted that introspective, John Muir experience.

But Dylan and I seem to hit it off. While the conversation is stilted at first, eventually we discover that neither of us feels like we *have* to talk, so we settle into a conversational rhythm as smooth as our hiking pace, only speaking when there's a need.

I'll later reflect how odd it was that we met right at the start of our hikes. And of all the hikers I will meet in years to come, he's the only one I hike with for any extended period.

It's like the time my dad taught me how to ice skate at Sunset Park when I was seven years old. He held my hand for a few laps around the ice. Then he released me to skate solo.

Eventually, we arrive at a tree with a blue rectangle painted on the bark. The blue-blazed rectangles signify AT side paths, which lead to a shelter or water source. (White-blazed rectangles, painted on trees or boulders every hundred yards or so, indicate the official AT.) This blue-blazed path leads to our first shelter. Most AT shelters are five-sided structures, including a wooden sleeping platform and roof, and with the front side open to the elements. They're located about a half-day's hike apart, usually near a spring or stream, and they have overhead cables for "bear bags." (Hikers are urged to put their food and waste in sturdy bags and tie them overhead at night, at least ten feet high and four feet from the nearest tree.)

Here at Hawk Mountain Shelter we meet three guys on a Labor Day weekend hike: Stan, his son Derek, and their friend Ed. I talk with Derek and find out he plays trumpet for his high school marching band in Gwinnett County, Georgia. Good-looking kid, dark hair, with a cheerful naiveté and shyness typical of many teenagers. With his stocky build and bushy hair, he reminds me of my son, Nick, at that age. I feel the slightest twinge of homesickness.

Derek's dad, Stan, is quiet and sullen. He's slightly overweight, rarely smiles, and looks out of place in the mountains. I can picture him wearing a white shirt and tie, crunching numbers in an office. Not wearing Patagonia clothing, and hiking in the forest.

Their friend, Ed, is just the opposite. Younger than Stan, he smiles frequently and is either gazing upward at the treetops, or energetically adjusting some piece of equipment, his tongue clamped between his lips. Ed is the first hiker I've seen to carry dual, aluminum trekking poles rather than a wooden stick. I assume Ed is related to Stan. Or maybe a client of his.

I also see the blonde woman I'd seen at Springer Mountain. Her name is Jenna, and she lives in Fort Benning, Georgia, though her hometown is beautiful Lake Tahoe, California. She's slightly chunky, in an attractive, athletic way. She has a self-assured manner, like most of the solo women hikers I'll soon meet, and when she talks, she takes her time to choose just the right words. I ask her if she's the infamous Rainbow Slug, but she laughs and says no, that she isn't much for trail aliases. Dylan and I have dropped our aliases, too. They don't seem appropriate for us section hikers.

Trail aliases are convenient for marathon backpackers, who often reunite, share campsites and shelters, and exchange news about other hikers. They provide color and anonymity, as well as distinction. (Keeping track of a half-dozen people named "Zach" or "Lindsay" could be difficult on a thru-hike.) Still, I've always thought they were a bit silly. They remind me of a fraternity I knew in college. The members all wore bright green t-shirts that had pet nicknames printed on the backs, like "Zonker" and "Brillo Pad." It was a kind of sub-cultural affectation.

I spend some time poking around the shelter vicinity. About forty yards from the shelter I come upon a large fire ring, about ten feet in diameter. There are a few charred logs in the center, and a small pile of kindling just outside the ring. Evidently some hikers had recently built a nice fire. I also notice trash. A metal cap from a fruit or preserved meat can, and some partially charred foil, leftovers from a freeze-dried meal.

Back home, I volunteer on the 78-mile Little Miami Scenic Trail northeast of Cincinnati, where I do a lot of running. I'm an adopter of a four-mile segment, so I do a lot of tree planting, brush cleanup, limb trimming, and trash pickup. I'm often bewildered why so many people don't seem to give a damn, even in a state park. Every weekend, on my Saturday morning run, I scoop up discarded water bottles and gel packets from littering pedestrians and bicyclists.

My running friend, Baxter, is a co-adopter like myself, as well as a trail board member. And, like me, Baxter has a streak of misanthropy. Between complaints about fickle volunteers and the side-effects of his pre-diabetes, Baxter often speculates what he'll do if he ever catches one of these slobs in the act of littering. I can imagine the local headline: "Trail Volunteer Pummels Bicyclist for Dropping Candy Wrapper."

Baxter and I find common ground on a lot of things. One of my most memorable conversations with him centered around a Caribbean cruise Lynn and I took. Baxter didn't understand the appeal. We both object to the carbon emissions and well-publicized waste violations of cruise liners, but Baxter goes even further than me. He hates the excessive hedonism and believes a vacation should be earned, that one should work for one's leisure.

"Well, we worked our regular jobs all year for this vacation," I explained to him. "So, didn't we earn it?"

"No, I mean you should have to work *during* your vacation, as well. Like run a marathon, or spend a week volunteering on the bike trail."

Baxter admitted to me once that he's an "anal-retentive proctoid." So maybe his opinion doesn't count.

I look for a trash receptacle but can't find one. *Guess that makes sense. A trash can in the forest will only entice bears and other hungry critters. Don't want a bear near my tent.* I have a trash bag for my own use, but don't have the stomach to pick up someone else's bug-infested mess. I just shake my head, then return to the others.

We all have a respite at the shelter, sharing trail mix and candy bars. Jenna then decides to hike with Dylan and me.

Sometime in early afternoon we get drenched when a thundershower strikes while climbing Sassafras Mountain. Rain is especially bothersome on a distance hike, because it's so difficult to dry your belongings when they're stuffed all day inside a backpack. Judging from the others' packs, mine is an outdated model. I think I bought it when Jimmy Carter was president, and last used it during the Reagan era. Maybe it's why everything inside gets wet. Cotton clothing is another problem. I should've bought some good wool socks, because my athletic socks become increasingly dirty and smelly, and never completely dry out the entire hike.

I tell myself this journey through Georgia is my Backpacking 101 course. It's like so many learning experiences, some of which are in the classroom, but most of which are not.

1978—ATHENS, OHIO

At Ohio University, Randy and I live on the same dormitory floor. He's two years ahead of me. He's also ahead of me intellectually and socially. He's majoring in pre-med, carrying a perfect 4.0 GPA.

*(I'm undecided and struggling to keep a 3.0.) He's
also able to move fluidly on a dance floor, chat up
attractive women, and sometimes coax them to his
dorm room. (I can't dance, I'm still uncomfortable
with women, and they only knock on my door by
mistake.)*

*But Randy's a nice guy. When he's not studying,
he lets me hang out with him on weekend nights in
his room. His room is a refuge, away from the
campus hordes. It's like a cozy tent on a bed of pine
needles. His room is dark, with just a soft yellow
glow from his study lamp. It has a thick shag rug,
and a musky odor of vanilla pipe smoke and roasted
coffee. My other college friends all listen to generic
arena rock. If there's no party going on, they're
playing pinball in the student union. But Randy
listens to English folk-rock like Lindisfarne and
Pentangle, and progressive jazz musicians like Pat
Metheny. He introduces me to Fleetwood Mac, but
not the commercial Buckingham and Nicks stuff,
rather the earlier and heavier Peter Green and
Danny Kirwan versions of Mac. And instead of
playing pinball, he prefers to just talk and mellow
out with music and a joint.*

*One Saturday night, Randy and I go out on the
town. I'm underage, so Randy's buying me tequila
sunrises all night long. We're sitting at a small table
in the upstairs foosball room, and Randy meets a
woman. She's dressed in a business suit. She has a
fake intellectual air about her. She's not
attractive...to me, at least. But Randy's smitten.
Eventually, we end up at the woman's apartment at 3
a.m., where one of the woman's friends keeps trying
to get me interested in her (I think). But I'm not
attracted to her, and I'm dog-tired and just want to
go home. But Randy drove, so I can't leave. Every
now and then, I get Randy alone and plead with him*

to take us back to the dorm. But each time, he smiles
complacently, puts his hand on my shoulder, and
gives the same response:
        "Think of this as a learning experience."

I curse silently about my smelly, dirty, wet cotton socks.
And curse at myself for not preparing as well as Dylan and
Jenna, who are much younger than me, and who should be
following *my* lead.

Sassafras Mountain is my initiation into straight, steep
ascents. The amount of carbon-dioxide I expel getting to
the top is incredible. I notice that each of us adopts a role.
Dylan is the strongest, so he leads. I come next, about fifty
yards behind. And Jenna is somewhere downslope behind
me. But there's teamwork and encouragement.
Occasionally Dylan stops, perhaps at a scenic overlook,
while I catch up. Then the two of us wait for Jenna.
Sometimes I stop and wait for Jenna. We pull each other
along, uphill, through the pelting water. Occasionally, we
share groans.
    One thing that strikes me about hiking a long trail is the
frivolousness. My boy, Nick, loves sports. When he was
small, he once asked me after a particularly nail-biting
ballgame "Dad, why are sports so important?" I struggled
for an appropriate answer, then came up with the off-the-
cuff "Well…they're *not* important. That's why
they're…uh…so much fun." Later, I realized it was
actually a pretty good response. Homework, job, and
paying bills are all important, but hardly enjoyable.
    I'm now with two strangers, who are much younger,
with very different backgrounds, one a different sex, and
we're sharing an activity that makes no sense: walking over
mountains, far from home, in the rain. *What?!* At first
glance, this pursuit seems totally senseless. It's like sitting

on the beach in a yoga position and counting waves. But we're actually having a lot of fun. And I can't think of many activities where you can share senseless fun with total strangers.

The rain has stopped, but in the quiet of our private struggles up the mountain, my eyes take in the water-laden leaves. Large raindrops dangle from the tips and edges. They're like shiny, translucent Christmas baubles. Watery ornaments everywhere, hanging delicately, but dispersing into spray as soon as my clothes and pack come into the slightest contact. Christmas ornaments, when they shatter, have a jarring sound, but raindrop shattering is silent.

Exploding raindrops. How often do I think of such things at home?

By the end of the day, Dylan figures we've covered fifteen miles. Tack on another mile for my backtracking from the forest road near Springer, and sixteen total miles is impressive—although I remember Rance saying to expect only seven or eight miles after the first day.

We overnight at Gooch Mountain Shelter, meeting up with Stan, Derek and Ed, as well as a few other hikers. The shelter itself is full, probably due to Labor Day Weekend, so Dylan and I pitch our tents about fifty yards away. He gets a good fire going. Then he pushes some sticks in the ground near the fire and drapes his wet socks over them. *Great idea.* I do the same for my socks and sneakers. But all I manage to do is singe the rubber sole of one of my sneakers.

Dylan, whose mane of hair requires more maintenance than mine, mentions he could use a bandana, so I give him an extra one I have. Bandanas are handy pieces of clothing on the trail. During marathon runs I employ a bandana as both hairnet and sponge, and on the trail, it serves these purposes, and becomes a satchel and potholder.

Dylan returns the bandana loan by letting me sample some of his homemade cherry-blackberry wine.

19

At home I'll typically have a beer or two after work, and I rarely drink wine—usually only with Italian cooking. But his nectar tastes so good out here in the forest. Alcohol dehydrates, and we lost a lot of water today, but somehow this juice is invigorating. Maybe because we *earned* it. It's the best vino I ever tasted. There is nothing like a shot of cherry-blackberry wine after an exhausting backpack trip.

As the fire crackles and the wine warms our insides, Dylan and I begin to warm to each other. Although we've hiked together the better part of the day, our conversation occurred in spurts. He was usually at least ten feet in front of me, and because of our exertion and concentration on roots and rocks, our talk consisted mainly of mundane trail observations. Of his home life, I know little, other than he likes to rabbit hunt, go fishing for flounder with his older brothers in the saltwater coves around Augusta, and hang out with his girlfriend. I ask him whether he works or goes to school.

"I can't afford college," he says. "I work as a production assistant in a turpentine factory."

"How do you like it?" I ask, immediately thinking it was a dumb question.

"It's not bad. The pay's good, and I like the people I work with. The worst part is I have to smell turpentine all day, and it stays with me after I go home."

His confession jolts a memory of a factory job I had one summer between college quarters. The work consisted of placing steel augers in a holding fixture, then taking a large metal file and striking the auger tines to knock off little metal bubbles that had formed during forging. This labor was supplemented by occasional sanding with the file, then bending the tines with a wrench device so they were perfectly aligned in the fixture. I never asked where the augers went, or why it was important to scrape bubbles and bend tines. The work was tedious and soul-killing, to the point where I looked forward to my monotony-breaking bowel movements. Despite my mom throwing my grey jumpsuit in the washing machine every few days, the smell of factory grease and metal shavings never totally disappeared. Even today I smell it.

Unlike Dylan, I wasn't forced to keep my factory job. The money I made didn't go toward food and rent, but textbooks and beer. My parents weren't wealthy, but they sent me to an expensive boys' boarding school, and me and my two brothers to college.

But I've worked blue-collar jobs, even after college. I still have friends I met while working them. So, unlike a lot of my peers, I think I can relate to working class folks like Dylan. Can't I?

I tell Dylan about my work as an aviation technical writer. I tell him I appreciate my job, "but the work can be dry. That's why I like escaping to places like this," I say, waving my arm. "Where it's *wet*." He laughs. "I'd like to do more writing related to alternative energy and transportation. It's mostly gas turbine, though. Oh well."

But he says it must be "cool" to write about aircraft engines. I try to self-deprecate.

"Gas turbine technology is just fan, compression, combustion, and turbine. Or, as we say in the business: suck, squeeze, bang, and blow."

He laughs again, then passes over the Mason jar of wine. A log cracks in two, and a few sparks from the fire shoot high in the darkness. *Lewis and Clark once sat around their own campfires, like this, long ago, on the other side of the continent.*

I think of how society has changed since Lewis and Clark. *While they were plowing through wilderness and river currents from 1804 through 1806, most people worked where they lived, usually right on their homesteads. Some were my Tupper ancestors, farmers, foundry workers, and family doctors who lived on former Cayuga land in the Finger Lakes section of New York. They could never have imagined the coming Industrial Revolution, which brought the assembly line, cotton gin, and mechanical reaper. Then a technological revolution, with the telephone, automobile, airplane, television, computer, and now iPhone. We're more productive because of machines, and we have more leisure time to enjoy nature (or, in many people's case, to enjoy punching buttons). Nature is now thought of in the abstract. It's something we gaze at dreamily, or sometimes frolic in.*

The down side of machines is that we're now geographically separated from our workplaces. Unlike my forebears Benjamin, Josiah, and Asa, we don't see where our goods come from, and a connection to land—the earth's resources that sustain us—has been severed. We cut, strip, and drill those resources to propel our machines, with little thought of consequences.

I take another gulp of wine, then pass the Mason jar back to Dylan. He shoots me a glance with his narrow Cherokee eyes in the glow of the firelight.

There is enormous faith that somebody else will take care of things. Including our lawmakers. We hope they make the right decisions about limiting air and water pollution, passing workplace safety laws, and going to war. But politicians never have to fight the wars, or work in turpentine factories.

"Squeeze, blow…suck…then bang?" Dylan asks, after a few minutes of quietness in the firelight.

"Sort of," I reply.

He takes a gulp of the wine, then looks at me with a smile. "Sounds like I could enjoy that!"

That must turn his mind to something else, because he then asks me what I think of Jenna.

"Well, she's a strong hiker, and she has a nice personality. Good-looking, too."

Dylan doesn't respond. He's slapping one of his socks against his shorts to put out the flames.

Perspectives

Earlier, I mentioned Ed, the hiker with the trekking poles who gazed at the treetops. As opposed to his sullen friend Stan, Ed had a cheery way and seemed to absorb as much of his surroundings as possible. I'm not the cheery type, but I was out here to absorb nature, too. And because we're always drawn to our own sort, I hoped I'd get an opportunity to talk with Ed.

The following morning—after shaking off the rain puddle from the top of my oblong tent, and untying my bear bag to discover an adventurous mouse had made a pilgrimage from the shelter to the woods, then scaled a tree, then tightrope-walked the limb that held my bear bag, then gnawed a hole through the nylon bear bag, a plastic baggie, and several granola bar wrappers—I see Ed descending down the hill to the stream. I follow him.

I arrive at the stream while Ed is filling his filtration bag with water. I get my first good look at him. His yellowish hair is close-cropped, he has a square and sturdy jaw covered with blond beard stubble, and some of the bluest eyes I've ever seen. Tall and athletic-looking, he reminds me of Aussie tennis star Sam Groth.

I also notice a large whitish patch on his long neck, about the size of a napkin; a burn scar. It extends down under his shirt collar.

I sidle next to him by the stream and begin filling my canteen.

"Top-o-the-mornin'!" he says cheerily.

"Hi," I respond. "Did your tent happen to get as soaked as mine?" I ask, shifting my stance on the stones so my sneakers don't slip off into the water.

"Yeah, that was a helluva rain we had. Lost a lot of food, too, from those mice," he admits, stretching the plastic tube of his filter. "Oh well. God, isn't this forest beautiful?"

"Yeah, it is. Sorry to hear about your food loss," I say. "I lost only part of a granola bar. Wonder how Dylan, Derek, and Stan made out."

Having completed his water replenishment, Ed stands up straight and does a few things to his filtration device. *Too much technology for me. I'll stick with water purification by pill. Yeah, great trail alias: "Pill Popper."*

"Not sure about Dylan or Derek, but Stan's stash got hit pretty hard, too," he reveals.

I picture sullen Stan with his scowl. I imagine a few curse words coming from him after discovering the midnight mouse mobilization.

"Poor Stan," I say, which gives me opportunity to find out about him and Ed, who seem such opposites. "Do you guys work together?"

Ed chuckles. "Not exactly. We served together in the Iraq War. We were in the same platoon. Rough business."

"Yeah," I respond wanly. Not having been in the military or fought in combat, and aware of the scar on Ed's neck, I refrain from pressing for details. But Ed continues.

"Stan can be a little surly, as you've probably seen," he says. "He hates the government and is pissed off about being sent to Iraq. And I don't think he enjoys being out here in the mountains. But he's a good man. He and his son Derek, and Derek's mom back in Gwinnett County, are good people."

I wonder if Ed's married. He's a good-looking guy, with a pleasant personality. He seems like he really loves hiking and nature.

I'd like to learn a little more about Ed, but I don't want to be nosy. We head back to our respective tents. I see more scars, on one of Ed's legs.

The mouse's invasion of my food stores reminds me of the time some kids entered my unlocked car one night to snatch my sunglasses and some coins from the coin holder. A minor crime, but a violation nonetheless. We sock away our wealth, cover it, lock it, and hide it from view. Then while we're asleep, under cover of night, the smallest of creatures will pinch a bit of it. Just like in the cities and suburbs, in the woods it is survival of the fittest.

By the time Dylan and I fold our tents, Jenna has already left. I think I sense some disappointment in Dylan. *Can't say I blame him. He could've hiked with a hot blonde. Instead, he has to drag along a guy old enough to be his dad.* Dylan and I eat a quick breakfast of stale bagels and pull out just ahead of Ed, Stan, and Derek. As we reach the intersection where the blue-blazed side trail meets the white-blazed AT, we see an elderly man approaching us. He has a face like brown corduroy, and hair like vanilla icing. He doesn't have a backpack, and he's carrying only a partially filled garbage sack.

"Hello young men," he says with a trace of Southern accent.

I look around, but only see Dylan.

We stop to talk, and discover this old-timer is a part-time trail volunteer. He periodically drops in on the shelters to pick up trash, and generally tidy up things. I remember the trash I'd seen at the fire ring at Hawk Mountain Shelter and mention it to him.

"Yes, it's hard reckoning some folks. Maybe they assume since there's no authority figures in the vicinity, they can behave as cavalierly with their trash as they please. They don't live here, so they figure, why not?"

"Maybe their homes are just as sloppy," Dylan says with a grin, which brings a chuckle from the old-timer.

I tell him it's nice to meet another tree hugger like myself.

"Tree hugger?" he asks. "No, I'm hardly a tree hugger."

"Oh," I respond, feeling a wave of mild disappointment.

"I'm actually a tree *fucker*," he says, staring intensely at me.

His intensity shakes me, and I glance toward Dylan. Hearing that word from someone so elderly, and who speaks like he's pretty well-educated, is a shock.

"I never met a tree I didn't like," he continues, in a lighter tone. "Although I've met some adult *people* I didn't like."

He sounds a bit like Baxter.

"Trees are stoic and understand quiet. They're humble. The young ones might slap around in the wind sometimes. The old trees, like me, creak occasionally. But the only outside stimulation they require—unlike us—is soil, sun, and rain. They demand *nothing*, they're content with *nothing*. They set a good example."

It's a short lecture, but it resonates with me.

He then reaches into his pocket and hands Dylan and me a couple small pamphlets. They're titled "Leave No Trace."

"Don't feel obligated, but if you get a chance—maybe as post-dinner entertainment following your tasty freeze-dried fare—give these a look-over."

We thank him for the pamphlets and tell him we will. Then we continue down the main AT, me in hot pursuit of my daily mileage, Dylan in hot pursuit of Jenna. The old-timer, undoubtedly, in pursuit of a cleaner earth to leave his grandkids.

I feel pretty strong, at first. Occasionally we pass day hikers, easy to identify due to their light packs. Some have their dogs with them. I'm wearing an old marathon t-shirt, and a few folks ask me which is harder, marathons or AT hiking. I reply "Well, it's hard to compare, they each use different muscles." By the end of my hike I have a more definitive answer.

I soon notice, though, that I'm falling slightly behind Dylan. I'm certain he's trying to catch Jenna. But I also think my lagging is because I'm not as fresh as yesterday. The last thing I want is for him to feel like some old man is holding him back. My biggest problem at this point is my left shoulder. But I discover it helps if I shift the pack weight to my right one. Also, reaching back with my left hand and pulling up on the frame eases the load a little. You find little things to help you when you're backpacking all day.

Somewhere near Woody Gap we encounter our first "wild" animal. He's on a mountainside and staring a hole in us as we pass: a little white Jack Russell terrier. I also notice occasional spots of red, green, yellow and blue in the dirt. *Someone's trail mix has leaked. I guess this little guy is waiting for us to move on so he can continue licking up M&Ms.* I think of my own dog, Sheba, a border collie mix that Lynn and I found at an adoption center. Also, Brownie, my Australian shepherd who died a few years earlier.

I discover Dylan comes from a family of dog lovers.

"My dad has a little dachshund," he says. "It's a great little dog. Sometimes I catch him whispering to the thing, like he's sharing a secret or something."

"I know how your dad feels," I tell him. "When your kids grow up, it can be hard. They move away physically, and often emotionally. But your dog never leaves childhood."

2008—MARYSVILLE, OHIO

Lynn always tells him to calm down. "Brownie, calm down!" she pleads. Of course, Brownie ignores her, same as he does on weekend evenings, when all four of us are gathered together in the family room, and she tells him to stop licking the carpet. It doesn't bother me. Brownie is happiest when the whole family is together, and I just assume licking the carpet is his way of licking us all at the same time.

Today, I open the front door and step onto the tiled hallway floor. I grasp the brass doorknob of the coat closet, turn the handle, then reach in and shuffle the hooks on the coat rack. Before draping my jacket over the wire, I hear a flurry of rapid clicking sounds on the porcelain. By the time I hang my jacket, he's lunging at my waist, panting heavily, gaping jowls and eyes afire.

After changing into my running clothes, I lead Brownie out the front door on his leash. This time, however, he doesn't prance in front of me. The leash becomes taut. I turn around. Brownie sits like a lump on the front walk. Something's wrong.

"I'm leaving Brownie inside tonight," I yell inside to Lynn. "I don't think he feels good."

As I walk down the driveway, Brownie gazes after me through the glass, his fluffy ears upright as if to say "Why aren't you taking me with you?" I walk slowly until I'm outside his range of vision. Only then do I start to run. When I return home, my best friend is waiting for me by the driveway. While I stretch my legs on the grass, he ambles over to me, his head lowered. The vet later said that the moisture under his eyes was probably caused by a fever from the massive tumor growing inside him. But I don't know.

Dylan and I feel sorry for the terrier, being way out here by himself. Whether the dog lives nearby, or was abandoned by a thoughtless owner, we never find out.

"Jack Russell" gets me to wondering if I'll get lucky and see a black bear. Yogi and Boo-Boo and Gentle Ben were frequent television companions when I was a kid. And Smokey the Bear is an enduring symbol of forest fire prevention. Even without these lovable animal icons, who wouldn't want to see, in their own habitat, one of the largest mammals east of the Mississippi River, and a symbol of unspoiled wilderness? No backpacker wants to tangle with a bear, but all hope to see one.

I've only seen one wild bear in my life, out in the Rockies of Colorado. I'd love to see one on the AT, but I need my eyes glued to the ground. I can't risk, while sightseeing, spraining or breaking an ankle from a hole, or a protruding rock or tree root.

According to the International Union for Conservation of Nature (IUCN), black bears (*Ursus americanus)* are one of only two of the eight major bear species not globally threatened with extinction. Their total U.S. population is estimated at around 350,000 to 450,000. Although common around campgrounds, especially in state parks where there are lots of garbage cans with discarded food, they're fleetingly seen in the wilderness. Rance told me he's only seen a few. On our shuttle to the trailhead, he described once seeing a bear hanging at the top of a thin tree, with both bear and tree bent halfway over the road. Evidently the critter had misjudged his own weight!

Lately, some states have proposed permitting and/or expanding the hunting of black bears, since bears are increasingly showing up in populated areas. I'm not against hunting animals for food, if their numbers are healthy. But there are humane ways to remove bears from populated areas without declaring open season on them. And then there's the way bears are traditionally hunted—using packs of dogs. It seems to me there are better ways to control bear populations, assuming there's even a need.

A similar scenario plays out in ranch-heavy Western states where small wolf populations are recovering.

I guess my love of bears, wolves, and other wild animals, stems from my love of dogs, beginning with the collie we got when I was nine, and later, Brownie and Sheba. Many of us have domesticated animals in our homes, and we often treat them like members of the family. Why can't we extend this devotion by protecting *wild* animal populations? Wildlife and environment rarely get discussed during televised election debates. I have a feeling that if our love affair with dogs and cats could be extended to the wilds, America would be a healthier country.

Best of luck to you, Jack Russell.

In the afternoon, while taking in a glorious view on Ramrock Mountain, we see Ed whisk by, grinning and swinging his trekking poles. I can't understand him. He looks like he's on a casual, mid-morning stroll across the hills of Tuscany. *This guy would be great in one of those Rick Steves travel shows on public television.* Stan comes next, looking raggedy and glum. *Definitely not Rick Steves material.*

"Hey Stan!" Dylan yells. Stan lifts his head and flashes a weak smile, the first I've seen on him.

"Oh. Hey guys. *Damn* these blisters." He keeps walking.

As soon as he mentions blisters, I feel a burning in my own feet. *There's something going on down there, and it doesn't bode well.*

Then Stan's son, Derek, comes shuffling up, bent over to where his backpack is almost horizontal. His red t-shirt is totally wet, and strands of wet black hair are plastered against his forehead. He gives a half-hearted wave of the arm, then continues tagging his dad over the ridgeline.

Later, at Woody Gap, we see Stan and Derek resting at a picnic table. Ed is nowhere around. I want to just wave and keep going, but Dylan strolls over to the table. I follow.

"You guys resting?" Dylan asks.

"No, we're going home," Stan mutters. "We've got a shuttle coming in about an hour. This mountain man stuff is for the birds."

Derek has unloaded his pack and ambled over to a slope by the treeline. Dylan and I plop down at the table opposite Stan. His scowl is even more scowl-like. I notice dark rings under his eyes.

"Not a good time on the AT, eh?" asks Dylan.

"Nope."

"What brought you three out here?" I ask, still curious about Ed's relationship with Stan.

Stan shakes out a wet sock, then gently presses his finger against a blister on the bottom of his foot. He keeps his head down.

"Derek and I invited Ed," he says. "He's been having a tough time at home."

Dylan and I are silent for a while. Stan doesn't say anything else. I look over at Derek, who's stripped off his wet shirt and is laying on the ground, his bundled shirt acting as a pillow for his head.

Then I recall the large burn scar on Ed's neck. Then Stan continues.

"Ed and I were in the army," he says haltingly. "We were in Fallujah back in 2004. "Operation Phantom Fury" was the name they gave it. One day, we entered a booby-trapped building. A house, someone's home. Long story short, I missed most of the blast, but Ed got hit pretty bad." Stan waits a few seconds before continuing. "It's not just the burns, or prosthetic. His wife left him. He's battled with a lot of PTSD. He's been in more psych wards than I can count."

I'm stunned. I glance at Dylan, who's staring at Stan openmouthed.

"Anyway, Derek and I thought some time in the woods would be good for him. I read about a group of vets who hike the Appalachian Trail for therapy. Supposedly, a guy can get his head together a little out here."

31

Stan is now rubbing some ointment on his blister. "I've got it a helluva lot easier than him. He took the brunt of the blast. If I'd have gone through that doorway before him, it coulda been me."

Dylan and I merely offer a few weak comments like "Jeez," and "Man." My biggest image of Ed is him gazing at the treetops and smiling.

"Wanna know why he went first?" Stan asks us. Without waiting for an answer, he chuckles strangely, then says "He cut in front of me. Said he had to piss real bad."

There's a short silence. Then I summon the courage to ask Stan where Ed is.

"Oh, he's continuing on. He's not ready to quit. He's really enjoying being out here. Maybe it will help him. I think it is. I hope so."

Dylan and I soon say goodbye to Stan, telling him to give Ed our best wishes. For the second time, he smiles. I wave over to Derek and tell him to keep practicing trumpet.

We surmount Big Cedar Mountain, then see a sign for Woods Hole Shelter. We've hiked thirteen miles, better than what Rance had predicted. On the path to the shelter, near a stream, we meet two new people: a real talkative, ex-army guy from Savannah named Chad, and his wife, Aviana. We make small talk for a while. It doesn't take long before a "Caution" sign goes up inside me.

It starts when Chad stares at my backpack. *What's he looking at?* Then I glance at Dylan's pack, and notice how different the two backpacks are. Mine is much taller and bulkier, the frame consisting of a large, upside-down metal U, reinforced by tight cording and nylon fabric. It's stiff and vertical, with only a few pockets, but large ones. Dylan's pack, however, is soft and doesn't extend over his head. It rides lower on his back, more on his hips, and it has smaller and more numerous pockets and zippers.

Chad is now smiling. "It's funny, I still see a lot of outer-frame packs," he says to Dylan and me. "I love the big pockets. My inner-frame Osprey Xenith 88 has an interchangeable hip belt and custom molding, which I like, but sometimes I think I'd prefer a good, basic outer frame." *I have no clue what he's talking about.*

He and Dylan then start exchanging backpack data and brand names. I feel like a complete ingénue and outsider. Chatty people like Chad often make me uncomfortable. Now, it's compounded by my feeling ignorant about the latest backpack technology. *This bulky pack must make me look like a total freak. Wonder how many snickers I've already gotten.*

I head to the shelter, which is another quarter-mile further. Here I meet two people I recognize from the previous night's shelter: a young woman from Orlando, Florida named Teri, and her friend, a dark-hued man with a foreign accent and a name that sounds like "Bouillon," as in the soup cubes. I can't help but think this is a name just begging for a trail alias, unless "Bouillon" is already his alias.

I pitch my tent in a flat area about fifty yards from the shelter. Next to my tent is an elaborate contraption with multiple metal hooks and a long wire cord that extends horizontally between trees, about twelve feet above the ground. It's a device for holding bear bags. *Hmm, is this place notorious for bear activity?* Dylan sets up his tent closer to the shelter. *Hope they don't think I'm being anti-social by choosing this distant spot.*

The seven of us convene at the shelter, and I push myself to talk with chatty Chad, even though his extroversion turns me off. His effervescent demeanor has already endeared him to the others. In fact, he aptly bestows upon Bouillon the trail alias "Gold Bond" due to some chafing that Bouillon's been suffering around his groin.

While on the surface, Chad and I are totally different—he's extroverted, and I'm introverted, he enlisted, and I went to college—I discover we have one thing in common: we're both originally from the farm country of Richland County, Ohio. In fact, the schools we attended are only about ten miles apart. We joke about our hapless Cleveland Browns, and I offer him one of my cheap cigars.

As we puff away and talk sports, I think how great it would be if AT shelters came equipped with kegs of cold beer. The cigars, conversation, and Ohio connection that Chad and I share are great tools in warming the chilliness I'd felt during his earlier scrutiny of my backpack. A mild beer buzz could only add to the warmth.

Hiking solo in the mountains seems like a lonely enterprise at first glance, but the reality is that, especially at shelters, where hikers often convene, you're pushed to be social. It's no wonder that thru-hikers quickly become absorbed into a mini-society on the trail. Some of them develop lasting relationships with other hikers.

While I'm talking with Chad, Dylan and Jenna are opposite each other at one of the picnic tables. They have an intense look, as if mentally unraveling the DNA double helix.

Today was hot and sticky, and I'm really looking forward to a sponge bath. So, while the others prepare for their individual suppers, I create an itemized list in my head for freshening up at the stream. *Might as well eat there, too, since I can boil the stream water for my noodles, preserving what's in my canteen. Let's see, cookstove, noodles, canteen, washcloth, soap, towel, fresh underwear...anything else? Oh yeah, can't forget matches.*

Before heading over, I tell the others my plans, just so the ladies don't come upon me when I'm *au natural*. The exchange is a little awkward.

"Well, guess I'll head over to the stream to bathe."

Silence. I suddenly remember that all of us use the same stream for drinking water. I try to nudge my idea forward a little.

"I'll make sure I stay downstream of the pool."

Jenna makes a funny sound. I interpret it as a nervous laugh. Then I glance toward Teri. She's humming to herself, legs crossed, while reading instructions on a macaroni box.

Boy, did I screw that up. And it was going so well with Chad.

I walk the long distance to the stream, hoping I haven't forgotten anything. I climb over a large downed tree trunk, into a small shady area on the side of the hill, next to the stream. Not a lot of room here, and I can't seem to find a dry, level spot for my belongings. The open spot is mainly wet mud, with mud impressions of the soles of countless hiking boots. Eventually I find a large flat stone and use this as a combined clothes table and kitchen counter.

Stripping off my dirt-stained clothes, I'm one with nature. No garments to shield my private parts, no man-made threads as a barrier to the wilds. I'm a shiny white stick of tender human flesh, feeling tremendously vulnerable and completely out of place with the hard, jagged rock and rigid, rough wood surrounding me. I tenderly step into the pool of icy water—really just a few inches of moisture covering pebble, rock, and sand—and feel the cold, cold water sting my feet. Goose pimples cover my skin, and my heart pumps faster. I submerge my raggedy washcloth and sop up the water, then rub it over my crotch and upper body. *Brrrrr!* Then quickly rub some organic soap over my skin. Then rinse off with more cold water. This all occurs in about ninety seconds, while squatting on my haunches. It's probably the quickest, most crude bath I've ever taken.

After drying off, I spread the holes in my underpants and carefully guide my muddy feet through. Slide on my dirty shorts and t-shirt. Then rinse off my feet, then guide my stinky socks over them. Then put on my sneakers. The dressing takes twice as long as my bath, 'cause I have to balance myself while standing up to dress, the area here being too wet and dirty to sit.

Suppertime! Just so I haven't forgotten how to ignite my cookstove, I glance at the instructions on the fuel tank. *I think I've got it. Here goes.* I open the valve, pump ten times, then shut the valve. Open the fuel knob, strike a wooden match on the matchbox, hold it over the stove, and turn the knob gently. *Great, got a flame going.* Now open the valve, pump for a full minute, then shut the valve again. Then adjust the flame. *Good job, Pete.*

Next, I dip my saucepan in the stream—making sure it's upstream from my bathing spot. Pluck out a few pieces of dark brown leaf that float at the surface. Pour the water slowly into my saucepan. *Not too fast.* More balancing, as I adjust the stove on the rock so it's not tilted. Then wait until the water comes to boil.

While waiting, I fold my washcloth and towel, lay my soiled underpants on top, and lean back against the tree trunk. *Oops, forgot my hairbrush. Oh well, I'll brush when I get back to the tent.* A few bubbles appear on the surface of the water. *Man, this is satisfying. It's a lot of trouble, but worth it. Can't wait to taste those noodles.*

Before long the water is at a rolling boil. I tear open the ramen noodles packet. I swallow some saliva and my stomach groans loudly. Then I dump the noodles in and...*Oh shit! I forgot my fricking spoon!*

For a brief moment I debate whether to use a stick to stir the noodles. *Don't think so.* I pour in the seasoning and watch the contents boil, cursing at myself for my forgetfulness. *There's no way I'm walking another mile just for a spoon.* I decide to wait for the mixture to cool, after which I'll sip it straight out of the saucepan. Another five minutes go by. My stomach continues to moan. After I think the mixture has cooled, I carefully stir it with my finger. Then I gently put my lips to the saucepan and eagerly suck the mixture into my mouth. Much of it drips down my chin and onto my t-shirt.

I'm glad nobody's here to see this.

Next morning, I spend about a half hour cross-legged on the floor of my tent, swabbing and bandaging the sore on the inside of my right heel. I can hear the others chatter while they pack up. I know I'm lagging behind, but this sore worries me, as I still have a lot of mileage ahead of me. Then I hear Teri's voice.

"You may be without a partner today" she says, evidently addressing Dylan. "Looks like he's sleeping in."

Dylan mumbles a reply. Then Teri laughs. My temples throb slightly. Jenna left early again, and I'm surprised Dylan hasn't already left with her.

I finish bandaging my sore, then throw on my socks and shoes, unzip the tent and crawl out, hoping to catch up with Dylan. While rolling my sleeping bag I see Chad and Aviana strolling down the trail. Chad waves a trekking pole toward me and yells loudly "Go Browns!" Then he yells back toward the shelter "Good luck with that rash, Gold Bond!"

Teri and Gold Bond soon leave, too. I'm the last to pack up, but Dylan waits for me. *Hope he's not upset. Hope he doesn't feel obligated to hike with me instead of Jenna.* We head down the blue-blaze till we come to the stream. Dylan says he'll be right back, and that he needs to fill up on water. As he saunters uphill toward the pool, he turns his head and says with a smile "Now you get to wait for me, dude!"

My worrying was unfounded. Everything's alright between us.

The specter of Blood Mountain looms next. The name alone scares me. At 4,458 feet, this is the highest point on the Georgia AT. Dylan had dropped the name several times, in a voice filled with trepidation. He's lived in Georgia all his life, and he has me convinced Blood Mountain is Georgia's equivalent of New Hampshire's unpredictable—and sometimes deadly—Mount Washington.

"Pete, it won't be long, and we'll arrive at…BLOOOOD MOUNTAIN! Do you think we can summit?"

"I don't know. I sure hope so."

"Come to think of it, we're going to have to. Whether we want to or not."

"You know, that's a very good point."

We arrive at the base and discover it's a straight ascent. The northbound hike up Blood Mountain is actually quite easy, albeit rocky and steep. In fact, I soon find that, although tiring, mountain ascents are easier than descents. Maybe something about the physics of the human body, a heavy backpack, and the slope of the ground. Ascents seem more natural to my sore, tired feet than descents, where my feet always seem to be dangling in mid-air.

Dylan has a good lead on me, but he waits for me at the rocky peak. Here, there's an impressive shelter made of stone. It looks like a fireplace had once even graced this sturdy domicile. I walk over to a ledge on the wall, where there's a damp notebook: the Blood Mountain shelter journal. I open the journal, leaf through it, and see a recent entry from three college guys who are thru-hiking—"Dirty Mike and the Boyz," they call themselves—and whose blog I'd occasionally read on my home computer (it was subtitled "Hiking the Appalachian Trail so *you* don't have to"). I remember their blog as being slightly off-color, and this journal entry is no different:

> *Thanks for the love shack. Great guy-*
> *on-guy sex. Mike ran out of Vaseline.*

AT journal scribblings cover the gamut. Some are crude, like that of Dirty Mike and the Boyz. Others are matter-of-fact, or lightly humorous, or religious, or philosophical. I try out various types during my AT trips, but never find my own voice, and eventually give up writing in them altogether.

The journal entry, read in my tired state in the wet and dark gloom of the stone shelter, causes me to laugh hard. Dylan approaches to see what the joke is. I read the entry out loud. He offers a half-smile, but there's nothing more. Then he turns away.

Hmm. I thought the Dirty Mike and the Boyz journal entry was funny. Crude, yes, but better than the "I'm challenging myself" or "I'm trying to find myself" banalities I usually see. Maybe Dylan's a trifle conservative. Or maybe he didn't understand the Vaseline part.

As with Springer, Blood Mountain is too foggy for a view. I need a bathroom break, so I suggest Dylan go on ahead and I'll catch up with him. Dylan seems more than eager to. With Jenna just ahead of us, I think I know what's on his mind.

While the ascent was quick and uneventful, the descent is different. Twisting, turning, with scattered boulders everywhere. The white blazes, normally reliable, go every which way. It's also busy due to a stream of Labor Day hikers. At a sharp bend in the trail, I see a white-haired, white-bearded man climbing up toward me. I step to the side to let him pass. He looks about 70 years old, but really fit. He also appears very tired, breathing heavily after hauling the weight of his pack up this steep mountain.

Suddenly, I don't feel so old. I ask him where he's hiking from. Between breaths, he tells me he hails from the Ozarks, and has hiked all the way from Fontana Dam, west of the Smokies, ninety miles. This is the greatest distance of any hiker I've yet met. *With some luck and good living habits, maybe I'll be emulating this Ozark mountain daredevil, after my own hair turns white.*

I survive Blood Mountain, enter Neels Gap, and find out why it's so special: a highway, and better yet, a hiking-related store that has food, supplies, and even hot showers. It's part of a cluster of stone buildings known as Walasi-yi, but the store is called Mountain Crossings, run by Winton and Marjorie Porter. Other than an occasional road crossing, this is the only slice of civilization on my entire trip.

I limp across the highway pavement, which is a slight shock after trail dirt and rock. Crossing the parking lot, I suddenly hear my name called out. It's Chad. He, Aviana, and Jenna are standing next to a small van. I soon learn that they're shuttling home. I didn't get to talk to Aviana much, but I really enjoyed Chad and Jenna's company and I'm sorry to see them leave the trail. I then realize that Dylan will no longer have Jenna to chase.

Did he get to talk to her here at the gap? Maybe they arranged to hike together again. Maybe he got her phone number. Maybe she told him to get lost. I never find out.

We all say goodbye, and Chad tells me Dylan has some pizza waiting for me on the patio next to the store. Then Jenna cryptically tells me to "take care of Dylan."

I walk up the sidewalk as cheerful Chad yells "Stay away from tight shorts, Gold Bond!" Then I walk into the store.

Mountain Crossings has everything related to hiking: boots, socks, non-perishable food, gifts, mail supplies. In the front of the store is a large wooden barrel filled with shiny, prefabricated, designer walking sticks. *Do people really part with their money for these things?* I think about my own walking stick, Kip, now leaning against the stone wall on the patio outside. Not long ago, back on Springer Mountain, he was homeless. An anonymous, less-than-perfect fallen tree branch at the edge of the trail, with a cloak of tender bark, and half-covered by leaves.

I can't wait to tell Kip about this barrel of elitist walking sticks.

I also discover that Mountain Crossings provides tourists an opportunity to gawk at the exotic species known as AT distance hikers. Here, distance hikers are celebrities. At one point, while sitting on the patio with Dylan, I look up from my pizza and see an attractive, middle-aged woman beaming at me as if I'm Robert Redford. I smile slightly and feel a self-satisfied rush of blood, a sensation I haven't experienced in probably twenty years. Being an AT distance hiker, even a section hiker like myself, is the only time I know when you can look and smell like a pig, yet still get treated with admiration.

The shower facilities at Walasi-yi aren't Hyatt Regency quality, but I'm not about to complain. Along with food, sex, and The Beatles, hot water is one of the great pleasures of life.

Just before hitting the trail again, I violate my non-digital policy and call Lynn. It's partly to reassure her, but also to quell some homesickness I'm feeling. The last time we spoke was when the Greyhound rolled into the McDonald's in Dalton. It's only been two days, but it feels like much longer.

After she answers, I come close to introducing myself as Bob Redford but decide against it. It's good to hear her cheery voice. Sometimes her penchant for worry irritates me, but then I think I'm lucky to have someone so concerned about my welfare. I tell her I'm doing fine and that I've made a trail friend "with straight, sandy-blond hair like yours...except it's even longer." She tells me that makes her feel much better.

Then she asks if my new friend is a man or a woman.

The Inner Clock

Time seems more a concept than a reality. We assign numbers to our lives to quantify and give them order. Our inner clocks don't necessarily reflect the numbers we use to record the passage of time.

About six years ago, I had an interesting conversation with my friend Don at work. Over the weekend, he'd accompanied his wife Mary Jo to her high school class's 50-year reunion in Lima, Ohio. Since I've never been to a high school or college reunion, I asked him what it was like.

"Very strange," he said.

"In what way?" I asked.

"There were about a dozen people from my wife's class. Within that group, there were about three or four smaller groups. And for most of the evening, these smaller groups rarely intermingled. There were the jocks and their wives. There were the popular girls, I'm guessing cheerleaders. Maybe a couple other groups. Despite the passage of fifty years, the people all gravitated to the same cliques."

I told him that doesn't sound unusual, that it's natural to cling to what we know, based on our memories.

"Yeah, I know, but I just had to laugh," he responded.

"Why?"

"Well, there was one guy who didn't seem to fit into any group. He spent a little time here, a little time there. But for most of the reunion, he seemed to be on the edge of things, clutching his drink for security. I felt kind of sorry for him."

"Did you or your wife talk to him?"

"We did. He was real friendly, and completely unassuming. He's a climate scientist. I looked him up after I got home, and discovered he's internationally known for his work. He travels all over the world. There was a photo of him with his kids and his wife, who's Asian. His wife is stunning. I also discovered that he's friendly with billionaire Richard Branson."

"That's pretty wild," I said.

"Yeah, and the reason it's so funny, is that Mary Jo said that when he was in high school, he was the class geek. He was totally nonathletic, really awkward. A complete wallflower. And at the reunion, these jocks and others, some of whom have never left Lima, still shun him. They have no clue about the universe he sails through."

Time can play tricks.

Dylan is the first to leave Neels Gap, telling me he'll wait for me at Baggs Gap. He plans to finish his hike at Unicoi Gap, further on up the trail, where his parents will pick him up. *He's moving awfully fast for someone who took a week's vacation to hike. He could face the very real horror of daytime television if he finishes too early.*

Teri and Gold Bond leave about five minutes after Dylan. "Grandpa" holds up the rear about ten minutes later. (But not before Kip and I have a good laugh about that barrel of walking sticks.) The trail passes under a stone arch of the building, then along a wide pathway, then up another steep slope and into the woods.

Something about moving forward just feels *so* good. And now that I'm fresh and clean, it feels that much better. Just north of Neels Gap I meet a friendly African-American woman from nearby Blairsville who's on a casual Labor Day stroll. She slows up when she sees me and starts asking questions about my hike. Eventually, I realize that she's pegged me as a thru-hiker, probably due to my large pack and beginnings of a beard. For a split-second I think of playing the part so as not to disappoint her. *I can do a pretty good Robert Redford.* But I come clean and tell her today's only my third day of a very short hike. Surprisingly, she's even nicer and more inquisitive than before. *It pays to be honest.*

Near Wolf Laurel Top I see a sunny clearing to the right. *Time for a rest.* I slip off my canteen and pack and take a couple photos of a nice valley view. Then I plop down on a bed of grass, my back resting against a large log. I rest until my breathing gets slower. Then my muscles relax, my vision becomes more focused, my head much clearer. My inner clock slows down. I let myself sink into the greenery and warm sunlight, as if sinking into a soft marshmallow that's melted into hot cocoa. I've never consciously meditated, but I imagine this to be as close to a meditative state as is possible, for me, like certain marathon races I've run, where my breathing, heart rate, and body movement all become as fluid, melodic, and rhythmic as music.

Suddenly, a guy in a black t-shirt comes puffing into the clearing. He's breathing heavily, like he's been half-hiking and half-jogging. There are creases in his forehead, as if he's concerned. *Odd.*

I stand up, and we exchange a few words. I find out he's anxious to get to Tesnatee Gap, so he can get to his car, so he can get home to get ready for work the next day. Then he hurries onward.

I'm now like a hard marshmallow that bobbed to the surface of lukewarm chocolate.

Earlier, I mentioned that the second-hand AT guidebook I bought online was years out of date. Fortunately, just before hopping the bus to Georgia, I'd located a very detailed, more recent guide on the AT website WhiteBlaze.net. I'd printed out the pages I needed and zipped them up in one of my backpack pouches. I now check these notes, and notice I'm very close to Baggs Creek Gap, where Dylan, Teri, and Gold Bond said they would rendezvous.

Sure enough, while moving swiftly along a soft and level stretch of sun-dappled mountain laurel, I suddenly hear my name called out. Looking to the right I see the three of them. They're pitching their tents, even though it's only four o'clock.

"Hey guys! Didn't think I'd see you so soon!"

"We decided to get our tents up in case of rain," Teri replies. Like at Gooch Mountain Shelter, she's sitting with her legs casually crossed, like she's ready to read a book, or do some crochet work. But this time she doesn't avert her eyes from me, like she did when I mentioned bathing in the stream.

"Is there rain in the forecast?" I ask, guessing they got a weather report back at Walasi-yi.

"It's actually Dylan's forecast," she replies with a laugh.

I glance over at Dylan, who's sliding his tent poles inside the hems of the fabric. He looks up at me and winks.

"Oh," I say.

I remember that Dylan had taken a whole week off.

I need to think quickly. *I hate having to split from my trail partner. Together we've had some good talks, good climbs...and good wine. But there are still over three hours*

*of daylight left, and I have my goal of Franklin, North
Carolina and my reunion with Lynn and Holly.*

I look over at Gold Bond. He's sitting on a boulder,
leaning on his walking stick, with his legs splayed wide,
gazing at his crotch.

"Well folks, I think I'll probably cover some more trail
before I camp. Maybe we can hook up at Unicoi Gap."
(This was the location where Dylan had asked his parents
to pick him up.)

Teri smiles and says, "Sounds good."

Gold Bond waves his walking stick and says in accented
English "Great, brother. We see you there."

Dylan doesn't say anything but continues to poke his
poles into his tent fabric. As I walk back to the main AT, I
turn once and see him now looking at me. He tilts his head
back as if to say "Sayonara, my friend."

I know, and I'm sure he does too, that we probably
won't meet again.

Descending into Tesnatee Gap I see something all
backpackers dread. The path at this point consists mainly of
rocks. About halfway through, I notice what looks like a
large shadow on a rock, about twenty feet ahead. As I
approach, it is unmistakable: a snake. And no ordinary
snake. A timber rattlesnake—*Croatalus horridus*—which,
along with the eastern diamondback and eastern coral
snake, is the most venomous reptile in the U.S. southeast.
Ironically, the timber rattler is a handsome snake. Thick
black stripes on a sleek, silver-grey background. I'd seen a
western diamondback once while visiting Colorado, and
this snake is much more colorful. However...

My shock is relieved a little when I see he isn't coiled.
Neither do I hear the distinctive rattle. To make sure he's
no threat, I poke him with Kip. No movement. Since the
rattler looks freshly killed, I wonder if the black t-shirted

man maybe startled him in his hurried state, then killed the snake and left his conquest on display. It then occurs to me that, just before leaving home, I'd opted to wear my comfortable running shoes instead of sturdy, high-topped hiking boots. I resolved to henceforth employ Kip at every step. I don't want to be Rance's next "I shuttled one guy who..."

Most backpackers wear hiking boots. Since the backpacking boom of the early 1970s, hiking boots have not only provided excellent support for traipsing long distances over sometimes violently rugged terrain, but they're also fashionable and are worn by non-hikers.

But recently there has been a movement away from heavy, lug-soled boots. Many hikers are opting for weight minimization over ankle support and style. The Appalachian Trail Conservancy keeps a lot of data on the AT, and it reports that more and more hikers, including thru-hikers, are choosing trail running shoes over boots. Not only are these lighter and more comfortable, but their treads are much gentler on the trail than lug soles, which eat into softer trail sections and contribute to erosion. The key to picking a good shoe is to find one that offers stability. And to make sure the shoe is already broken in (although not too broken in).

But as the rocks become more jagged, and particularly after seeing this dead timber rattler, I wonder whether I made a mistake not investing in good, sturdy boots.

After Tesnatee Gap I reach the colorfully named Hogpen Gap. Here, there's a nice spring that's located down a blue-blazed path not far from the trail. I fill my canteen just as my thirst is peaking. Two middle-aged guys have arrived here, too. The one man appears to be holding sentry duty at the head of the blue-blaze. I say hello and make a comment about the spring being a lifesaver. But he says nothing. The other man is near the spring and only slightly friendlier. He tells me they'd covered an exhausting twelve miles that day. Covered in sweat, he can't wait to get his hammock strung up, so he can plop down for a rest. The sentry-duty guy then quietly slips by to set up his own hammock. I have the feeling that, maybe in their fatigue, they'd had an argument.

It feels like a dark cloud is approaching. But I shrug it off.

A couple miles later, on Poor Mountain, I find an open camping area next to the trail and break camp just before nightfall. I realize that I should've called Mom at Walasi-yi. She'd been almost as worried about me as Lynn, asking time and again about bears and wolves. So, after my mac and cheese dinner, I call to reassure her I haven't been eaten by a psychotic black bear, or a confused timber wolf that had drifted 2,000 miles from Yellowstone. I'm surprised that I still have cell service. This will soon change. I'm heading deeper into the mountains, and eventually there will be no connection to the outside world. Also, Labor Day weekend is over, and a lot of the backpackers have returned home.

My night on Poor Mountain is a little breezy, so I hang my socks on a tree branch to dry out. But mountain dew trumps mountain breeze. The clincher comes in the morning when I'm rolling up my tent and a sudden squall hits. If I'd have stayed in my tent, I'd have remained dry. If I'd have rolled my tent just five minutes sooner, there would be no soggy wet mess to carry.

I scribble a quick note to Dylan, Teri and Gold Bond. I take some extra time to single out Dylan. I see a lot of myself in him. He loves the wilds like I do. I remember him telling me how much he wants to get out of the turpentine factory. He hopes to one day visit Colorado. Maybe even move there. I now remember the Bob Dylan song I was humming the first time we met, near Springer Mountain. I tell Dylan to stay forever young.

I grip the shiny grain of my walking stick, Kip. *Kip moved West to live in the mountains. He was living in thin air on evergreen slopes near the Continental Divide. Hiking, skiing, making music...swimming through life instead of treading water. Maybe Dylan will do the same. I hope he does so before he loses the capacity to swim.*

JUNE 1983—LAKE CHELAN, WASHINGTON STATE

I climb on to the ferry boat, dragging my backpack alongside. I feel the eyes of the passengers on me. They're much older, most of them retirees headed for the isolated lodge at Stehekin, at the northern tip of the lake. One of the passengers isn't retired, though. He's a middle-aged man, accompanied by his wife and children. As the ferry chugs up the blue ribbon of water, framed by the snow-capped Chelan Mountains of Wenatchee and Okanogan National Forests, the man approaches me and asks me where I'm hiking. I tell him. Then he wants to know how old I am, where I'm from, what's in my backpack, etc. He's very curious about what I'm doing. His questioning makes me uncomfortable, so I try to turn the table and find out about him. I learn that he's from Brownsville, Texas, and he and his family are starting a week's vacation at Lucerne, on the western edge of the lake. But he seems reluctant to talk about himself.

While we ride the ferry, he ignores his family, who are at the stern. Instead, he sits near me at the bow. He wants to make sure I have everything for my hike. I balance my backpack on the deck, looking ahead, trying to make out where the trailhead is. The man sits near me the whole time. He pops occasional questions: "Do you have (this)," Have you (done that)?" He glances up at the white peaks, his eyes squinting in the bright sunlight. When the ferry

*arrives at Prince Creek, I'm the only person to
disembark. The man helps me with my backpack.*

*As the ferry pulls away, I see him, a solitary
figure, standing in the bow of the boat, looking at
me. I feel a twinge of sadness.*

I stuff the note to Dylan along with an old business card
in a plastic baggie, then skewer the bag on a tree limb next
to the trail, where it's visible, before hastily vacating camp.
I curse for the next ten minutes while sloshing through
blinding rain, but fortunately it's only temporary—just
enough to get me soaked. At Low Gap Shelter I replenish
my canteen and fix some bitter instant coffee and hot
oatmeal. This perks my spirits a little until I remember I'd
left my socks on the tree branch. Which means I'm down to
my last pair.

Low Gap is a dark, wet, lonely place, so I don't stay
long.

*Has it been that long since Dad taught me how to ice
skate? Dylan's no longer here for a safety net. Now that
I'm alone, can I skate solo? Are things really as wet and
lonesome as they seem?* Several things happen after Poor
Mountain that start me questioning the wisdom of a solo
hike.

First, there's the downpour. To stay hydrated, I'm
drinking over two quarts of water a day. But I want water
in my *canteen*, not in my shoes or my backpack.

Secondly, it's the only day in which I see not one person
all day. *Nobody.* Possibly the only time in my life this has
happened. Late in the day I hear a plane overhead and think
There are actually people up there. I often play make-
believe, deceiving myself that I'm completely self-reliant.
Beautiful lies I can live in. Truth is, the world is a joint-
stock corporation. Almost all humans have a burning need
for other humans' companionship. A few days' solitude in
dark, sprawling mountain forest drives home that reality.

The third issue is the blister/sore on my right heel, which forces me to stop several times to change gauze pads. My hiking stride is now replaced by a goofy one-legged tiptoe. But every time I begin to feel sorry for myself because of my blister, I think of Stan and *his* blister, which causes me to think of Ed.

Herman Melville's first novel, several books before his classic *Moby-Dick*, was *Typee* (for over seventy years, until the "Melville Revival" in the 1920s, *Typee* was a bigger seller than *Moby-Dick*). In *Typee*, the main character (Tommo, based on Melville himself) jumps ship in the Marquesas Islands. For several months, Tommo lives an Eden-like existence with a tribe of cannibals in an isolated valley on one of the islands. He eats succulent fruits, basks daily in sunshine, enjoys unlimited sex with the most beautiful maiden on the island, and is treated like a god by the natives. But the entire time, he struggles with an annoying leg injury from a tumble down the mountainside. Increasingly, Tommo worries that the only reason the cannibals are so benevolent is because they're lulling and fattening him, so he can be served as a ceremonial entrée.

Some literary scholars believe Tommo's leg injury symbolizes the fall of Man, the concept of original sin. Even in the garden of Eden, a snake is lurking.

While I'm reveling in this stunning Georgia mountain forest—with its weird and mysterious rock outcroppings, incredible stillness, and ancient trees that thrust high in the sky yet root deep underground—my blister and my one-legged tiptoe remind me that perfection is illusory.

At Chattahoochee Gap I start to dry out, and I celebrate by plopping down on a large tree root and treating myself to some protein-rich, sodium-soaked, foil-packed salmon. The pink meat is delectable after all the handfuls of sticky, raisin-peanut-M&M trail mix I've been gorging on. Trail mix is great for quick energy, but it quickly gets monotonous. And just before arriving at Chattahoochee Gap I discovered something in the trail mix bag that almost caused me to lose my oatmeal breakfast: a mouse hair. The little critter back at Gooch Mountain had not only pierced my granola bar, but burrowed into my trail mix. *God, how many handfuls of mouse candy have I eaten since Gooch Mountain?*

I dine on salmon at the base of a tree until the daddy-long-legs around my legs begin forming small battalions. A blue-blazed path on the right leads downhill to Coon Den Ridge and Chattahoochee Gap Spring, which I've heard is the source of the Chattahoochee River. So, I struggle to my feet and follow the path, leaving my pack leaning against the trail post. It's a steep descent, but I've never before visited the source of a major river, so I follow the path, stepping gingerly on rock and root to avoid scraping my blister sore.

After a couple curves in the path, I arrive at a campsite. It's just a patch of mud with a few charred logs scattered around. Next to the campsite is a trickle of a stream, about two feet wide. I look to the right and see a small pool poking out of a hole in the ridge. The pool is no bigger than a shallow bathtub. But the water from this pool dribbles quietly past the campsite and disappears into a patch of ferns on the edge of the ridge, then tumbles down the mountain. According to my guide notes, this narrow stream will grow and evolve into the great Chattahoochee River that provides drinking water to all of Atlanta and half the state of Georgia. I straddle Chattahoochee Gap Spring, envisioning myself as King Neptune.

How long would it take for a drop of water from this spring to spill out of a faucet in downtown Atlanta? Water moves at different velocities. A mountain rivulet moves faster than a valley stream. There's no telling how long. Besides, water is liquid, and a water drop is only a drop when it's isolated from a larger body of water. And besides, like the proverbial piece of string, how big is a "drop" of water, anyway?

I sit on the path next to the spring and become increasingly flustered thinking about water. As with my inner clock, there's no reconciling where water has been, where it is now, and how soon it will evaporate.

.

Deeper into Green

My guide notes call it Red Clay Gap/Blue Mountain. By now the trail is less a trail than a narrow, twisting rock slide.

Swollen feet, blisters ready to scrape at every rock. Nobody to help if ankle goes one way and foot the other. Rattlesnake concerns. Once I conquer the rock slide, the trail descent into Unicoi Gap is interminable, running parallel to a road but never getting any closer. I can hear an occasional car in the distance, but can't reach the road.

One of my many "learning experiences" on this hike is that difficult trail segments—a steep ascent or a treacherous, rocky segment—should be tackled in the morning. You do not want to encounter these sections in late afternoon or evening, when your muscles are taxed, and you're anxious to pitch camp.

There's a shelter at Blue Mountain, and I'm tempted to rest here to nurse my blisters, but I'm so anxious to get to Unicoi Gap, I zip past it. I leave some candy bars on a rock for the folks behind me, since I assume they'll be as tired as me after the rock slide, and I just plow forward.

Literal rock bottom is when I'm about a half-mile from the road. A massive tree had fallen and is blocking the path, and on the steep ridge there is no opportunity to circumvent it. This is what is referred to as a "blowdown." On many occasions during my hike, I'd marveled at the human effort that went into upkeep of the trail. On steep sections, I'd climbed staircases whose steps were made of sturdy log beams. I'd seen extensive drainage ditches, some made of huge rock slabs and others made of logs, designed to divert heavy rains from washing away the trail (and which require periodic unclogging of debris). Some portions of the Georgia AT meander through dense groves of rhododendron. These require periodic cutting and contouring.

All this work is accomplished by local volunteer organizations, in this case, the Georgia Appalachian Trail Club. I think about the old guy with the Leave No Trace pamphlet back at Gooch Mountain Shelter...the "tree fucker." He's probably retired and wants something to do to keep busy in his golden years. But he may have also been a backpacker who now feels a need to give back to those mountains that had given him so much. I'll see this stewardship again, on the Continental Divide Trail. The more I hike, the more appreciative I am of the backwoods ethic shown by these volunteers.

Fixing blowdown problems requires hauling out some serious equipment. At minimum, axes and handsaws. But the biggest trees usually need a couple of chainsaws, leveling bars, and lots of human gusto. The monstrous tree near Unicoi Gap is the biggest blowdown of my entire hike. This tree was probably a few hundred years old and may have plummeted to the ground only days before my visit. Although the volunteer crew hadn't yet been able to get up here, after returning home and contacting the Georgia AT Club, I learned that they'd already climbed Blue Mountain and cut and cleared the obstruction...probably only a day or two after my encounter.

I somehow manage to hoist myself and my heavy pack on this whale of a tree trunk. Then I do a Karl Wallenda balancing act for several yards. Solid ground is probably five feet below me, which is a substantial height when you're carrying thirty-plus pounds of gear. I think about my situation for a few seconds and decide the best course of action is not to think, but just jump. So, I jump. Despite the awkward weight on my back, I'm able to land solidly on two feet. *Yes!*

But not long after, I become so frustrated with the endless descent I jam Kip into the ground. Too hard, it seems. He cracks in two. *No!*

I'd had my walking stick since Springer, and I feel awful. He'd provided support, balance, rattlesnake detection (and a few palm blisters). We'd even shared a few laughs. I remember reading in Bill Bryson's book *A Walk in the Woods* that, after the author forgot his stick, his friend (Katz) offered to backtrack four miles to retrieve it. And I can't forget Gold Bond's panicked look when he almost forgot *his* stick back at Mountain Crossings. It sounds silly, I know, but you become attached to your walking stick.

But when at rock bottom, things can only get better. I find another stick when I reach the road at Unicoi, this one even smoother and straighter than Dylan's stick. I name it Kip 2. On the other side of the road, about a half mile up, I encounter a mountain brook with a water pool just big enough for my bathing needs. As it's getting dark, I pitch my tent on a slight slope right next to the trail, then break out the organic soap for a refreshing bath. I have to hoist my bear bag in darkness, but things are looking up.

It was a rough day. But as I crawl into my sleeping bag, a barred owl sounds out its eight ghostly syllables as if to say "Yooo will-be snoo-ooz-ing soo-oon." He's right. Along with the babbling brook, his singing lulls me to sleep.

I'm skating solo.

The next day breaks beautifully. The silver morning light streams in, and my bear bag, which hangs directly over the AT like a giant chandelier, is undisturbed. I decide that, as long as the ground is fairly level and smooth, mountain streams offer better camping facilities than mouse-infested shelters. I don't need a campfire, and I make sure I leave these areas clean and undamaged (other than forgotten socks on tree branches). I still haven't read that Leave No Trace pamphlet that the tree fucker had handed me. But so far, I think I'm being eco-responsible.

I hike up and over Rocky Mountain feeling rejuvenated. Despite yesterday's trials, I still managed almost twelve miles.

On the descent from Rocky Mountain, I stop to snap a photo, and bump into my first person since the hammock duo. He's a retired fellow named Tom, from Huntsville, Alabama. Tom and his wife have a condo in nearby Helen, Georgia. Tom enjoys taking brief day hikes, on his wife's condition that he accompany her on shopping trips.

Tom and I talk for about fifteen minutes, then shake hands goodbye. On the other side of Indian Grave Gap, I come upon a large water pipe jutting from the mountain at about chest height. I slip off my bandana, soak it in the water stream, and douse my upper body. The cold water invigorates me after the uphill hike in the heat. My guide notes say there's an abandoned cheese factory nearby. Some transplanted New Englander had established it many years ago. Maybe this pipe is a remnant, but I don't see any factory ruins.

I've heard that some older New Englanders can be a bit eccentric. But why would a guy build a cheese factory in the middle of the Georgia mountains?

Soon after, I cross paths with a middle-aged man with a bundle of tawny, unkempt hair. His trail name is Comus, and he's on a southbound section hike. He just recently finished a stretch in the Smokies. Evidently, Comus's wife shuttles him to various points on the AT for his hiking pleasures. I try, but I can't envision my Lynn agreeing to something like this.

Comus's destination is Neels Gap. *Is it my imagination, or is everyone destined to go there?*

"Ah yes, popular Neels Gap," I say, recalling my hot shower, hot pizza, and the hot woman who was staring at me.

"Check this out," he says, giggling with excitement, and pulling out a dogeared paperback book from his pack. The title is *Just Passin' Thru*, by Winton Porter, the guy who runs the Mountain Crossings store at Walasi-Yi. "I'm gonna get him to sign it!"

At Mountain Crossings, the distance hikers are celebrities to the tourists. Winton Porter is evidently a celebrity to the celebrities. I can't help but think that we're all celebrities, in some manner.

Gazing at the worn paperback Comus is holding, I ask him what he knows about the history of Walasi-Yi.

"That's an old Civilian Conservation Corps project," he explains, then giggles again. "At one time it was buzzing with Depression-era workers. Then it was a restaurant. Then an artist colony. These days it serves tourists and backpackers. Looking forward to it!"

I'd heard of the Civilian Conservation Corps, or CCC. I knew it to be one of President Franklin D. Roosevelt's New Deal programs during the 1930s and 1940s. My dad had been a CCC worker up in Pennsylvania before going off to war.

The CCC was perhaps the most popular of Roosevelt's New Deal programs. It provided jobs for young people, like building and improving structures, stocking lakes and streams with fish, implementing erosion control, blazing footpaths, planting, and more. Thirty bucks a month was pretty good for a young person during the Depression.

Under the CCC, almost three billion trees were planted, and 800 parks established.

The CCC faded when World War II struck, but it spawned other conservation programs that exist even today.

"Where you camping tonight?" Comus asks me.

"I'm shooting for Addis Gap. Still ten miles ahead, and not sure I'll get there before dark."

"Hell, that ain't far! Except for Tray Mountain...(man, you gotta snap a photo from *there*)...it's level hiking. Want any reefer? It'll help you get over Tray." Comus hurriedly digs into his backpack.

"No, no, that's ok, thanks anyway," I quickly respond, before he has a chance to fish out his marijuana bag.

"Oh," he responds dejectedly.

"Nothing against it," I quickly interject, "but it's been a long, long time."

"Hey, no problem, brother. I *totally* understand!"

After we part, I think how Comus's wife must be very patient and devoted, chauffeuring him from trailhead to trailhead, while he reads books and giggles in the passenger seat.

At the base of Tray Mountain, near a forest service road, I meet a young couple who'd done an overnight hike. *Jeez, today is like a Turkish bazaar compared with yesterday. Including the hashish.* I surmount Tray Mountain much easier than expected. Like Comus promised, it offers a sweeping panoramic view. I rest here, eat some tuna-on-bagel while swatting sweat bees, air out my clammy feet, and move on. *Got to make Addis Gap.*

Then I enter a long, level stretch called the Swag of the Blue Ridge. I keep seeing dug up earth on the side of the trail, and wonder if bears were here recently. *Maybe these are signs of bears scratching for grubs?* I like the swag because, despite my heel sore, I'm able to make good time. *But what the hell is a swag," anyway?*

The swag goes on and on. Then I think I see another hiker about a hundred yards ahead. Except he's not moving. *Is he sitting on a log? Must be resting.*

But as I get closer, I discover it's a huge, faded, plaid parka draped over the sawed end of a large, fallen tree trunk. Some burly backpacker had probably become overheated and discarded it months ago, in the spring or previous fall. But the sight of this solitary coat is a little disturbing. I'm in the middle of nowhere, and the trail around here is vacant. Who is the owner? Can he be hiding? Is there a North Pond Hermit hunkered behind hemlocks and boulders in the dark woods, hoping a Little Debbie snack cake might fall from my pack? I half expect the coat to rise up in the air and start dancing around, like in some cheap horror movie.

I take a quick photo of the coat then skedaddle, occasionally turning around until the spooky thing is out of vision.

The hiking along the swag continues flat and easy. A couple miles further, the trail suddenly widens out. I enter a large open space that looks very similar to Chattahoochee Gap. I figure this might be Addis Gap. Then I see a wooden sign with "ADDIS GAP" etched into it. Comus was right. I reached my destination, and with time to spare. There's a large, open campsite on the left, just next to the trail. *Uh, a little too large for me, and no water here.* A second wooden sign with "Water" etched into it points down a graveled road to the right. I recheck my AT guide notes to learn that this is an abandoned fire road, and a primitive camping area is located about a half-mile down. I'm tired and sore, and I hate to even walk another yard, but it's imperative I find water, since I've only a few drops in my canteen, and tomorrow I have steep Kelly Knob to climb. So down the road I go.

It's a wide road, and it winds through the forest seemingly forever. I hear a raccoon trilling in the distance, and I think of my childhood pet coon, Rascal. The trilling becomes louder, and soon I hear a rushing stream. Then I arrive at a curve in the road, with a large mound of gravel to the left. Just beyond the curve, on the right, I see what looks like a large camping area in a hollow, about a hundred feet below where I'm standing. The stream rushes through a culvert under the road. To reach the camping area, though, I have to continue further down the road. *Shit, I can't go another step.* But there's a tiny spot on the left, cozied up to the edge of the stream, and with a little landscaping effort, I might be able to squeeze my pup tent in. After stomping on some poison ivy vines and bending a few saplings, I barely manage to maneuver my tent in. It's at the foot of a short hill about fifteen feet below the road. *I'll bathe in that pool over there, and the miniature cascade can later sing me to sleep—just like at Unicoi Gap.*

I have a refreshing bath, fill my canteen, then climb up to the gravel pile to fix my dinner. After getting a flame on my cookstove, I manage to burn my thumb knuckle on the hot metal. But I also have the pleasure of entertaining some company. Sometime during my feast, a curious squirrel shuffles up to my ramen noodle dish. He switches his bushy tail and takes a few sniffs, then suddenly scurries away in fright. ...*Wait, come back! You haven't tried my famous noodle au jus!*

As the forest begins to darken, and the crickets and cicadas begin their nocturnal symphony, I look around the neighborhood. I notice that the fire road continues even further, eventually disappearing into the woods. *God knows how far it goes.* I briefly ponder how nice it would be to follow that road, then perhaps plunge into the woods for some truly primitive hiking...an off-trail American walkabout...and allow myself to get swallowed up by this beautiful greenery and dark mystery. I could wander through this lush forest for miles, maybe trekking all the

61

way to the eastern seaboard. Without trail markers, though, I would never know my exact whereabouts. Neither would anyone else.

My previous campsites were either at shelters with other people, or were smack on the edge of the AT. This is the farthest I've yet wandered from the main trail. Dylan's far in the rear, and I'm totally alone down here.

Then I think of the ghostly coat back at Blue Ridge Swag. I think of Lynn's worries about my safety. And my mother-in-law's humorous assurance that "If there are any kooks, Pete will just outrun them."

Despite trying to fight my overactive imagination, my thoughts drift to what I've read concerning the few murders that have occurred over the years on the AT. The first documented homicide happened very close to here, in 1974, at a shelter. Then in the summer of 1996, two young women were found inside their tents near Skyline Drive in the Blue Ridge Mountains. Their bodies had been bound and gagged, and their throats cut. The killer was never apprehended.

I'd prepared well for this hike, but my thoughts of murder in the wilderness cast a pall on my night at the fire road campsite. I zip up my sleeping bag and hope morning arrives soon. Normally, I'm confident and comfortable when I'm alone, even in the wilds. But not at this moment. Maybe it's because I'm removed from Addis Gap and the main trail. The AT is a highway of human activity. Even on a quiet day, one knows that sooner or later another friendly hiker will arrive. The trail is isolated in many areas, but it's also a conduit to civilization. The irony being that civilization is far more unsafe than the woods. The crimes perpetrated on the AT during its long history are miniscule compared to what happens in a large U.S. city.

But if by some far stretch something *does* happen to me here, it would be a lonely, isolated fate. And it might be months before anyone finds me. Or even years.

*Abandoned roads, side trails, walkabouts...fine for
experienced hikers, Pete. But remember, this is your first
extended hike. You don't even know how to use your
compass properly. Maybe you're overreacting, but better
stay closer to the main trail next time.*

My goal for day six is to reach Plumorchard Gap
Shelter, just under ten miles away. But this is minimum.
The AT seems to lull one into progressively shorter daily
mileage. I'd started at sixteen miles and had dropped to
eleven. I'm worried I won't make Franklin by Sunday
evening. Therefore, I decide to strike back.

Next morning, I awake and proceed through what is now
a familiar routine: replace blister bandage, pull on dirty
clothes, lower bear bag, transfer food to pack, roll and pack
sleeping bag, lower then fold then pack tent, boil water for
oatmeal, eat, read guide notes, snap photo of campsite, slip
on bandana, hoist pack on back. The routine usually takes
about an hour. Then I move.

I trudge up the gravel road towards Addis Gap, my
thoughts of bushwhacking into oblivion having faded with
the moon. It's a new day and the sun is shining. What a
glorious day to be breathing in the mountain air and
moving forward on fresh trail!

At the Addis Gap clearing, I turn right onto the main AT
and immediately begin climbing steep Kelly Knob.
Halfway up I see a blue windbreaker on the side of the trail,
a telltale sign of another winded and overheated hiker. At
Kelly Knob summit there is a clearing with a breathtaking
view of three states: Georgia at the base; Standing Indian
Mountain in North Carolina to the northeast; and Table
Rock Mountain in South Carolina in the misty distance to
the east.

I snap a photo... not that it means anything. My digital camera isn't powerful enough to capture the dim outline of Table Rock Mountain, the most distant peak.

No matter. A photographic artifact is only a colored shadow of the moment, anyway. One of my favorite musicians, Syd Barrett (the founder and one-time leader of Pink Floyd) was also an abstract artist. After leaving the group, he lived like a hermit with his mother, and he created hundreds of paintings. But only a few survive, because he continually painted over paintings that he'd just completed! For him, it was the thrill of creation that mattered. His audience was his mother and himself, and preserving his art held no appeal.

After preserving my colored shadow, I find a boulder and recline against my backpack. I look to my right and see a small grove of mountain laurel—*Kalmia latifolia*. This attractive plant is located throughout the Appalachian Mountains, from Maine to Florida. It's a broadleaf evergreen that blooms with dainty pink and white flowers. I've seen a few other groves of this attractive plant, but the one here on Kelly Knob almost seems like a gift, a thoughtful reward for climbing the steep slope. I feel an urge to run to the field and roll in the foliage. Instead, I marvel at how even a hard, rocky terrain like this can spawn such a beautiful and gentle thicket. It's amazing how thrifty nature is. If left alone, it rewards us with color, texture, and sustenance.

I also encounter patches of lichen, which are symbiotic plants that result from algae living in fungi. Lichen come in numerous sizes, forms, and colors. The ones I've seen at Acadia National Park in Maine are crunchy and cream-colored. These lichens are sea-green colored and look like little mounds of coral. Supposedly, it takes decades for certain species of lichen to recover if trampled upon.

Then I see a movement and look to the right. A winsome little chipmunk! He's sitting upright on a piece of fallen timber, head cocked slightly, tail twitching. He chose a great place to burrow his nest: near a field of mountain laurel, with a spectacular view of three states. I carefully unzip my bag of trail mix, reach inside, pluck out a raisin, and toss it towards the critter. He zips over, examines it, snatches it quickly, then bolts into the brush. Chipmunks stockpile their nonperishable food in early autumn, so maybe he'll store this in his burrow for the winter. *If I were him, though, I'd eat it right away.*

    The highlight of today's hike, and one of the most intriguing people I'll yet meet, occurs at Dick's Creek Gap.

    A two-lane highway passes through this gap, connecting Hiawassee, Georgia to the west and Clayton, Georgia to the east. I approach it via a series of switchbacks, which are zigzag trails on the side of a mountain. Switchbacks are much easier to negotiate than straight ascents and descents, but they're very time-consuming. Some people prefer switchbacks. But being an impatient sort, a recreational marathoner who likes an occasional physical challenge, I prefer the straight ascents.

    On the way down I see several mammoth, elderly trees. One of them has knife carvings so old they're indecipherable. A lot of folks are unaware of this, but tree graffiti is not only a violation of trail ethics, it's also illegal. Seeing it on display in the wilderness can be stomach-churning, but these old carvings aren't nearly as offensive as spray-painted boulders or fresh hackings on younger trees. I scan the bark for any words of legibility…maybe something along the lines of "Joe Carter 1941." But the carvings are as dark and gnarled as an old cowhand's knuckles, and I can't make out any words.

    While traversing the switchbacks, my left shoulder starts whispering to me, but I make a vow I won't unload my unwieldy pack until I reach the gap. *Damn these switchbacks, let's get to the bottom.*

Right when the whispers are screaming, I descend upon a snug little clearing that faces a miniature waterfall. A slightly tilted wooden sign is sunk in the middle of a rhododendron patch on the hill above the water. The playful lettering on the sign reads "Carnes' Cascade." A small, green, wooden bench sits in the shade facing the waterfall. The scene is like a slice of real estate plucked from a miniature golf course, but without the putter, ball, and green felt.

I'm smitten by this postcard oasis and, though I haven't hit the gap yet, I can't ignore an opportunity to linger. So, I take a few moments to relax. I unload my pack, soak my bandana in the cascade, fill my canteen, then sit on the bench to munch a candy bar. *Who the heck is this Carnes? Probably a dedicated trail volunteer who lives nearby.* I gaze at the water that tumbles down the hill, striking the rocks at the bottom. I listen to the percussive sounds of the water's impact on the stones. This hike has opened my eyes to a lot of little things that I never would have appreciated before. One is the orchestra of notes created by water striking jumbled rock. If one moves the rocks slightly, the water strikes at different angles and offers an entirely different tune.

I like the tune that plays here at Carnes Cascade.

After about ten minutes, I reluctantly rise from the bench and mosey over to my pack. Slinging the stiff, brown load over my back, I thank the mysterious Carnes and continue downhill to US-76. I soon discover the highway is only a few hundred yards further. *Carnes—or his admirers—didn't have to hike too far.* Although it's still rural Georgia, I hear a lot of helicopters. The distant airplane on Blue Mountain was assuring, but I wonder the reason for this racket.

These incessant copters are a real intrusion on the peacefulness of the forest. Did Lynn report a missing husband? Oh God, what did she do now.

This thought worries me. So, near the highway I slip off my pack and try to call her. But my flip phone reads "NO SERVICE." *Oh well. Let 'em keep searching.*

Scanning my guide notes, I see that I'm at Dick's Creek Gap in the Nantahala Wilderness ("Nantahala," like "Amicalola" and "Unicoi," is a Cherokee word. It means "Land of the Noonday Sun." The Cherokee Nation, of course, was forcibly marched from their southeastern homeland by the U.S. army and state militias, after gold was discovered, to present-day Oklahoma. The removal was part of the "Trail of Tears," when an estimated 4,000 Cherokee men, women, and children died from freezing, starvation, or disease. The reality of so many U.S. geographic names in the U.S. being derived from the Indians, after we waged war against them for their land, is a cruel irony that's never escaped me).

While reading my notes, I see a guy on the other side of the highway, himself reading the wilderness kiosk near the trailhead. He has a huge mustard-colored backpack, long baggy pants, bushy hair, and a dark beard. *Hmm. I might meet my first thru-hiker.*

I cross the highway at the same time as the hiker dips into the woods. I'm afraid he'll get away, since he's the first human I've seen since the couple at Tray Gap, and I could use conversation. But instead of following the trail, he seems to be flitting back and forth in the woods.

I nonchalantly approach the kiosk, and out of the corner of my eye notice the hiker has seen me. He immediately descends into the clearing.

"Dude, I'm glad you're here, I think I got dropped off in the wrong spot!" he gushes.

He looks very young, maybe nineteen or twenty. He has a black U-shaped beard, like an Amish farmer, and it's contrasted by a wispy, dirty-blond moustache.

"What spot are you looking for?" I ask.

"Dick's Creek Gap," he replies.

"Well, this is it."

"Really? I can't find the shelter."

I tell him that not all gaps necessarily have shelters. We chat a little, and he tells me he needs to get to Henson's Bed and Breakfast to get a supply package. But he doesn't know where Henson's is.

I look at his map, which is not very good.

"Wait a second," I tell him, as I once again unload my pack. "Let me get out my trusty WhiteBlaze guide."

"Dude, thanks man."

We read the information for supply and mail locations near Dick's Creek Gap, but Henson's isn't listed. I'm worried that maybe his mail drop isn't legitimate. I read the instructions on his map.

"Ok, it should be here." I point at a spot in the air just off his map, indicating its proximity to the well-known Blueberry Patch hostel. "Your place isn't on the map, but it should be located here, according to your instructions."

"I swear I went that way, but didn't see it," he says. "Is that the way to Hiawassee?"

I point westward and tell him, yes, Hiawassee is eleven miles that direction. I make sure I point toward Hiawassee. I warn him do *not* go eastward, or he'll end up in Clayton. "That's where that banjo picker in *Deliverance* lives," I say. But he's evidently too young to know what I'm talking about.

"Why is the direction arrow for the trail going this way?" he asks, pointing to the AT logo on a nearby boulder. This logo is an upside-down V with a T underneath.

"That's the Appalachian Trail logo, it's not a direction arrow," I explain.

"Dude, I didn't know that!"

We talk some more, and I learn his name is Chester and that he's from Tyler, Texas. When I ask if he's a thru-hiker, his face lights up.

"No, but I plan to do one! This is just a 13-day hike for practice."

If he's been hiking less than thirteen days, he must have been cultivating his beard long before he started. Probably to look the part. I wonder what Chester's home life is like, and what his parents might think of his being way out here. Or even if he has parents. I think of when I was young, and the oft-troubled relationship with my own parents. They were as confused as to how to deal with me as I was confused about myself. Fortunately, the three of us eventually found harmony…years later.

I then tell Chester I hope to soon meet my wife and daughter at a motel in Franklin.

"I stayed in a motel a few nights ago and didn't like it," he says excitedly. "The air conditioning was way too cold. I prefer being out here."

Why didn't he just turn the knob on the air conditioner register? Better not ask.

"Have you gotten lost yet on the trail?" he asks, explaining that he, too, is northbound, but that he had some difficulty back at Blood Mountain.

"No, but I've heard complaints about the blazes on Blood Mountain," I answer.

"Yeah, they need to do something about that, man!"

I tell Chester I'd love to join him on the trail, but I have to make time and need to continue hiking north. After we say goodbye, I watch him walk toward the road, hoping that he'll point his thumb in the right direction. I think of a character in *A Walk in the Woods*, an old man, who was even worse than Chester, wandering thirty miles off-trail. Maybe this type is common on public trails, a hiking subgenus, people with disordered minds drawn to the gorgeous disorder of Nature. Opposites attract, but so do likes.

I like Chester. I also think he's brave for striking into the wilds at such a young age. But I can't help wondering that section hiking, let alone thru-hiking, maybe isn't the best idea for him.

The Old Man in the Trail

After a few hours of up and down climbing, I arrive at another intersection in the woods. A shelter sign points to the right. Plumorchard Gap. It's getting late, and I'm torn between staying here and moving further. I decide not to water up at the spring, but see if any people are in the shelter, then push on to Wheeler Knob, about two miles further. Supposedly there's a campsite and water there.

Plumorchard Gap Shelter is empty, so I continue to Wheeler Knob. At the base of this mountain I cross a gravel road, and I hear a vehicle crunching gravel in the distance. *Hunters, maybe?* I've never understood why hunting and hiking can coexist in national forests. Most hunters are responsible, but there's always the possibility of some trigger-happy amateur mistaking a hiker for a deer.

I disappear into the woods before the vehicle arrives. For the first time, I notice some large conifers; a sure sign of North Carolina, which is just a few miles ahead. As the forest light begins to dim, I see a wide camping area on the left, in the middle of a large arc in the trail. I stroll around and discover a second, smaller camp spot tucked in a hidden area toward the back. I've since learned the importance of maximizing the glow of daylight, so I do the chores that need sunlight: pitching tent and filling water.

But the water is just a slow drip coming from a narrow underground pipe. My washcloth absorbs more mud than liquid. It's a big letdown, because today was very hot and sticky, with numerous intricate sprays of silver silk spider web stretched across the path. If anyone would've seen me they'd have thought I was nuts, since I constantly swung Kip in front of me, up and down, like a crude magic wand, to knock down these pesky webs.

Fortunately, I have enough drinking water in my canteen to last until sunup. After digging into my pack for my dinner supplies, I hobble to a large fire ring to relax, air out my smelly and swollen feet, and enjoy some freeze-dried red beans and rice.

As with Hawk Mountain Shelter, there's trash. Many hikers and campers think foil packets will burn. They won't. Foil singes and chars, but doesn't burn.

Disgusted with my previous tenants and their mess— and sticky with sweat—I eat a quick meal, but this time I'm not in the mood for a post-dinner cigar. Instead, I crawl into my tent. I'd brought a collection of Jack London stories to read, but tonight I choose non-fiction: the Leave No Trace pamphlet.

Although lacking the plot, character, and action of *Call of the Wild* and *White Fang*, the pamphlet offers sage advice for responsible camping and hiking. Here are the seven basic principles of Leave No Trace:

1. Plan ahead and prepare
2. Travel and camp on durable surfaces
3. Dispose of waste properly
4. Leave what you find
5. Minimize campfire impact
6. Respect wildlife
7. Be considerate of other visitors

Pretty simple. I think about how closely I've adhered to
these principles. Except for not buying wool socks, I've
planned and prepared well. But I've violated the "camp on
durable surfaces" rule, pitching my tent too close to the
streams at Unicoi and Addis Gaps (Leave No Trace
recommends pitching your tent at least 200 feet away from
water). My waste, including the cigar butt leftover from my
football discussion with Chad, is in a plastic bag at the
bottom of my pack. As far as "Leave what you find," the
only things I found were a few sticks for walking, and these
stayed in the woods. Dylan started the only campfire, but it
used an existing fire ring. I've respected all wildlife. I've
respected other visitors.

I feel bad about the wet socks hanging at Poor
Mountain, but that was an accident. I *did* resolve to camp
farther away from streams, however. This is important,
because riparian wildlife is real tender. I've seen a number
of fenced-off areas near streams, which are attempts to
reestablish vegetation.

Reading the Leave No Trace pamphlet is another
"learning experience." If only my old college buddy Randy
knew of all my learning experiences.

I don't sleep well at Wheeler Knob. I'm too excited
about crossing into North Carolina.

I roll out of my tent at first light, quickly pack my
belongings, and sling my pack on my back. Actually,
"sling" is the wrong word.

I'm carrying thirty-five pounds. Although this is light
compared to many hikers' packs, it's too heavy a load for
casual slinging. By now, I've perfected a technique.

I prop my pack against a tree or boulder, preferably
where the ground is sloping, so I can take advantage of
gravity. Then I plop my butt on the slope in front of my
pack, then slip both arms through the shoulder straps. I lean

forward slightly, trying to make my back as horizontal as possible, and slowly hoist myself erect—carefully, or my oversized sleeping bag will spill to one side. Lastly, I buckle the waist belt. This belt has become increasingly loose, because my waistline has shrunk, so I occasionally need to tighten it. The goal is to support as much weight as possible on my hips, so my shoulders feel less pressure. For some reason, however, I'm never able to fully master this concept.

If there is no sloping ground nearby, a boulder or log at knee-to-waist height often helps. If there's no sloping ground, boulder, or log, then I have to improvise as best I can, and light comedy results. (I still recall Dylan's muffled giggles back near Big Cedar Mountain.)

Once my pack is on my back, my arms are through the straps, my pack belt is tight, and my staff is in my hand, I feel fulfillment. I'm not sure why. It just feels good, and right. Earlier I mentioned "Buddhism in the woods." There's something satisfying about the simplicity of hauling your home on your back and having nothing but an open trail (or road) ahead. All the responsibilities, all the urban and suburban bullshit is gone. Backpacking in the woods is a psycho-societal cleansing.

And, with me, there's also contentment knowing that what's *in* my pack are the only items I *need*. Maybe it's because she's the daughter of a grocer, but Lynn buys way too many food staples, including duplicates and triplicates, and these foods often linger beyond their expiration dates. We also have too many clothes and fripperies. In fact, our whole house is cluttered with crap we don't need.

This is stressful on people like me who are drawn to neatness and organization. When I hike, I know what I need and don't need, and where everything in my pack can be easily retrieved. My cold-climate emergency clothes are stacked neatly on the bottom. At the top are my bed (my sleeping bag) and my house (tent). In between, neatly folded, are my lighter clothes. Stove and cookware are atop those. My foodstuffs are tucked in a large outer pocket, and smaller items (flashlight, matches, jackknife, rope etc.) are in smaller pockets.

Simple. Organized. Non-stressful. Minimal BS.

After leaving Wheeler Knob, it's a brisk two-mile jaunt to the state line. I almost miss it. The indicator is a large tree at the edge of the trail. It has a rusty metal tube nailed to it, and a simple wooden sign, no bigger than a shoebox, with "NC/GA" carved in it.

I made it!

Goal accomplished. What a *huge* relief. I've hiked over seventy-five miles for this. A blink of an eye for a thru-hiker, but a marathon for me. The rest of my hike will be an afterthought…or so I think.

There's a small, worn area opposite the tree where previous hikers have rested or celebrated. I stand here and take a photo of the wooden sign to commemorate the occasion. It's my own quiet ceremony. No cheering crowd or laurel wreath, but who cares. I completed my modest task, and that's my reward.

Then I continue to Bly Gap, only 0.2 miles further.

Bly Gap is on a slight incline at an open trail intersection. About fifty yards from the intersection is a large, gnarled, live oak tree with its trunk stretched on the ground, as if tired from holding its heavy load.

According to my guide notes, this tree is believed to be the oldest in the Carolinas. It was used at one time "to spot the line between Georgia and North Carolina." I later learn that the colonial line was drawn in 1663. Shit…before the Founding Fathers were even born! Two years after Charles II restored the English monarchy. During the French reign of the Sun King, Louis XIV. Goodness knows how many years the tree had lived *before* 1663.

The old fellow allows me to prop my pack against his scarred and withered trunk. I sit down and rest my back against his deep wrinkles. I've been pushing myself for days, have only occasionally stopped for reflection, so I devote some time here. A large meadow dips into a valley in front, and the sun comes streaming in. A few feathery clouds grace the turquoise sky. I think about the old oak, and the thousands of AT hikers who've also rested here over the years. I also think of how lucky I am to be healthy enough to do this.

Mostly I think about Dad, who's been gone for almost seven years. I don't think of him as much anymore, but I still miss him a lot. He liked history and passed it to me. He also loved camping. In one of our last conversations, we bemoaned how materially muddled our lives had become. He told me "I could live in a hut and be happy." (Then we agreed that, with wives who enjoy possessions, this would be difficult.)

I know, wherever Dad is, he's pleased with my small achievement.

Dad died in late November, when the air was cold, and the sky a melancholy grey. His death was a shock, and it felt like winter should go on forever. Then spring came. The sun came out, the clouds broke up, and the birds chattered again. It felt awkward. I still grieved and wanted the weather to grieve too. *It's painful, sometimes, when seasons change. But time drags us along, whether we like it or not.*

I tilt my head back and gaze at the streamer-like clouds. One of them I pick out for Dad. *Is he up there? Watching me?* I also concentrate on the large meadow before me. There aren't many such sunny, open areas along this southernmost section of the AT. So, this is a treat. Most of the meadows back home in Ohio are privately owned, fenced off on large home lots or farms. But this meadow is public land.

Public land is owned by all Americans, but it's not necessarily protected. A lot of National Forest and Bureau of Land Management (BLM) land is unprotected and vulnerable to road-building, oil and gas drilling, coal extraction, grazing, and commercial development. The U.S. Forest Service has been relentless in selling large tracts of our public land to commercial interests. Only land that has been designated as "Wilderness" by Congressional legislation is protected from extraction and exploitation.

In 1964, Congress passed the Wilderness Act. It preserves the last areas "where earth and its community of life are untrammeled by man, where man himself is a visitor who does not remain." The act protects wild places that private interests might otherwise carve up for tract housing or gasoline. These places receive the highest level of federal land conservation protection. The AT passes through some Wilderness land; I've already walked through a bit of designated Wilderness at Blood and Tray Mountains.

As of this writing, only three percent of American land is designated Wilderness.

I recline against my pack, gaze at the meadow in front of me, and think about wild places and the Appalachian Trail. If we want our descendants to experience the same serenity we experience while in untrammeled nature, we need to designate as Wilderness as many places as possible. But even if man never treads on these wild places, shouldn't they be allowed to exist on their own terms? There's a purpose for protecting wilderness, but does that purpose have to be linked with human use, whether it's camping, trail-hiking, or even bird-watching?

Bill McKibben, in his landmark book *The End of Nature*, advocates a radical shift in thinking. He observes that, for too long, we've had an *anthropocentric* rather than *biocentric* agenda. Man has thought of himself as being the center of the universe, of having dominion over all other forms of life. And now that we've subjugated nature enough to actually *change weather patterns* and detrimentally affect all plant and animal life, we've come to a tipping point. McKibben proposes we shift to a more biocentric view. In other words, maybe we should take a step back and change how we view ourselves as a species.

Before I start discussing philosophy with the ghosts of Hank Thoreau and Johnny Muir, I say goodbye to grandfather oak and begin another ascent. This one is very steep, and I have to stop at least a half-dozen times to catch my breath. One thing I notice in North Carolina is the sudden disappearance of poison ivy, which I'm real susceptible to. It's all over the Georgia AT, but thankfully not as prevalent here.

I eventually reach the summit—the last major summit of my hike—and soon enter Sassafras Gap, a long, flat stretch with lots of overhanging rhododendron that offers a nice, shady canopy. Rhodos are pretty, and all over the trail down here, but the low-lying branches continually snag my bulky backpack. Big is not necessarily better.

Feeling good, I start humming again. I've already done the entire second album by the Band, which has a lot about climbing down off mountains, rivers changing direction, and whispering pine trees.

Near Muskrat Creek Shelter, I see some open azure off to the left. A side path meanders toward what looks like a vista, about thirty feet off the main trail. I follow the path, through some overhanging rhodos, and emerge into a pool of sunlight. Directly in front of me is a sweeping valley. In the center are a number of distant buildings, little Lego-like shapes popping up here and there amongst the greenery. *I wonder if this little village is even on the map. There are probably people milling about, though I can't see them. Wherever they are, they're totally unaware that I'm spying on them.* Then I glance left.

Whoa. A sea of peaks and valleys, varying shades of blues and greens, rolling wavelike, southward into the mist. And I've walked all of it. *Have I really walked over all those mountains in seven days?* I feel warm and luxurious. This rocky outcrop, and these mountains, have been here since before man. For a few days, I've rested inside their blue-green belly. For a few moments, I have doubts of things earthly, and whispers of things heavenly.

Don't over-romanticize, Pete. Don't forget the timber rattler. Don't forget your little blister. I recall reading of mountain men like Kit Carson, Jim Bridger, Jim Beckwourth, and explorers like Meriwether Lewis, Zebulon Pike, and John Colter. They had more to deal with than blisters and timber rattlers, out West in unsettled, high-altitude, sub-zero country, often in complete solitude, where over the peak or around the river bend might lurk a hungry grizz or band of hostile Lakota. My 21st-century section hike is hardly perilous.

Still, I bask in the lie I've fashioned for myself. At this moment, I choose a solitary tent on a bed of pine needle over a tract house in a suburb. And a narrow, dirt path over a four-lane highway.

After Muskrat Creek, I hit another stretch of jagged rocks, which reminds me of the rock slide at nightmarish Red Clay Gap. Near the beginning of this headache, I hear voices up ahead. It's two young guys with trekking poles, headed my way. The one in front looks very tan and is wearing a large, red head scarf. His partner is short and squat, with a big black moustache. He appears to be doing most of the talking.

"You mean there are actually some other people on this thing?" I yell out as we near each other. They laugh, as I skirt to the edge of the rocks to give them passing room.

We exchange small talk, and I learn they're on a southbound section trek to Tray Gap. I tell them I've just come from there, and that they're the only people I've seen other than one person at Dick's Creek Gap. (I later calculate the distance between Tray Gap and here to be twenty-five miles.) They're surprised, telling me they hiked the AT once before and came across "hundreds" of hikers. *Is this a mind game they're playing with me?*

Another thing I haven't seen in a while is a mirror. Several times on my hike I'd remembered a scene in the Steve McQueen prison-escape movie *Papillon*. McQueen has been sent to solitary confinement on Devil's Island. One day he pokes his head out of a small hole in his prison door for a lice check. He sees the inmate in the cell next door, who's been there for years, much longer than McQueen. The guy looks ghastly. White hair, pale skin, hollow cheeks, bloodshot eyes. He asks McQueen "How do I look?" McQueen turns away in horror and slowly answers "Fine. You look fine." A couple days later the man's lifeless body is carted off.

I tell these guys about not seeing a mirror in a while, then ask them how I look.

"Ya look pretty darn good!" laughs the short guy. *Is he laughing at my question, or because I look like the dead prisoner in "Papillon?"*

It's good to meet these two, as I was really missing human company. It's also good to find out the rock slide will soon be coming to an end.

Before we continue our hikes, I mention Chester. "There's a young guy with a large pack and a sort of fluffy beard. His name's Chester. He may be northbound. If you see him, tell him Pete said hello."

"We will," says the short guy.

"Also, he may need some trail help. He seemed to be a little confused back at Dick's Creek Gap."

The two guys look at each other. Then the short guy turns to me.

"Was his beard real funny looking? Baggy pants, his pack an ugly yellow color?"

"Why, yes."

"Yeah, we saw him yesterday evening while driving through Clayton. He was at the side of the road, reading a map."

Chester had gone the wrong way.

Reunion

A few miles ahead I reach USFS 71, at Deep Gap, and I have lunch at the most sophisticated diner since Walasi-Yi: a gravel parking lot. A lone SUV with Orange County, Florida plates sits in the lot. I wonder if this vehicle belongs to the guys I just talked to.

I pull out my guide notes and study the remaining mileage. Standing Indian Campground is 3.7 miles ahead, at the end of a blue-blaze called Kimsey Creek Trail. The AT itself, however, loops northeast 21.8 miles, taking in both Albert Mountain and Standing Indian Mountain before joining the campground road.

As much as I'd like to remain hooked to my lifeline— the main AT—I decide to take the Kimsey Creek shortcut. I'd reached my goal of completing the Georgia section. I'm bruised, burned, blistered, dirty, smelly, and I miss 21st-century comforts. I'll be finishing a day early, on Saturday. But if I can contact Lynn at the campground, maybe she can change our motel arrangements in Franklin.

I pop open my flip phone and again see "NO SERVICE." I'm running out of time. This means waiting till I reach the public campground, which according to my WhiteBlaze notes has a pay telephone. I kept my flip phone battery only reluctantly, at Rance's urging, for emergency purposes. *But this is a minor emergency, isn't it? Damn, I hope I can get her in time to change the motel reservations.*

Kimsey Creek Trail starts innocently enough; a wide path along a pretty stream. But it soon becomes narrow, and for the first time I have to remove my pack and carry it in front of me. The trail then empties into a grassy service road. I follow this until it merges with a paved road. After twenty minutes without any blue blazes, I realize I'd made a mistake, and backtrack. This involves a mile of needless walking.

I return to the grassy road and only then see a blue blaze on a boulder, where an overgrown path is barely visible. *Come on, folks, how 'bout a little trail maintenance?*

Just a little further, I descend into my last grove of rhododendron, and the largest I've yet seen. It's in a tiny glade nudged against burbling Kimsey Creek, which is actually more of a large stream than creek. A great silver maple had fallen here, and there's a soft, loam clearing in front of the trunk, just big enough for a pup-tent. *Perfect riparian camping spot.* Though I'd intended to overnight at the public campground a few miles ahead, I'm pulled toward this woodland haven, with the orange glow of sunlight reflecting off the thick and shiny rhododendron leaves, and the clear water trickling over rocks. So, I become Bilbo Baggins, and pitch my tent in this secluded Shire. This time, however, I follow the Leave No Trace principle and make certain I'm a good distance from the stream.

I still want to call Lynn as soon as possible, though, so I decide to walk—without backpack—the couple miles into the campground to the pay phone, then return later. *Heck, no one is coming by here anyway.*

So, I walk. And walk. And walk.

I've violated my own maxim: ten miles on the bike trail back home is equivalent to one mile on the AT.

On the brink of tears, I give up and—once again— retrace my steps. Another half-mile of needless walking.

The good news is that this is my last night of sleeping on dirt and eating cardboard. Formal night. I've saved my best meal for tonight: Mountain House freeze-dried chili mac.

I take a cold bath in the stream, then brush my hair to make myself presentable. Dip my saucepan in the stream, then boil some water, which I mix into the chili mac packet, using my bandana as a potholder. Then gobble greedily while seated on a small birch log. Hoist my bear bag, smoke my last cheap cigar in the Gentlemen's Club by the massive maple, make my diary entry, then crawl in my tent to read Jack London by headlamp. After about an hour I click off the light and listen to the calls of the wild. Then drift to sleep. My last thoughts are of the millions of stars overhead, sparkling jewels that make the blackness less frightful. *How many millions are beyond those that my eyes can speak to me?*

The Kimsey Creek site might be the best camping location I've ever enjoyed. But the air is so succulent with mountain dew, when the drops smack the hard rhodo leaves, they sound like tiny rubber bands snapping. They're a most unusual alarm clock, and I'm awakened long before morning light.

Since I'm already familiar with part of the day's hike, having traversed it the day before, it goes quickly. Near a wooden bridge on the ground is a canister of Raid and a piece of plastic-encased notebook paper where someone scribbled "Yellojackets Under Bridge. BEE Carefull!" Then a second bridge with a directional arrow to the campground. Then a series of railroad ties, partially submerged in marshy water. Then a small meadow. After this…terra incognito.

Terra incognito turns out to be another long slog, and I have to continually search for blue blazes to make sure I'm on the trail. At the end of a long grassy road I see an outdoor amphitheater through some trees to my right. Other than occasional road crossings, this is the first sign of human society since Mountain Crossings six days prior. My blood begins to pump quicker.

After a few frustrating wrong turns, I stroll into a large open area filled with RVs of varying shapes and sizes, and my blood pumps harder again. *Back to modern living.* A few early-birds are outside and tending small morning fires. I imagine the others peering open-mouthed through their trailer windows, wondering about a bedraggled, wild-eyed mountain hermit who's probably looking for a free breakfast.

One of the trailers has a handsome, polished wood-grain sign, with the words "RIP BURDICK'S THE NAME, FLY FISHING'S MY GAME." I round the corner of the trailer and see an elderly man in a white t-shirt, sitting in a lawnchair in front of a fire. I approach him hesitantly, so as not to startle him.

"Excuse me, sir, but do you know where the campground office is?"

"It's back that-away, other side the river. Ya musta made a wrong turn."

Why didn't this bit of information surprise me?

"Oh, ok, thank you," I reply.

"You been hikin'?"

"Yessir, for about eight days."

"Seen any bears?"

(This is one of the more common questions AT hikers get from non-hikers.)

"No, but I saw some bear footprints, and bear scat."

"Oh. No bears though?"

He then asks if I was in the woods the whole time, or if I rested in any towns. I tell him Blairsville and Clayton were the two closest towns, but that I didn't visit.

"Clayton's where that banjo boy in *Deliverance* lives," he tells me, as if the banjo boy is a major Hollywood star.

"Yes, I know," I reply.

Then the door of the camper opens and a pleasant-looking, silver-haired lady emerges, holding a cup of coffee.

"Would y'all like a cup of coffee?" she asks.

"Oh, no, thanks ma'am, I just need directions."

Then the man interrupts. "He's been hikin'. Ain't seen no bears though."

"You sure you don't want a cup of coffee?" the woman asks.

"Well...sure, maybe I will after all," I answer. She hands me the foam cup and I take a long sip. The liquid is hot, but not scalding. I let the warm, syrupy elixir slide down my throat. When it hits my empty stomach, I feel a warm tingling. *Liquid sunshine. Just like Dylan's wine, the best coffee I've ever tasted.*

"That tastes so good, ma'am. Thanks very much."

I want to reassure her that I'm not just a roaming drifter, a scraggly mountain bum who periodically descends the hills for free coffee. I want her to think I'm just a "nice young man" who is concluding a short backpacking trip...even though I'm not that young, and not as nice as I like to think.

I tell her "Sorry for my appearance. I probably look a sight."

But all she says is "You look like you needed a cup of coffee."

I backtrack again and continue over the river. Before long I see a little white, clapboard building. In front is a small garden of perennials, with painted stepping stones, a ceramic frog, and a small statue of Smoky the Bear. I approach the front door and see a sign with the words "CAMPGROUND STORE," just above a colorful, wooden thrift-store clock that indicates the store opens at 9 am. I have about twenty minutes, so I slip off my pack and plop into one of two big wooden rocking chairs to the right of the door.

Soon, a man comes along to unlock the door. I recognize him because I'd seen him walking a little poodle near the "Rip Burdick" camper. Part of his face droops, as if he's had a stroke. But he has a nice smile.

I rise out of the rocker and ask directions to the pay phone. He tells me they'd removed it due to vandalism, but that I can use his cordless phone. He asks how I'd arrived at the campground, and I tell him about the trail.

"You know," he slowly drawls, "if you'd have taken that service road by the amphitheater, you'd have cut off about a half-mile."

I just take a deep breath and count to five.

Well, I finally reach Lynn, who's able to change the motel reservation. I know she's been worried, since she hasn't heard from me in five days. It's the longest we've ever gone without talking to each other.

After hanging up, I have to practically force some money on the proprietor for the long-distance call. I then step through the screen door and see a white-haired man sitting in one of the rocking chairs. I nod at him, then drop to the ground and go through my usual acrobatic maneuvers for strapping on my pack. While this is happening, the proprietor comes out and sits in the second rocking chair. Once or twice I glance at the two. Fortunately, they don't smile as I go through my routine. Instead, they stare open-mouthed, looking slightly concerned at my struggle.

I wave goodbye to the old geezers and head up the campground road, where I pick up the AT again at Wallace Gap. Despite our occasional disagreements, the AT and I by this point are like old friends, and it feels good and right to get off pavement and tromp on trail dirt again.

From Wallace Gap it's just a couple easy miles to Winding Stair Gap, then US-64 to Franklin. I leave Kip 2 leaning against a rock wall. *He'll make a superb companion for some future hiker.* I then hitch a ride with a ruddy-faced man wearing an Ole Miss ball cap, who takes me straight to the Hampton Inn.

Franklin is a town that's used to seeing AT hikers, so the motel employees aren't too freaked out when they see me. In fact, the desk clerk is extremely nice. She goes out of her way to be hospitable to a Neanderthal, even ringing my room later to see if I'm alright. It takes me a few hours to wash up, pamper my feet, get some *real* food—well, Taco Bell anyway—and dry my wallet contents, which are still damp from the first day's rain shower.

I lie back on soft pillows. I stretch out my tired legs on the spongy mattress and let my throbbing, shoeless feet catch their breath. I flick on the TV and switch between channels. *Same old nonsense.* I decide that evening info-tainment is the least offensive program going, so I leave it on local WLOS News 13. The anchor is talking about North Carolina House Bill 74, which was signed into law by the governor only two weeks prior.

This bill, passed by a Republican governor with a Republican House and Senate—the first time the party has had such a monopoly in North Carolina in over a century—introduces sweeping reform of state environmental regulations. It loosens laws concerning state landfills and highway billboards. It delays for three years cleanup of polluted Jordan Lake, located in the most populated region of North Carolina and which provides drinking water to over 300,000 residents. It eliminates protective boundaries for sensitive wetlands and streams. It also eliminates a popular, though purely advisory, Mountain Resources Commission (MRC).

I groan, then angrily click the mute button on the remote and sink deeper into my pillows. *What's the matter with these people? Why would they jeopardize the natural resources of their own state?*

Curiosity gets the better of me, so I click the mute button to restore the sound. I hear "...fracking.... extraction process...jeopardize drinking water, public health, environment..."

I click the mute button again to turn off the sound. This time, I leave it off.

(After returning home, I did some research and learned that the now-defunct MRC received no financial compensation for its work. But it was successful in obtaining non-state funds for economic development information important to the mountain regions of North Carolina. According to the North Carolina branch of the Sierra Club, "eliminating this commission will have a negative impact on the preservation of natural resources in Western North Carolina and will not save any state money."[1]

And after NC House Bill 74 was signed into law, the non-partisan *NewsObserver.com* referred to it as a "sledgehammer and blowtorch" to derail sensible environmental regulation, criticizing it as being "illogical and dangerous" and for offering numerous concessions to developers and polluters.

> The beauty of the state and the consistency of the laws that protect it are what have attracted businesses, newcomers, students and tourists. The wholesale stripping away of regulations is a misguided effort to liberate business from limits on pollution and excessive development and hardly seems like a formula for making North Carolina more appealing.[2]

---

[1] "North Carolina Sierra Club Legislative Report on 2013 Legislative Session," NC Sierra Club

[2] "McCrory Signs Regulatory Overhaul Plan, 32 More Bills," August 23, 2014, www.newsobserver.com, August 23, 2014

"A Reckless Law on NC Regulations," www.newsobserver.com, August 28, 2013

Wasn't I one of those "newcomers" and "tourists," backpacking my way through a beautiful part of the state?)

The TV sound remains off, but the screen images flicker, and my eyelids become heavy. I drift into a hazy alpha-state, dozing lightly, then waking, then dozing again. Strange dream scenes come and go. There's one scene that keeps recurring: several scrawny black bears, huddled in a fire pit, crunching on a mound of cardboard and taco shells. Outside the fire pit is a crowd of grey-suited, somber-looking men.

Then a loud knocking on my door. I yell "Just a minute!" then walk to the door, open it, and my daughter Holly wraps her arms around me. Lynn immediately follows, with a beaming smile. Then hugs and kisses everywhere, and a comment on my beard growth. It's so good to see them after eight days in the woods, and I forget all about House Bill 74, politicians, hungry bears, and taco shells.

We later treat ourselves to an all-you-can eat buffet at a nearby restaurant. During the meal, I admit to Lynn that "I don't think I'm a mountain man," and her laughter and chattiness tell me it's just what she wants to hear. The buffet food is delicious, a substantial improvement from what had sustained me on the trail. The only thing missing is some cherry-blackberry wine.

Thus ended my hike on the southernmost section of the Appalachian Trail. No, I didn't see any bears. Didn't even see a thru-hiker. But I hiked over ninety miles, traversed over twenty mountains, and averaged over twelve miles per day while carrying my home on my back. I saw beautiful mountains *from the inside*, bathed in mountain streams, and visited scenic waterfalls, a river source, and trees so ancient they sent chills up my spine. I saw bear tracks, a red salamander, an Eastern fence lizard, a dead timber rattler, and a flock of wild pheasants. I heard three barred owls, a whippoorwill, and a lonely raccoon. I saw exotic plants and colorful mushrooms.

I also learned about Leave No Trace and met hiking Samaritans who can teach us all something about selflessness and outdoors stewardship.

For the first time in my life, I didn't just *see* nature, but *felt* it.

And I made several friends. One of them is a young guy with long hair who works in a turpentine factory and has a girlfriend back home who wants to get married. Some day he hopes to visit the Rockies of Colorado. He's someone whom I can easily envision planning and completing his own thru-hike. I wonder if he'll ever do this.

Another is a young guy from Texas who hopes to complete a thru-hike. I can't envision him doing this. But I give him credit for trying.

Oh yes. I also saw a little white dog guarding a trail of candy droppings near Woody Gap.

The Appalachian Trail—Shenandoah National Park

The oldest and strongest emotion of mankind is fear, and the oldest and strongest kind of fear is fear of the unknown.

—H.P. Lovecraft

Where the Wild Things Are

Shenandoah National Park is in central Virginia. It extends along the Blue Ridge Mountains, with the Virginia Piedmont on the eastern side, and the beautiful Shenandoah Valley to the west. It was designated a national park in 1935, only two years before the AT was completed. The AT enters the park at its southernmost point, just north of Waynesboro, Virginia, and it meanders along scenic Skyline Drive to Front Royal, the northernmost tip of the park. This green Eden encompasses over a hundred miles of oak, maple, hickory, and tulip poplar trees, mountain laurel, ferns, and plentiful deer so tame you can almost touch them, as well as one of the largest concentrations of black bears on the entire trail.

The bears are particularly populous due to the large collection of public campgrounds that dot Skyline Drive. Public campgrounds mean lots of people, and lots of people mean lots of food waste. And lots of food waste draws animals, including bears.

After "Aren't you afraid to hike alone?" I often get the question, as with Rip Burdick at Standing Indian Campground, "Did you see any bears?" People love hearing bear stories. Not because bears are large. Buck deer can get large, but hikers are never asked about them. Also, it's not because bears are seldom seen, or we'd be asked if we saw any weasels. We're asked about bears, of course, due to fear.

Fear is a powerful emotion. One traumatic experience in childhood, no matter how outwardly insignificant, can dog a person for life. Adults construct all sorts of metaphorical cages to protect themselves from fears, some rational, but many equally irrational, stoked by our relentless and ever-exploitative news media. It's why certain politicians get elected who otherwise wouldn't. Fear is one of the reasons why the gun industry and its lobby, the National Rifle Association (NRA), are such a powerful force in American culture. (And we're now paying a horrific price for all those guns.)

I won't forget the burly ex-soldier I met at Red River Gorge in Kentucky. He stumbled into my campsite after dark, while I was sitting on a large rock outcrop next to a stream and puffing a stogie. He asked if he could share my camp spot. On his belt, in clear view, was a huge handgun.

"Do you mind if I stretch my hammock here?" he asked me.

"No, go right ahead," I answered.

"Thanks. I'm having trouble finding a spot. All the sites are taken, and people seem real nervous. I guess it's my gun."

Uh, yeah, that could be it, dude. Is there a reason for the weapon? After crawling in my tent later, I made sure not to crawl back out until morning, even though my bladder was full. I didn't want to startle the man.

Irrational fears extend into the safest places imaginable: the woods. Maybe it's the stories we read as children: *Hansel and Gretel, Peter and the Wolf, Where the Wild*

Things Are. Later came feature films: *The Wolf Man, Night of the Living Dead, The Edge, The Grey*. Be it bears, wolves, cougars, giant venomous snakes, bloodthirsty bats, witches, goblins, headless horsemen, zombies, Texas chainsaw killers…forests and the isolated outdoors have become metaphors for danger and fear.

Again, the reality is that the country and the forests are safer than the cities. But humans can't seem to shake certain embedded fears. And of all creatures in the woods, nothing seems to worry people more than bears.

Bears are big. An adult American black bear averages 125-550 lbs. Its cousin, the more aggressive grizzly bear (*Ursus arctos horribilis*), averages 400-750 lbs. Some freak grizzlies grow even bigger. Both species are omnivores, eating both plants and animals. But a grizz standing on its back feet can reach over nine feet in height, and can take down large mammals such as bison, moose, elk, and caribou. His claws can grow to four inches in length.

Also, although extremely rare, bear attacks do happen. The most infamous occurred in Glacier National Park on the night of August 12, 1967. On that night, two young women, Julie Helgeson and Michele Koons, were dragged from their sleeping bags by two hungry grizzlies…unbelievably, in separate incidents nine miles apart. Their bodies were eventually located by searchers. Helgeson hung on for a few hours before succumbing to blood loss. Only portions of Koons's body were found.

But nightmare incidents like August 12, 1967 occurred back when little was known about bear behavior, and campground bears were still feeding at open-air garbage dumps. The two grizz that killed Helgeson and Koons were later tracked down. One had glass imbedded in its molars, and the other had a torn paw pad, probably from stepping on broken glass. Wildlife officials speculate they were in extreme pain when they attacked.

(Soon after this happened, I read the story and saw photographs in the magazine *LIFE*. For a long while, I was convinced that all grizzlies were malevolent monsters. Films like *The Night of the Grizzly* didn't help.)

The only grizz in the lower forty-eight states are in Yellowstone and Glacier National Parks, and in small pockets of Montana and Idaho. However, there are a lot of black bears along the AT, because it skirts many Shenandoah campgrounds. It runs alongside Skyline Drive, crossing this thoroughfare a total of twenty-eight times.

Two years after my excursion through Georgia and North Carolina, in September 2015, I decided to backpack a piece of the AT in Shenandoah National Park, just north of where my family camped when I was fifteen and hiked The Priest. When I told Lynn my plans, she said angrily "I thought you said you weren't a mountain man!"

I told her I wasn't exactly a valley man, either.

In Shenandoah, I would not be lacking for human companionship, and there was a better-than-average chance I might enjoy bear companionship. Like many people, I was hoping to see a bear on my hike. On this hike, I not only saw one, I shared my campsite with one.

So, if Mr. Burdick from Standing Indian Campground is reading, here's my bear story.

I park my car at a public lot behind a Ming Garden Buffet in Waynesboro, Virginia. I'm transported to the trailhead at Rockfish Gap by my shuttle driver, Durgood Prufock Jr. (more on this colorful individual later). The first day I cover six miles, some of which finds me slogging through a relentless rainstorm. Near Beagle Gap, just after descending from a large hill crowned by an ugly cell tower, I walk under a several mature apple trees, and enjoy a tart afternoon snack.

I camp near a five-foot-high cairn that's in the middle of the trail at the top of Calf Mountain. My campsite is right next to the trail, and reminiscent of my overnight on Poor Mountain in Georgia, with good, flat stones for setting up my campstove, and just enough tree branches on which to drape my soggy clothes.

I get an early start the next day, and later water up at a spring near the shelter halfway down the mountain. While filling my canteen, I meet a hiker coming from the shelter. She's a middle-aged woman who is trekking the entire length of the trail to Manassas Gap. She calls herself "Owl." *Hmm. Shouldn't she be hiking at night?*

It's kinda nice to see someone close to my age on the trail. She moves on ahead while I fill my canteen, but I hope to meet up with her later, so we can discuss baby boomer topics like Huckleberry Hound and telephone booths. Unfortunately, I later see her ambling down a side trail off the main AT. Maybe I spooked her back at the watering hole. Later in the day, I discover my damp tighty-whities are still drying on the outside of my pack.

At the base of Calf Mountain, at Jarman Gap, I officially enter the park. It's located at a fire road near a huge gnarled tree, maybe the oldest I'd see on this entire hike. Later, at Sawmill Run Overlook, I gobble some trail mix and provide a curious spectacle to a few tourists who are cruising along Skyline Drive. My backpack is propped against a large tree as I squat on the ground, so my underwear is at least partially obscured. But if they know anything about backpacking gear, they're surely humored by my ugly, brown, outer-frame pack, which, along with my tent and sleeping bag, all of which extend high into the air, resembles a stack of Marshall amplifiers on a rock stage.

At Turk Gap, I meet my first thru-hikers: a college-age couple who'd started way up in the piney woods of Maine months earlier. They are headed for the Springer Mountain trailhead in north Georgia. They represent the advance guard of southbound thru-hikers, and they have the lean, muscular look of swift, veteran hikers. In the past, whenever anticipating a possible meet-up with a thru-hiker, I'd expected a mixture of pungent smells. But despite getting within several feet, these two are odorless. They also look clean and manicured—even the man's red beard looks shapely.

Near Riprap parking area I meet a young woman. She works as an emergency nurse in nearby Charlottesville, and she's out enjoying a sunny day hike. Then I lunch at the edge of the parking lot, where I meet another solo day hiker. I'll bump into him again, the following day, at Loft Mountain campground. His name is Jackson, a high school senior from Richmond, Virginia. Jackson's bouncing around in his pickup between campgrounds, doing short hikes on the AT, and squeezing in some summer kicks before the school year starts. Nice kid, long blond hair, really laid back, and reminds me a lot of my Georgia trail partner, Dylan.

I notice Jackson's truck has a license plate frame that says, "DON'T TREAD ON ME." But he seems too young and mellow for politics. His parents probably let him borrow their truck. Maybe they christened him after famed Confederate General Thomas J. "Stonewall" Jackson. Judging from his dour expression, Stonewall seemed like a "DON'T TREAD ON ME" kind of guy.

As I approach Blackrock Mountain, my mouth and throat begin to feel like they're caked with sawdust. But my canteen only has a few gulps of water left. I recall the many streams and springs I encountered in Georgia. Comparatively, Shenandoah is very dry. Climbing the straight ascent up the side of Blackrock taxes me. I have to stop every few minutes to regain my strength, pressing my tired body on Kip 3 as I gulp oxygen. A few sweat bees buzz around my slicky, sweaty legs.

After about twenty minutes of alternate walking and resting, my upper body hunched forward, I hear pounding ahead. I lurch my neck up as two vigorous and fit-looking hikers appear, almost out of nowhere, stomping down the steep descent. Another male-female tandem, only older.

"Oh...hi..." I gasp. Almost...didn't see you...real tired."

"Hey, you're almost there!" yells the man, in one of the cheeriest voices I've yet heard on the AT. "Just around that bend up ahead, and a little way further, and you're at the summit."

He looks about forty or so, with salt-and-pepper whiskers. His wife is heavily tanned, with aqua blue eyes, a long pigtail hanging down her back, and ample breasts.

"We're the Honeymoon Hikers!" the man chirps pleasantly, as if expecting me to recognize the name.

They explain that they're doing a southbound thru-hike...having earlier accomplished a *northbound* hike for their wedding honeymoon. In my exhaustion, I try to comprehend this feat of strength and will, but my attempt withers.

"Can you, uh...tell me...how far ahead the next...water is?"

The man tells me Dundo Picnic Grounds is only a few miles ahead, and it has a water pump. They ask if I've met any other thru-hikers, and I tell them about the red-bearded man and his companion. The woman wants to know how far ahead they are. "Oh, about a...half-day's hike...I guess." I get the impression that they're familiar with the couple, and are trying to catch up. I thank the Honeymooners for their help and turn back to the trail. *Wonder if they'll catch up. They've probably shared a shelter or two with the other couple.*

Before we part, Mr. Honeymoon asks me to look up their online trail journal if I get a chance. After I return home, I take him up on it. It's a daily diary of their hike, dry and matter-of-fact, but sprinkled with references to God, with each entry followed by the commandment to "Walk with Jesus."

99

I'm fairly certain that "Jesus" isn't the trail alias of a hiker the Honeymooners have met.

The trail is a liberal democracy and open to all sorts, including hikers who want to share their religion. Later, in the White Mountains, I meet a religious zealot of a different stripe.

I've always liked Emerson's simple dictum that "Nothing is at last sacred but the integrity of your own mind." And I get much of my spirituality—not religion necessarily, but spirituality—from dark green and brown old-growth forest, or white water rushing between red canyon walls, or a broad plain of blue ocean.

At the risk of sounding trivial, I'll just share that I think nature is a good church, and its furry, finned, feathered, and flowered parishioners can't speak for themselves. They need humans to take turns in the pulpit.

So, in the spirit of the Honeymooners...Walk with Truth and Beauty.

Blackrock Mountain summit was aptly named: huge, dark boulders stacked a hundred feet high, like a scene from the movie *Planet of the Apes*. I rest on one of the rocks, catch my breath after the long uphill climb, then savor a smooth downhill trek into Dundo Picnic Grounds.

Dundo isn't a campground, merely an extended ring of picnic tables for auto tourists. Except for one elderly couple enjoying an early supper at one of the tables, I have the grounds to myself. In the center of the grounds are basic bathroom facilities, with a hand water pump in the grass outside. I take about a half hour or so to drink up, fill my canteen, change my socks, and scrub down my sticky skin.

Before exiting the grounds, the elderly couple circle their Subaru over to the water pump and kindly offered me some granola bars and bananas. I've eaten so much granola already, I decline the bars, but I do accept one of their bananas. They slowly pull away, both wearing warm smiles. I think how we tired and disheveled hikers often provoke feelings of compassion. It's a shame it can't be like this off-trail more often. A warm smile and a generous piece of fruit are quiet virtues that go a long way.

Now it's time to find a campsite. I'm envisioning a nice, quiet, trailside site similar to Calf Mountain. But at Browns Gap, where Skyline Drive again crosses the AT, there is only an empty parking lot and a couple lonely fire roads that meander into the woods. The bright sunlight is becoming dimmer and dimmer. A few cars whizz by on Skyline Drive. I start to clear out a primitive tent site near the parking lot, while a curious whitetail deer observes me from only twenty feet away, but this cramped, very public location just doesn't feel right.

When all else fails, hit the trail. So, I start up another incline. About a half mile up...voilà! There, on the left, is my home for the night: a clearing, moderately used, with flat ground for my tent. And at the far edge of the clearing are two skinny trees, about ten feet tall. A horizontal log beam rests on two forks carved at their tops. The contraption looks a little like a pole vault bar. Someone had obviously built this thing to hang his or her food bag so marauding bears wouldn't get it.

Usually, backpackers will seek out a single tree that has a high, horizontal limb on which to hang their bear bags, then tie their rope to the tree trunk. But it can sometimes be a struggle, finding a good size tree with a limb at just the right height, and sturdy enough to hold a few pounds of food. This designer bear beam, then, is very convenient. *Surely this construction project took a lot of time. But why would someone devote so much time and energy to building it? Maybe a ranger built it.*

I pitch my tent in this clearing about twenty yards from the AT. Then unroll my sleeping bag, and toss it inside the tent, along with my nighttime needs: flashlight, foam pillow, some fresh clothes, my journal, and a yellowed copy of *The Adventures of Huckleberry Finn.*

I set up my stove on a flat rock, then find a bigger rock to use as my dinner chair. Quickly get some water boiling, dump in my packet of ramen noodles, and hunch over the pan with my spoon poised. Then I hear a noise behind me.

Turning around, I see a young woman stepping swiftly down the trail, swinging two trekking poles. She either doesn't see me, or decides to ignore me, because she continues toward the road crossing a half mile away. By now the evening's half-light has become quarter-light, and I wonder if she'll be able to find a decent campsite, since I hadn't seen much between here and Dundo Picnic Grounds several miles back.

Ramen noodles aren't vitamin-enriched, and I've never seen them on a restaurant menu, but, for me, strings of yeast in hot, flavored water is a gourmand feast. I'd covered over seventeen miles that day, and I'm as tired and sore as an Arizona pack mule. I also have some serious chafing on my inner thighs due to sweat-soaked underwear. After supper, I hang my bear bag high up on the log beam, and scrub my skillet, using my fingers and a little water. I then pack my skillet in my backpack, which I lean against a tree. The skillet has a slight residue from the noodles. But I'm not concerned.

I smear some antiseptic lotion on my thighs, then crawl into my tent. Too tired to read about Huck and Jim, I wait for darkness to fall while lying spread-eagled on my back. Then I click off my flashlight, as a multitude of nocturnal insects begin their nightly symphony.

It's a long while before I fall asleep. I'm still buzzing from the day's activities, and one alpha cricket keeps an incessant screeching for hours on end. But eventually I fall into a deep, deep slumber.

At home I wear earplugs. They help me sleep more soundly. But I promised Lynn I wouldn't use them out here in the woods. So, the gruff sound that awakes me is loud and unmistakable.

Still spread-eagled on my back amid some weird, puffy dream, my eyelids suddenly shoot open.

Oh, boy. That's no cricket outside my tent.

The sounds are various: sniffs, snorts, and grunts. Beastly and guttural. They're directly outside my tent's mosquito netting, which is at my head. (Later, I recall the animal as sounding like a bad-tempered, overweight hog. But there are no wild pigs in these mountains.)

I slide down toward the foot of the tent. I listen to the snorting for several seconds. The only animal around here that could make those baritone notes is a large bear.

From my sleepy haze, I recall something I'd read about loud noises helping to scare off bears. About going on the offensive. Not showing fear.

By now, I'm fully awake. And I do feel fear. Mainly because I can't see the thing, and we always fear the unknown, and the things we can't assign shape to. I don't know how big he is, how close he is, or his personality. But I don't want him clawing his way into my tent.

I take a deep breath. Then I take action.

"HEY, WHAT'S GOIN' ON!" I yell in a shaky voice, obviously not expecting a reply.

There's a spooky silence for about a second. One second of fraught intensity that I'll never forget.

Then I hear what sounds like a locomotive crashing through forest. Then...silence again.

I lie still for about five minutes. I turn on my flashlight. I pull out my flip phone from my shorts, push the button, wait a short while, and then glance at the time: 3:02 a.m. At this point, I'm no longer scared, but I suddenly feel very groggy. The bear had awakened me from one my best sleeps in several days. But, after about five minutes, I'm awake enough to venture outside. I strap my flashlight to my head, unzip the mosquito netting, and step into the clearing.

103

I first check my backpack, which is about thirty feet from my tent. *Looks ok.* Then I walk a short distance to the right, over to the bear beam. I shine my flashlight into a void of blackness. *Bear bag is undisturbed. Everything seems fine.* I hear the rhythmic drone of the crickets. But there are no other sounds.

I duck back into my tent, hoping to get another few hours of sleep. But I remain awake.

What if he comes back? Do bears do that? I'm lying stock still on my back with my arms pinned to my sides, like I'm having an MRI in one of those closed machines. *Black bears aren't grizzly bears. They don't attack humans unless it's a mother protecting her cubs. There's no reason why I can't go back to sleep.*

Then I notice something: the crickets are silent.

Do insects get quiet when a bear is in the vicinity? How could they, they're not that intelligent...are they? Do insects even have brains? If so, how big are insect brains? Maybe the sun is rising. I think they get quiet once daylight arrives. Yeah, that's it. Still looks dark out there, though. How big is a black bear's brain? Is he smart enough to sense that I'm scared? Why should I be scared? Is it from lack of sleep? Are there bear cubs nearby? God, I wish daylight would arrive. Should I climb a tree? Black bears don't climb trees. Wait a sec...they do according to Rance. Maybe Rance was just bullshitting. Hell, why did I have to choose this campsite?

My insomniac thoughts become more disjointed and paranoid. Then I hear rustling in the brush.

Oh shit, bear's comin' back!

This time I don't yell out...not yet, anyway. I pull my headlight off my head, then flick it on several times so it's on flashing red mode. I quickly unzip the tent in case I need to make a getaway.

The rustling gets louder. Then I hear snorting. *Shit. Time to yell.*

"HEY! GET ON OUTTA HERE YOU OLD BEAR!"

But the snorting gets louder. *He ain't goin' away. Better skedaddle.*

I step out of the tent with my arms covering my head just in case I get hit by clawed rage. But the snorting is coming from the foot of the tent this time. I walk slowly backwards toward the fire ring, holding the flashing red light high. It's still very dark, and I can only make out the outline of my tent and a few nearby trees. Then I hear the grunts again. I'm able to pinpoint exactly where they're coming from.

Gotta think quick. I decide to take the offensive. Waving my light in front of me, I move toward the grunts and begin yelling at the top of my voice.

"AHHHHHHHHHH!"

At this point I'm at the edge of the clearing. Then, I hear bushes shaking, and the monstrous barreling-through-the-brush sound again. It only lasts seconds. Then all is quiet.

I stand in the same spot, frozen with indecision, for at least five minutes. But I hear no more noises. Then distant trees begin to appear, and the blackness softens. *I guess those insects sensed dawn before I did.*

I move back inside my tent, sitting cross-legged for about a half hour. It's the last I hear of Gentle Ben for the night.

Much later, I think of all the screaming I'd done, and emerging from my fabric cave with arms draped over my head, not to mention all my crazed insomniac thoughts.

Who truly was the "wild" thing on this night?

One of the many curses of aging is that the after-effects of insomnia are more brutal. My head feels like a bowling ball balanced precariously on my shoulders. The best antidote, for me, has always been exercise in cool morning air, and I know I'll be alright once I hit the trail.

Once it becomes light enough to see clearly, I gather my stuff from inside the tent, step outside, and hastily pack. After packing, I chomp on a Pop-Tart—while being observed by the same sociable deer from the night before—then look around for telltale signs of my other nighttime guest. The only evidence is a small patch of dirt that looks like it may have been clawed up during a search for grubs. It's about twenty feet from the head of my tent.

Must've occurred during his first visit. Hard to believe my head was that close to the beast.

I'm not sure why the bear got so close to my tent. Certainly, he smelled me and my sweaty clothes and skin (if not the antiseptic lotion). Maybe he was attracted by my skillet. I hadn't used soap on it, but it was still clean other than a slight noodle film on the surface, and I'd stuck it deep into my pack. He may have smelled my bear bag. I'd wrapped all my foodstuffs in either plastic or foil. But a bear can supposedly detect human food from up to a mile away. I'll never know the reason for his coming so close.

As I start down the trail, I have a humorous thought: *It's too bad I never saw him. We might have hit it off.*

I'm not more than a hundred yards from my campsite when I hear the now-familiar crashing sound. I look to the right and glimpse a large, black form pounding through the undergrowth, over the hillside. He never turns around. I stand in the same spot and grip my camera tightly for about five minutes, hoping he'll peek over the hill. But he remains hidden.

In hindsight, I'd probably invaded his feeding grounds earlier that night, and he was waiting for me to leave the next morning. The designer bear beam is there for a reason; others had probably also had their night dreams disturbed. I'm surprised there's no sign saying "BEAR LIVES HERE. TRESPASS AT YOUR OWN RISK. HE REALLY LIKES RAMEN NOODLES."

Later, I have a strange thought that maybe my experience is one episode in a recurring drama. Maybe the

Browns Gap bear does this with every overnight hiker. In fact, maybe that curious deer is his sidekick, his Boo-Boo. Or maybe the deer acts as a Greek chorus for this bit of woodland theatre, advising the bear and offering commentary on the action. Then again, maybe my imagination is running wild.

I'm glad we got to meet, if only briefly. He was an adult bear, and black as the previous night's darkness. He was the second bear I've seen in the wild, after the one outside Boulder, Colorado in 1983. But that encounter wasn't nearly as, shall we say, "intimate." Now I can claim to have seen wild bears on both sides of the Mississippi. Could there be a grizz in my future? Do I want one in my future?

Three days later, on Labor Day, I arrive at popular Skyland Lodge, the endpoint of my hike. Vehicles are stacked in the parking lot, adults and children enter and exit the restaurant and lodge like immigrants at Ellis Island, and the smell of bus exhaust stings my nostrils. I find a solitary spot away from the horde, under a maple tree, near the dumpsters behind the restaurant. While I can still hear the low drone of the tourists, my only companions are two young women leaning against the dumpster while on a cigarette break.

At about 7 p.m. outside the lodge, my shuttle driver, Durgood Prufock Jr., pulls up, his yellow pickup plastered with signs advertising his shuttle service. I load my gear in the truck bed and hop in front.

Durgood would be a great model for a character in a television sitcom. Short and pudgy, he talks with a sometimes-incomprehensible Southern accent, and sounds like he's chronically short of breath, occasionally grunting mid-sentence. He relishes conversation (and Coors beer), and at one time he served on the Waynesboro City Council.

("Ah never talk 'bout national pol-tics. Gits ya inta trouble.
But ah'll talk yer ear off 'bout local and state pol-tics.")

Durgood has been shuttling hikers for thirteen years, and
estimates he's hauled several thousand of them. On our
drive back to Waynesboro, he tells me about some of the
more memorable ones: the guy he picked up at the airport
who wore a three-piece suit and penny-loafers, and planned
to buy all his gear at Wal-Mart. ("He gave me the creeps.")

Also, the mysterious man who carried nothing but a
white duffel bag. ("He never said what wuz in it, and ah
never ast. He wuz creepy, too.")

He said the capper was a guy he called Rambo, who
wore full camouflage, carried a handgun, and had a knife
the size of a bayonet. ("Strange man. He looked like he
wuz goin' inta battle. We did'n talk much. Just 'bout the
weather.")

Thinking of the two young women who were murdered
near Skyland Lodge years ago, I ask him about the
incidences of crime on the AT in Shenandoah.

"Thar ain't much at all. Most of it's jes minor mischief,
and happens near a road crossin'. Horny teenage boys
who've bin drinkin' on a Saturday night, and go up the trail
a little ways lookin' for women (grunt). The further ya git
away from the roads, the safer ya are."

His comment triggers my memory of where I crossed
Skyline Drive at Browns Gap. I narrate my bear story,
hoping to entertain him. But I guess Durgood's heard it all
before, because he merely reciprocates with his own story.

"Ah shuttled two young women from Wisconsin one
time," he relates. "They wuz real 'cited 'bout hikin', but
tol' me the only thing they were 'fraid of wuz bars (grunt).
They had convinced themselves they wuz goin' to be
attacked by a bar."

I laugh.

"Ah said 'Lemme git some gas here, an ahm goin' to
setcha straight.' After ah got back in my truck, I tol' 'em
that black bars ain't the same as grizzly bars. They don'

attack people (grunt). Ah said that thar has never bin a bar attack on humans in the state of Vuhginia."

"What did they say?" I ask.

"You'd a thought ah lifted five pounds offa thar shoulders!" he said. "They wuz so relieved to hear that. They 'bout threw their arms 'roun me. Ah don't know what it is, but somewhere 'tween the Midwest and here (grunt, grunt) people git this notion that black bars is vicious man-eaters. It just ain't true."

I ask Durgood if he heard from them after their hike.

"Yep. They couldn't git over what ah tol' 'em 'bout bars. After they got home ta Wisconsin, they sent me a big block'a cheese. That wuz nice. But ya'll take a look at this fat boy here. Cheese is the last thing ah need."

The Appalachian Trail—White Mountains

"If future generations are to remember us with gratitude rather than contempt, we must leave them a glimpse of the world as it was in the beginning, not just after we got through with it."

—Lyndon Johnson

Peakbaggers and Presidents

Backpacking on the Appalachian Trail, or any hike on a long trail, can tinker with a person's expectations and sense of reality. I'd already discovered the cruel reality of mileage on the trail. There were moments when I was convinced that AT volunteers and mapmakers had conspired to play a mad joke on hikers. Time and again I experienced the uplift of seeing, for example, "Jack's Shelter 0.5 miles," followed by a trudge for what seemed like multiple miles and hours, before finally arriving at a blue blaze with a sign saying "Jack's Shelter 0.3 miles"

It was inconceivable to me that distances on the trail could be so seemingly elastic and arbitrary. I'd destroyed my walking stick on a peak in north Georgia during a peak of frustration. And many times since then I'd unleashed a flurry of expletives after having the rug—or trail—pulled out from under me.

After my Shenandoah hike, however, I felt confident. I'd shared a campsite with a black bear. I'd also set a daily mileage personal best: 17.8 miles between Browns Gap and Hightop Hut. And I'd finished Shenandoah much sooner than anticipated. I was becoming more assured about what to do and what not to do on a solo section hike, and was gradually working my way toward more demanding hikes.

Therefore, I decided to up the ante. Originally, I'd planned to gracefully end my Appalachian Trail romance with a tranquil hike through the Berkshires of Massachusetts, and maybe do a side excursion up Monument Mountain, outside the town of Great Barrington. This small mountain is where my favorite writer, Herman Melville, lunched one day with Nathaniel Hawthorne and Oliver Wendell Holmes, before writing his masterpiece, *Moby-Dick*. I was looking forward to lunching at the very spot where these titans convened. Monument Mountain is very close to the AT.

But after Shenandoah, I said *Why play it safe? I'm fifty-seven and not getting younger. Challenge yourself. Ramp it up. You'll be that much more prepared for the PCT and CDT.*

So, I changed my plans. In May 2016, I settled on a section of the AT that many veteran AT hikers consider the most scenic, as well as the most arduous: the White Mountains of New Hampshire.

The White Mountains are in the northern part of the state and include a string of lofty peaks called the Presidential Range. They're named after early American presidents (Washington, Adams, Jefferson, Madison, etc.) as well as one more recent president (Eisenhower) and some non-presidential political notables (Daniel Webster, Henry Clay, etc.). Just outside this range are a few other presidents and celebrities (Lincoln, Garfield, Lafayette, etc.). I like reading about American history, so walking through these names appealed to me, and I looked forward to "bagging" a few of them. It was also a little daunting. Was I up to the task of sharing space with Washington, Lafayette, Jefferson, and Lincoln?

Of the peaks in the Presidential Range, the tallest and most famous is Mount Washington. It's the second tallest mountain east of the Mississippi River, just behind Clingman's Dome in the Great Smoky Mountains. It's 6,288 feet tall, and the mountaintop is frequently obscured by clouds. The peak is infamous for its sudden weather fluctuations and is billed as having the most unpredictable weather of any "small" mountain in the world. Until recently, it held the world record for the highest wind velocity: 231 miles per hour, recorded in 1934. Mountain climbers preparing to climb Mount Everest and K2 use Mount Washington for training.

It seems perverted that a hiking trail dribbles over this menacing colossus of granite. But the Appalachian Trail, as well as sundry side trails, curls upward into the clouds to the pinnacle. So does an auto road, and a passenger railway. Therefore, despite several people each year dying of cardiac arrest or exposure on Mount Washington and neighboring peaks, the people keep coming. Now, it's my turn.

I explored the internet for some preliminary research and ran across a "Best Hikes" website that recommended a hike between Kinsman Notch in the southern end of the Whites, and the town of Gorham at the northern end. It seemed lengthy, but certainly could be accomplished in about a week, based on my two previous sections, and my daily hiking average of about fifteen miles.

I contacted a former hiker who still used his trail alias of "Golden Eagle," a resident of Gorham who operates his own shuttle service, and who agreed to transport me from Gorham to Kinsman for a modest fee. We arranged a meetup date over Memorial Day Weekend. This would give me two weekends, a holiday, and four paid vacation days in which to complete my hike.

But the more I read about the White Mountains, the more apprehensive I became. I read testimonials about broken ankles on the rocky trails, and saw photographs of boulders the size of garbage trucks and cliff faces that required ladders. I learned that, even in early June, temperatures above treeline could drop rapidly in a moment's notice. I read one story about a man half my age who became trapped on one of the mountains and succumbed to hypothermia. Near his curled, frozen body, rescuers found several dozen wooden matches, scattered like skinny cigarette butts, that he'd vainly attempted to light in the biting wind.

I called back Golden Eagle and told him I was changing plans and would be shortening my hike. Instead of Kinsman Notch, I would start at Franconia Notch, 10.3 miles further north. This would provide a time window in case I somehow became delayed.

Fondly remembering Chad's technology dissertation at Woods Hole Shelter in Georgia, I also decided to upgrade and bolster my moribund equipment. First came the pack. I purchased a bright-blue, inner-frame Gregory pack to replace my sickly, brown outer-frame model (the tag on my old pack was so faded, I couldn't make out the manufacturer). I liked the convenience of the old pack's space and pockets, and it still seemed strong and durable, but a softer, inner-frame design might prove less antagonizing to my shoulder. It would also force me to invest in a smaller sleeping bag, since now I'd have to stuff the bag *inside* the pack, rather than stacking it on top of an outer frame and frightening other hikers by my resemblance to a ten-foot-tall Frankenstein monster.

I found a good 25-degree sleeping bag that conserved space. Also, I got a new and improved sleeping pad in case I encountered cold ground, and a blow-up pillow for added comfort. I traded the bulky canteen for a 48-ounce Nalgene water bottle that I could also stuff inside my pack. And instead of a large, traditional camera, I decided to rely on my pocket-sized cellphone for photos. (I still don't own a computerized phone; I don't totally shun immersive technology, but I severely ration it—like the Amish). With the canteen and camera consigned to the dustbin, no longer would I have anything dangling from my neck to revive my shoulder problem.

Anticipating possible cold weather, I bought an expensive pair of heat-retaining, base-layer long underpants, and made sure to pack a winter cap and gloves. I also had an old pair of winter running pants that I performed surgery on, cutting out the heavy cotton lining and leaving the nylon outer shell. These would keep my legs somewhat warm without adding too much weight. My son Nick had bought me a good polyester winter jacket as a Christmas present, and I stuffed this in the bottom of my pack for emergency.

I never looked at myself in the mirror, but the transformation from 1970s dirtbag hippie to 2016 designer dude must have been striking. No longer would I hear "old school" from younger hikers, or see their eyes grow larger as my gargantuan pack approached them on the trail.

But although I looked a little different in some respects, the maverick hadn't completely sold out. I continued to shun handheld computers and GPS devices, and I determined that a good, solid walking stick, like Kip, was as good as or better than a pair of flashy trekking poles. (No offense, Ed.) And the dirty red bandana remained wrapped around my head.

I arrive at the parking lot at Rattle River, just east of Gorham, much earlier than expected. Golden Eagle has no other shuttles that morning, though, so he's fine with picking me up sooner than we'd agreed on. I rest against a boulder—the first of many I would encounter—and he soon pulls his van into the lot. He's much older than I anticipated, but muscular, with thinning hair and a short, tight ponytail.

On the drive to Franconia, I learn that Golden Eagle is 82 years old and originally from Louisiana, where he still lives during the winter months. In summers, he migrates to Gorham to escape the heat and humidity, where he lives in a trailer. I also learn that he was in the army, where he worked at deciphering Morse code. Then he worked in civilian life as a switchboard operator.

"Did you serve during Vietnam?" I ask him.

"Thankfully, no. I was after Korea, and left the service right when the Vietnam horror show started," Golden Eagle says, somberly. I think of Ed and Stan, who had to deal with the Iraq War horror show.

There's an awkward silence. I try to extend the conversation without being controversial.

"I was lucky and missed getting drafted into 'Nam by a few years," I finally offer. "My dad and I had a few conversations about 'Nam. He served during World War 2 and Korea."

"All wars are bad," he says in a low tone, "and only a few have been justified. America can't go twenty years without plunging into another one. Dwight Eisenhower warned of a growing military-industrial complex. It's here."

Golden Eagle's comment triggers thoughts of my own work for twenty years as an aerospace technical writer. The work has not always been commercial-related. I'm not a pacifist, and I'm aware of how America has defended democracy worldwide, but I also know how it's thrown its weight around, in Vietnam, Latin America, and many other places. I often feel guilty assisting it, if for only just a bit.

But the earlier awkwardness begins to soften, since I discover we think along similar lines.

Feeling confident, I continue the conversation. "My dad was always sympathetic to Vietnam veterans. He felt they were treated abysmally by our government, and the general

public. I agree, but I also think Vietnam protesters were
totally justified."

Golden Eagle doesn't say anything for a while, and now
I worry that I was overconfident, and maybe touched a sore
spot. Then, in a strong, confident voice, as if he's rehearsed
it and said it many times before, he neatly wraps up the
topic:

"I'm still waiting for the day when soldiers and veterans
can be respected without being glorified, and conscientious
objectors can be respected instead of stigmatized. Not sure
we'll ever get there."

Golden Eagle and I continue to chat in spurts during the
half-hour drive. Unlike my earlier shuttle drivers Rance and
Durgood, he offers no hiking advice, which I'm a little
surprised at, since the White Mountains have a reputation
for being demanding. I flatter myself that I must be
showing self-assurance and conveying experience. Then
again, maybe he figures I'll find out for myself how
demanding these mountains are.

Before long he pulls to the side of the highway. With
cars whizzing by, I drag out my pack, and pay our agreed-
upon fee. He gives me a strong, confident handshake. Then
I start down the incline toward Whitehouse Brook, which
flows under Interstate 93.

As I step along the well-worn path running along the
stream in the cool shade under the interstate bridge, I hear
the cars swoosh overhead. *Before long the only sounds I'll
be hearing are my breathing and footsteps. I wonder how
my shoulder will fare with this new pack.* I glance here and
there for straight, dead tree branches that might be lying in
the brush. Not only does a solid walking stick provide
stability, but it's nice to have a companion while hiking
alone, even if the companion is inanimate.

In less than five minutes I'm already climbing at a sharp
angle. It's early afternoon so I only have a few hours before
I'll need to make camp. My immediate target is Liberty
Springs Campsite about three miles ahead, although I'm

hoping to make it at least to the summit of Mount Lincoln, and maybe over the top of Mount Lafayette, which is a whopping 3,500-foot climb ahead.

Like most tentsites in the Whites, Liberty Springs charges a small fee, the proceeds going to the Appalachian Mountain Club, which helps maintain the trail. But eight dollars so I can have a wooden platform under my tent? Are AT hikers that opposed to spreading their tents on the ground? I grew up learning to camp in the woods and scraping away my own flat spot between roots and rocks, so I don't understand the appeal of a wooden platform. If it rains, my tent's going to get wet anyway.

But evidently a lot of backpackers today are drawn to these platforms, almost as much as they're drawn to shelters. I can't help thinking the reason is more social than comfort. Humans have an evolutionary yearning to be with other humans …ironically, even after we've made a conscious decision to submerge ourselves in wilderness and *separate* ourselves. We need a connection to society even if we pretend we don't. And the electronic devices we carry function as more than just communication and navigational devices. They also serve, like Linus's omnipresent blanket, as emotional safety nets. They remind us that we're "civilized" creatures who have succeeded in smoothing the rough edges of our indifferent and hostile universe.

I wonder what John Muir would think of today's creature comforts. He disappeared for weeks at a time, in wilderness far more austere than what exists today, with nothing more than a few pieces of clothing and some biscuits and tea.

After experimenting with several walking sticks and discarding them for various reasons (too curved, not strong enough, too thick, thin, short, long…) I find one that feels just right, like Goldilocks' porridge. *Ok Kip, it's just you and me on this crazy journey.*

As in Shenandoah, I encounter a lot of day hikers out for a holiday weekend stroll. It's easy to identify day hikers, because they're usually in groups of two or more, they converse a lot, their clothes are clean, and they carry smaller packs (if any). I expect they'll start to thin as I get farther from the road, and especially after Memorial Day passes. Depending on the situation, such as how tired I am or how many are in the group, I either nod and say "Hello," or I ask them where they're headed and where they're from (which sometimes leads to further conversation).

I may avoid tent platforms and shelters, but I'm not completely antisocial, and I do enjoy sharing time with nice people on the trail.

About a half hour into my climb of Mount Lincoln, I'm leaning on Kip to catch my breath. *Not a good sign.* My back felt strong in the weeks leading up to my hike, and thus far there's no stiffness or aching, but I shouldn't be getting this tired so soon. It's primarily a straight ascent, no switchbacking, and the farther I go the more rock I see.

Eventually, I arrive at Liberty Springs Campsite. It's on the left, several horizontal platforms wedged into the side of the mountain. There's already a hodgepodge of red, yellow, and blue tents pitched on the decks, with loud laughter and conversation. It's not what I'm looking for.

I continue my ponderous climb up Liberty Ridge, feeling like mercury that imperceptibly rises inside a thermometer. I'm now taking many breaks to catch my breath on the steep, rocky slope. Finally, I arrive at an open area with a tilted, wooden trail sign. My options are a sharp left on a slope down Old Bridle Path Trail, or an innocent-looking climb to the right on Falling Waters Trail. The formal letters etched on the sign say nothing about the AT, although someone has defaced the sign by carving "AT" on the wooden arm that points left.

Why doesn't this sign have official indication of Appalachian Trail direction? I learn later that all the White Mountain trails use more vivid and colorful local names instead of using the AT acronym. Many of these trails were blazed long before the Appalachian Trail was conceived, dating to the 1800s, and the Appalachian Mountain Club (AMC), which helps maintain the AT, honors these historic blazers by retaining the original trail names.

I'm for history and tradition, but now I'm confused as to which trail to follow. *Should I trust this carving? It could be some wag playing a prank.* Going left doesn't feel right, so I turn right. After about twenty yards, though, Falling Waters Trail doesn't feel right, either. I return to the sign.

I remove a plastic bag from my pants pocket, open it, and pull out a folded paper package: my David Miller AT guide. *It's probably time I learn how to use the various symbols and notations on this thing.* After my eyeballs roll over the paper for a while, it appears that I should, indeed, turn left on Old Bridle Path, which is what I do. Going right could have been disastrous. Next to injury or illness, my biggest fear while hiking is accidentally becoming diverted on the wrong trail. It's not only additional exertion that I don't need or want, a wrong turn would severely hamper my timing and logistics. *At the signpost, up ahead, the next stop...The Twilight Zone!*

For the next half hour or so it's a relatively easy flat stretch that feels good after the arduous climb. It gives me an opportunity to chew on the scenery. In addition to the omnipresent rock, I notice a lot of thick hemlock and azalea, and a goodly amount of shiny white birch. As I start to work my way above treeline, I see increasing amounts of low-lying bird's nest spruce. Eventually, even the shabby spruce disappears, and I'm scrambling on bare rock, steadying myself by poking Kip into the granite crannies and using my free hand to grasp nearby branches and pull myself upward.

I didn't know it at the time, but I'm following the same route as Guy Waterman did sixteen years earlier...before he deliberately lay down and froze to death.

Waterman is well-known to serious mountaineers in the Northeast. A complicated man of diverse talents, he was a speechwriter for Eisenhower, Nixon, and Ford, and played jazz piano in Washington D.C. clubs for fun and extra money. In the early 1970s, he abandoned the corporate world and purchased a parcel of land near East Corinth, New Hampshire. Here, he and his wife Laura built a one-room cabin and lived on vegetables and roots. Except for a Subaru for transportation (a vehicle they parked in an isolated spot a mile from the cabin) they shunned all modern conveniences. Their only money came from savings and occasional royalty checks from books and articles they wrote together, including their pioneering book *Backwoods Ethics: A Guide to Low-Impact Camping and Hiking*, one of the first to posit the Leave No Trace philosophy.

Both Guy and Laura were relentless hikers. Each had bagged all forty-eight of New Hampshire's significant peaks, on multiple occasions, from multiple directions, including in winter. Devoted to each other and their beloved White Mountains, they were revered by a tight-knit community of fellow climbers, hikers, peakbaggers, and wilderness advocates.

But Guy was also tormented by internal demons. He had three sons by an earlier marriage, but had a cold, troubled relationship with all. The two eldest, Bill and legendary mountaineer Johnny, ultimately disappeared without a trace into the whiteness of Alaska. And as he got older and began suffering the infirmities of age, Waterman began having spells of depression. He was also increasingly frustrated by what he saw as indifference to the wilderness ethics he promoted.

On the morning of February 6, 2000, Guy handed Laura a few pages of a memoir he'd written. She was in tears, since he'd already prepared her for what he was about to do. They hugged a long time, then he drove his Subaru to Franconia Notch (parking on the opposite side of Interstate 93 from where I started my hike). He hiked up Franconia Ridge toward Mount Lafayette.

Around noontime, a local hiker passed him on Old Bridle Path near where it connects with Greenleaf Trail, near an AMC hut. The hiker thought it seemed late to be making an ascent, especially with a sub-zero cold front approaching. He later described "a real Old Man of the Mountain," with a "thick, heavy beard, and some pretty old gear."[3] The hiker assumed the man was merely hiking to the hut, then would turn around. He didn't know that Waterman was headed to the summit. The nearby Mount Washington Observatory would record that night's low temperature at minus sixteen degrees Fahrenheit, with wind velocity between seventy and ninety miles-per-hour.

It was several days later that Waterman was located by friends. He was laying on his side just off the edge of the trail, near a sub-peak of Mount Lafayette. Next to him was his walking stick; a large, wooden staff he'd inherited from his father, the man who'd taught him to climb.

Waterman deliberately chose Mount Lafayette on which to end his life. It was the first peak he summited after quitting the city and moving to New Hampshire. It was also a mountain that he'd scaled while hiking with all three of his sons. And, over many years, he'd devoted countless hours to maintaining the trails leading up and over the peak: erecting scree walls and rocky cairns, constructing log steps, replenishing vegetation, shoring up erosion, painting discreet trail markers.

Waterman was a model of environmental stewardship. Seen in this light, the defaced sign I'd seen back at the top of Liberty Ridge was coldly ironic.

---

[3] https://www.outsideonline.com/1907636/natural-death

Glancing Back at Shangri-La

Old Bridle Path eventually turns eastward and becomes Greenleaf Trail. Near this curve is an AMC hut. These huts are nothing like the shelters of Virginia and Georgia that I was familiar with. They're essentially mountain hotels, maintained by a summer staff of young people, and they offer warmth, comfortable beds, bath facilities, and hot, hearty meals to upwards of forty people per night. Problem is, many require reservations, and there's also a substantial overnight fee (at least, substantial to a cheap sonofabitch like me). Later, I'll indulge in the luxury of one of these huts, but on my first night, I'm still strong, and I brought my tent for a reason, and there's still enough daylight left to get up and over Lafayette. So, I continue.

As I plunge deeper into the Whites, I notice that I'm yanking on branches more frequently to help get over the boulders or to steady myself on steep descents. I've never tried the dual trekking poles like I see so many other hikers using these days. Maybe they provide better stability...I don't know. But I would think they'd be a hindrance in rough terrain like this, which often requires a free hand. In the days to come, I'll slip and fall several times, and without a free arm to grab branches or brace falls, my scrapes could easily have been sprains or breaks.

Perhaps Guy Waterman would agree: holding a hunk of timber feels natural. The wood is much "warmer" than shiny, mass-produced, aluminum trekking poles. And a walking stick has individuality. Every walking stick I've used thus far has been slightly different. Kip 1 was slightly curved, Kip 2 was smooth, shiny, and straight, Kip 3 had a small knot at the top for grasping guidance, and my current stick is slightly tapered at the bottom end, to better fit into cracks and crevasses.

Just like people, natural walking sticks have their own physiques and personalities.

Eventually, I summit an unknown peak and reward myself with some trail mix and a few gulps of water. The view is less than stunning due to overcast skies. But the alpine landscape is strange and exciting. I haven't experienced such an alien setting since I climbed Long's Peak in Colorado back in 1983.

It is granite everywhere. Imposing granite boulders, granite rock washes, crunchy granite pebble underfoot. The fog and cloud soup surrounding me is grey, the rock is grey, everything's muted except a few spots of color in the distance indicating other backpackers. Occasionally, my head feels swimmy from the thinning oxygen, which accentuates the overall weirdness. *Is that Mount Lafayette up ahead?* I don't know, but I follow the cairns and continue to move skyward. Even at this great height I continue to see hikers, most of whom shoulder small packs that indicate either a short day-hike or one-nighter.

I amble through the rocky moonscape and eventually arrive at the tallest peak: Mount Lafayette. Here, I wander off-trail, then perch on one of the highest outcroppings to rest. There are a few couples sharing the peak with me, but they don't seem to want to converse, so I keep to myself.

Since all views are obscured, there's nothing much to do here except rest and reflect. But resting and reflecting is comforting. I've just bagged my first peak in the Whites, and it feels great.

I think about Greenleaf Hut to the west, buried somewhere in the cloudy mist. *Should I have stayed there?* But I'm still hoping to locate a tentsite below treeline. I dread having to set up my tent in the dark. I've done it before, and it's no fun struggling in a strange place in blackness to locate a flat and smooth tent surface, then having to pull out my gear and fix dinner in blackness. I usually aim for 6 p.m. as a curfew, though sometimes this extends to 7 p.m. I realize I'm running out of time, so I tread faster, hoping to soon get below treeline and find some good real estate.

(Note: it is illegal to camp above treeline in the Whites, and dangerous. Many hikers have been killed after being struck by lightning on exposed ridges. Still, there are hikers that do so, out of either necessity or ignorance.)

The climb down Lafayette is just as grueling as the climb up. I never expected so many rocks and boulders, and maintaining correct footing on this rough terrain requires all my concentration. But although there are no trees here in this nether land, the AT is well-marked, with periodic white paint bars on the boulders, and numerous rock cairns to assist hikers with direction. Guy Waterman and his gang of mountain goats performed a great service.

Under one of these cairns lie the hiking boots of Johnny Waterman, which Guy buried as a permanent memorial to his lost son.

As daylight ebbs and my muscles grow weak, I worry about finding an open campsite below treeline. The southbound hikers are thinning out. Other than one young guy just north of Lafayette, I'm the only solo hiker. Concern builds, and despite my tired muscles, I push myself harder. This is when backpacking can get dangerous: one misstep could result in a broken ankle, or worse.

Eventually, finally, I dip below treeline. The trail becomes narrow and dense with pygmy spruce once again, and the scree crunches under my lug soles. I glance left and right, repeatedly, for the next hour, but I'm unable to locate a wilderness lot big enough for my oblong tent. Occasionally, I step off-trail and kick around the brush, but there's nothing accommodating.

I soon enter a low, flat section where the hemlock trunks thicken. Still, no open spot. *Maybe just a little further.* No open stop. *Just a bit further.* No open spot.

I finally see an area to the right where I can barely squeeze my tent. Although the only water is a swampy area on the opposite side of the AT, and I'm less than the 200-foot minimum trail clearance recommended by the AMC, it's the best I can do. Darkness is approaching, and possible rain. So, I squeeze between a few seedlings, stretch out my tent, and prepare my sleeping quarters.

God, my legs are killing me! I don't think I could've gone a step further. In reality, I probably could have; one thing that recreational marathon running has taught me is that one's brain is stronger than one's body.

I manage a quick meal of noodles just as it starts sprinkling. I'm too tired to hang a bear bag, write in my journal, or do any reading. So immediately after my last slurp of broth, it's lights out. It had been only a half-day hike, but it was as grueling as I've experienced. I'm only at the northern base of Mount Lafayette...*what could lay ahead?*

Morning arrives with a stream of warm, happy sunlight. This is my favorite time for hiking. I'm still sore from yesterday's grueling ascent of Mount Lafayette, but I'm refreshed from sleep. All is dry except my tent covering. For the first time, I begin to think that a domed tent might be better than my oblong design, because the rain created a puddle in the middle of the covering. A dome would've offered better drainage.

I pack up and quickly devour a Pop-Tart. Another thing I've learned is that I don't like large, long breakfasts while hiking. When hiking or camping outdoors, I *love* a hot mug of dark-roast coffee in the morning, but the preparation involves too much time and logistics.

As I start toward Mount Garfield, I comfort myself with the thought that today should bring fewer rocks and boulders. I'm wrong.

The hike up Garfield is a difficult climb, with more steepness and boulders. At the top is a little, square-shaped, sepulchral stone building. I rest here, observing drifting, grey clouds that seem pulled by Lafayette's peak, or as if those clouds are curious why there's land so high. Once again, it's too overcast for a photo. So, I poke around the grim building, then make my way inside. There's nothing here, no furniture or mock fireplace, not even a visitor's register for hikers to scribble obscene notes like those of Dirty Dave and the Boyz on Blood Mountain.

After a ten-minute rest, I start down Garfield. I'm getting thirsty, and need to replenish my water; last night's camp spot had only pools of swamp water.

Just below the stony crypt, I arrive at a fast-flowing stream. The sign here indicates a shelter 0.2 miles ahead. Under normal circumstances, I'd check it out, but I don't relish more boulder-skipping, so I merely rest awhile at this stream. I'm supposed to wait at least a half hour after dropping in my iodine tablets, but I'm so thirsty I only give it about fifteen minutes (the Pop-Tart I devour here makes me even thirstier). A young couple I'd seen on Garfield summit passes me on their descent. Then a man with two young girls passes me on the ascent. They look upbeat, so I'm not too concerned about my climb down Garfield.

But, although I've done only a few weeks' worth of backpacking on the AT, this north side of Garfield, just below the water stop, is one of the most treacherous I've yet hiked. Several times, particularly since I see no white blazes on the rocks, I stop out of concern that I left the trail. It's not a trail, merely a boulder slide cascading down the mountain. And because the boulders are wet from the previous night's rain, their surfaces are slick. *How could that man and his daughters have been smiling?*

Here, I have my first serious wipeout. Because the boulders are at such a steep angle, I grip onto various small limbs to steady myself while seeking solid footing. This works for a while. Then, suddenly, my grip gives out. I fall backwards, slipping several feet on the rocks. Somehow, I'm able to extend my left arm and brace my fall with my hand, but I feel a jabbing in my wrist.

I lie on the slick, mossy rock for about thirty seconds. Then slowly turn my hand in circles a few times. *Whew, no breaks.* If the downward pressure had been any greater, I might have broken a wrist bone.

After an interminable period, I reach the end of the boulder slide, and a white blaze confirms that, yes, this is the Appalachian Trail. But how can they call this a "trail?" (Answer: a trail can be anything you *want* it to be.)

The next rest stop is Galehead Hut, which arrives just in time. I dine on some salmon and bagels on the front steps, and chat with several groups of day-hikers. Galehead is my first hut in the White Mountains, and it's beautiful. It's a huge, roomy cabin with about a dozen wooden tables for eating, a large kitchen, bathrooms, and a sleeping section with bunk beds. I arrive just before the summer employees do, and there's a big note from the caretaker welcoming the crew ("croo," in the AT dictionary) to their new summer home. There are also some blueberry muffins, and a large pitcher of lemonade, dollar a glass. *So* refreshing!

I sign my name in the register, then continue onward.

For NOBO hiking in the Whites, Galehead is strategically placed, because it comes right before a grueling ascent. Galehead is at the base of South Twin Mountain, a climb not as treacherous as the boulder spill on the north side of Garfield, where the rocks are cold and slimy, but nevertheless a relentless and steep ascent, almost a mile. My energy ebbs the higher I climb. Adding to my misery is the burning midday sun. Despite all the lemonade I drank at Galehead, my throat and mouth are soon as dry as desert tumbleweed. Over and over I have to stop, panting with exhaustion from stretching my legs to push over each chunk of rock. I come to the end of a fifty-yard stretch, turn the corner, then another fifty-yard ascent comes into view. This happens about a dozen times, and I finally stop looking ahead, for fear of another disappointment.

When I finally arrive at the summit, I almost collapse from exhaustion. But the fatigue is compensated by a panoramic view of the Whites. The scene is 360 degrees of light blue sky and rolling green mounds, with only a few puffy white clouds, high up in the blue, to add texture. Although South Twin is not the highest peak I've climbed thus far, it might be the most superb as far as view. Stunning, green, undulating mountain-scapes on all four sides, Lafayette included. Peaks upon peaks upon peaks. Deep valleys lie to the northwest, tiny structures and faint, string-like roadways are scattered far below.

I rest here a long while, drinking in the scenery. I meet a guy from Boston who likes to do short hikes just to "bag peaks." Just after I arrive, I'm joined by a young New Hampshire couple I'd seen at Galehead Hut. I'd left Galehead way ahead of them, and I'm astonished at how fast they scampered up South Twin, and how fresh and energized they are. Like the Boston fellow, they're both peakbaggers. The woman said that they're next headed to Guyot Shelter, which is the same place I'm going. But when we leave, I notice they start down a blue blaze path. When I inform them that the AT is "over here," the woman says they plan to hook up with the AT later, after they've "bagged one more peak."

I can understand these peakbaggers on one level. I'm a collector, too, amassing vinyl records and marathon medals. For a while, when I was into genealogy, I collected ancestors. These people collect mountains. Some of them, I'm sure, even have databases to store their conquests. (One hears the word "conquer" a lot when discussing the summiting of mountains. To conquer means to "vanquish" or "subjugate." But other than coal companies that tear off mountain tops to scrape at the coal, no one ever truly conquers a mountain.)

I can also relate to peakbaggers, and thru-hikers, on an athletic level. Summiting mountains and completing hikes of over 2,500 miles is a tremendous athletic achievement.

I'm sure not all peakbaggers and thru-hikers are dismissive of the aesthetic rewards of their activities. But it seems to me that, in their zeal to "acquire" and "achieve," many of these folks overlook or are unable to comprehend what the *real* treasure is.

Another thing that strikes me about these Massachusetts and New Hampshire backpackers is their passive acceptance of rocks and boulders. Hard, solid objects seem a regular part of their lives. Several times I've mentioned to them how prevalent boulders are in the Presidential Range, and how difficult they are to hike over. But I only get looks of puzzlement.

However, my biggest awakening is more personal: I think I'm losing stamina. I'm in an upper age bracket in these mountains, and I lack the strength and energy of these young New Englanders.

This realization gnaws at me. Although in better shape than probably most men my age, I'm starting to slip.

Too hot, tired, and sore to dig out and energize my flip phone for keepsake photos, I begin the hike down South Twin.

The descent isn't too strenuous. I then hit a long, level stretch, the first I've yet encountered in the Whites. Guyot summit is a benign hike, too. It's a bald peak, very open, and there's another shelter nearby, but it's still too early for me to retire. I round Guyot, and in the middle of the trail, in a little oval of sunlight, sits a plump little quail. Utterly fearless, he sits like a little sentry as I gaze down at him, only scurrying into the brush when I'm right on top of him. I haven't seen much wildlife at these higher altitudes, and the quail is a pleasant surprise.

More flat hiking, then a ponderous descent toward Zealand Falls Hut, where I plan to overnight. Along a muddy stretch, I see a huge bear print in a patch of mud, and while I stop to take a photo, two young women approach me in the opposite direction. They ask if I've seen any campsites, but I tell them the hut at Guyot is the only spot I know of, about two miles ahead.

As I continue hopping boulders toward the hut, I become increasingly tired.

I'm now thinking about cutting my hike short.

This Presidential Range is much more grueling than I envisioned. More thoughts about my age, as well as the lower back vertebrae problem (technical name "spondylolisthesis") that afflicted me over the winter. *I should have never shoveled the driveway that day. The snow was too wet and heavy.* I feel no pain or stiffness now, but my back recovery was slow, and *maybe I needed more time to recover and strengthen up.*

If I cut my hike short, I can visit my aunt in New Jersey. Maybe take in the Woodstock festival site, which I've never seen. There's also our childhood home in Wilbraham, Massachusetts. Why push myself? It's not worth it if I'm miserable.

The negative thoughts afflict me, becoming more forceful as I become more fatigued.

Eventually, I hear rushing water. I glimpse a building far ahead, through the trees. As usual, the last few hundred yards are interminable, and the incessant boulders continue almost to the front porch step. But I eventually arrive at Zealand Falls Hut. I'd hiked twelve miles that day. I'm as tired as I've ever been.

There's a novel and movie called *Lost Horizon*, about an isolated utopian community in the Tibetan mountains, called Shangri-La. Here, all the inhabitants are peaceful and blissfully happy. They're also immortal.

Stumbling into Zealand Falls Hut is like tumbling into Shangri-La. The actual falls are further down in the valley. The rushing water here, next to the hut, is Whitewall Brook, a series of small cascades that empty into a peaceful green valley with a small pond (which I later discover provides a home for a community of beavers). The water is clear and cold enough to sting. The boulders are no longer threatening; they're silky and smooth in an inviting, feminine way. Stately conifers rise above the clearing and hut.

The hut itself is buzzing with summer employees who've only arrived that day. In fact, I'm the first overnight visitor of the summer, and I have the entire "guest room" to myself.

It's self-serve only, because the employees are still setting up shop, which means they won't be cooking my supper. But this hardly matters. Freeze-dried beans and rice is fine with me, now that I have a roof and a soft bed. One of the volunteers, a freckled, chestnut-haired gal named Eliza, cheerfully takes my twenty-eight dollars and sets out a large pitcher of Gatorade on ice. And just like Galehead Hut, there are homemade muffins for a small fee. I drink about half the pitcher, then crawl into the guest room to plop my aching muscles on the nearest bed. I lay there so long that Eliza juts her head around the corner to see if I'm ok.

I wonder what she's thinking, seeing this whiskered old man with the dirty bandana stretched out, like a rotting corpse, in her newly adopted home. Can she smell me? Do I look frightening? I'm just too damn tired to hang out with this group of excited kids on their first day of summer camp.

Later, I meet Carter, with shirt tucked in and hair parted down the side, who looks like he's better suited for interning in a law office. And Josh, with round glasses, a mess of golden curls, and an "It's all good!" smile, who looks like he stepped out of the 1960s. And a witchy, mysterious raven-haired beauty wearing a black dress, whose name I'm unable to pin down. There are a couple other members of the "croo." They're all pumped up by their pending summer in Shangri-La.

Can't say as I blame them. What a dream, to be young and healthy and spend your summer vacation in a mountain forest, meeting interesting people, and playing songs for beavers each evening from the front porch. Why did I waste my summers working in factories and retail stores?

Since there's no shower, Eliza had recommended the falls as a good place to wash up. I eventually rise from the cot and trudge achingly to the stream. But the water is way too cold for a sponge bath, so I return to the hut, then use the washroom to clean up. I have the quarters to myself, so I drape my damp and dirty clothes all around the room. Just before retiring, I glance out the window. The croo is gathered on the front step, and Josh is casually strumming a guitar to the accompaniment of muffled conversation and soft laughter.

The morning is glorious. The sun is a giant orange ball, rising at the end of the long valley to the east, beckoning me to hit the trail again. The croo is still tucked away in the upstairs loft. I pull together my belongings, then gobble a blueberry muffin. I'm anxious to visit the beaver pond below. I've never seen a beaver, but would like to. I write a little note in the hut journal.

"Hi Eliza, Josh, and Croo. I'm honored to be the first overnight guest at beautiful Zealand Falls Hut in 2016.

135

What a great experience this must be for you. You'll have
an unforgettable summer. Wish you all the best...Pete from
Ohio."

Or something similar. There's a song called "Ooh La
La" by Ronnie Lane and the Faces about wishing we knew
certain things when we were young, rather than having to
wait till we get older. *Is it possible to do this? Maybe there
are a few very perceptive young people that can. I wasn't
one of them.* The song melody sticks in my head most of
the morning. "Ooh la la" at Shangri-La.

I start up the rocks at the back of the hut, then realize
I'm headed up the wrong trail. Seems to be a lot of trail
intersecting here. Eventually, I find the correct path and
work my way down to Whitewall Brook in the valley
below. My muscles are very sore, but I feel refreshed from
a good sleep. I'd mentioned to Josh about sabotaging my
AT hike, and he'd recommended some blue blaze trails to
quickly get me back to the main road. But this morning I
feel renewed, so I continue down the AT.

The beaver pond is only about a 20-minute walk from
the hut, and I follow an AT side trail, Zealand Trail, which
runs along the east side of the pond about fifty feet from the
shore. Spying an area where the trees thin out, I weave my
way to the shore. Although no beaver activity, I get a good
view of their dam: a low-lying, grey mound of sticks and
switches at the south end of the lake.

In my opinion, beavers don't get enough love from
humans. So, here's a short documentary and tribute. I'll
allow my wooden companion, Kip, to have the honors:

North American beavers (castor canadensis) are the
continent's largest rodent. They have four powerful
incisors, a potent lower jaw for gnawing wood, and a
large paddle tail. Their tails serve as rudders underwater,
to store fat in the winter, and as props to sit on. Beavers
slap their tails on the water as a warning whenever
predators are near. They have webbed feet for efficient

136

swimming. Their fur is also unusual, consisting of short hairs for warmth, and longer hairs for waterproofing.

Beaver dams are made of vertical poles and horizontal crossbeams. The dams stop up water to create ponds, and once constructed, beavers then build their large lodges, composed of branches and mud. These lodges are like little motels, harboring in the winter not only small beaver families, but also muskrats, mice, and frogs. Beavers don't hibernate, but survive the winters by spending most of their time in their lodges, eating the underbark of sticks that they've stored.

Beavers are impressive environmentalists, turning deserts into gardens by preventing stream evaporation through natural dam and lodge construction, increasing water depth and circumference, which encourages plant growth, and which then entices other diverse wildlife. They're very family oriented; they mate for life, and unlike many other mammals, male beavers actively volunteer in the raising of young.

At one time, the beaver population in North America was from 60 to 90 million. Beavers were at the heart of the American fur trade from colonial times up through the mid-19th century, their fur used for clothing and hats. Fortunately, the demand for beaver fur declined by the 20th century, and beaver populations made a comeback. Their numbers in Canada and America are now estimated at 10 to 15 million.

Well done, Kip!
Kip and I feel fortunate to have the opportunity to gaze on a beaver dam, just as we felt fortunate to share an overnight campsite with a black bear.

After turning back to the trail, I poke around in the underbrush a little, where I locate a perfectly gnawed stump tapering to a sharp, symmetrical point. I take a photo as evidence of the beavers' carpentry skills…and to prove I was there.

My hike for the next few hours is one of the most enjoyable of my entire AT experience. The trail meanders along the edge of a deep valley, with very little climbing and only a few boulders. It's just what I need after yesterday's tiresome plod. Scotch pine, hemlocks, and white birch abound. Near a granite cliff face, I glance behind me and see a little white speck on the side of the mountain: Zealand Falls Hut. *The croo will have read my note by now.*

Because the hiking is flat, there are some swampy areas, but volunteers have lain numerous wooden planks, or "bog walks," to assist the hikers. I soon arrive at Ethan Pond, where there's a shelter and tentsites. *No one around.* A sign indicates the caretaker will be arriving tomorrow, and another sign says something about trout fishing in the pond. It's a peaceful little bowl of dark, still water, the kind of placid tarn that we all imagine all mountains everywhere should have. The shiny morning sunlight and mountain backdrop only accentuate the idyllic setting. *Yeah, I can see why fishermen would trudge several miles to fish for trout here.*

After Ethan Pond, I begin heading downhill through a forest. The farther down I go, the more I worry about what I'll be encountering after I cross US-302 below. It's afternoon, getting hotter, and the overnight areas north of the road are sketchy. Mizpah Spring Hut and Naumann Tentsite are still well over six miles ahead. *Will there be a campsite available in the inevitable rocks I'll be facing? What about fresh water?* The doubts start creeping in.

At Crawford Notch, I cross some railroad tracks. Up ahead, a middle-aged couple is conversing on the edge of the trail. As I near them, the woman glances at me, then asks "Is that a silver maple?" while pointing toward a tree.

"Why, yes, I think so!" I reply, though I honestly don't know what maple it is.

I cross a parking lot and start down a long driveway toward US-302. About halfway down, the same couple pulls up alongside in their car. The man rolls down the driver's window, and both ask me, in British accents, if I need a ride. I thank them and politely decline. They smile and drive off. I notice their car has a Rhode Island license plate. *A nice state.*

I cross US-302, then unload my pack under a tree and try to call Lynn. Although at a busy two-lane road, I'm sandwiched between peaks, and there's no reception. I eat a quick lunch of bagels and salty salmon, which compels me to drink more water from my flask than I would like. *Getting hotter.* I cross a pedestrian bridge over Saco River. I start climbing Mount Webster. It's still almost six miles till Mizpah Spring, yet it's already 1:10 in the afternoon. Leaving the bright sunlight, the road, and the society of people, and pushing myself up a mountain in the dark shadows of trees just doesn't feel right.

I'm sore. Tired. Thirsty. Ahead of me is five thousand feet of boulder climbing to the summit of majestic Mount Washington, of which I've heard so many horror stories. *Do I really want to continue? If I turn around now, I'll always regret it. I've gotta get over Washington.*

I begin climbing. Suddenly, I see two little white balls sitting in the middle of the trail. *What the heck are these? Mushrooms?* I reach the white balls and see that they're two round rocks that someone has painted white, with two red and black eyeballs in the center. They're staring up at me.

This is strange and unsettling. *Do these eyeballs mean something? Are they a warning?*

I tiptoe around the eyeballs and continue up Mount Webster. After only a few minutes, I'm gasping for breath. I rest awhile. *Don't think of it, Pete, you'll regret it.* I climb onward. After a few minutes, I'm panting again. I stop to rest a second time. *You've quit many times before, Pete. Don't quit now.*

I keep going. After about a half mile of climbing, I collapse against a large boulder (*what else?*) and drain my last drops of water.

A feeling of intense loneliness envelopes me. I begin to think about what I can do if I curtail my hike. Visit my aunt. Visit our old house in Wilbraham. Sightsee a little.

I hoist my pack and take a long look at the trail ahead. I turn around and move downhill, past the eyeballs, toward US-302, and toward what we call civilization.

A Solid Hunk of Hickory

E very so often I have a nightmare. The details are
always different. The theme of the nightmare,
however, is the same: rage. I lash out at people,
sometimes becoming physically violent. The victims of my
anger can be strangers, friends, family members…it doesn't
matter. During these tantrums, and despite all evidence to
the contrary, I am convinced I am right. I'm like a car
careening down the highway, with no one at the wheel to
control it.

I've always blamed these disturbing dreams on being
picked on when I was young. I reached puberty late, and
during adolescence I got bullied by a few bigger kids.
Maybe the victimization came earlier. Patronizing things
Dad said. Or Mom pushing vegetables down my throat.

I don't think I'm unusual in this regard. There are
probably other men, and maybe women, who have the
same kinds of violent nightmares. I'm aware, too, that lots
of people suffer much deeper psychic scars: victims of
severe physical, mental, and sexual abuse. But I think my
nightmare is a reaction to not having spoken up, or not

having fought back when I should have. (In fact, maybe it's why I'm now a curmudgeon.)

When I backed down from Mount Webster, I felt the same kind of guilt as when I ran away from that asshole in junior high school.

From Mount Webster, it took only two rides for me to hitchhike back to my car at Rattle River. The first ride was with three grey-haired locals in a Subaru. The second was with a Chinese kid who'd just graduated from Boston University and was sightseeing around New England. His tiny hatchback was loaded with junk, but he insisted on squeezing me in. He was real curious about my AT hiking. When we got to Rattle River, we said goodbye, but instead of getting back in his car, he followed the trail into the woods, wearing rubber flip-flops. When I drove off in my own car a half hour later, he still hadn't returned. I guess the trail hooked him.

He was an interesting fellow, full of curiosity, and eager to learn. But my biggest takeaway came from my earlier ride, the one with the grey-haired locals. The man driving the Subaru was a New Hampshire native and veteran backpacker. He asked about my hike, and I confessed I'd cut it short due to fatigue, and that I felt guilty about it. He told me I had no reason to feel that way. He said that, every year, at least two or three people die while pushing themselves to summit Mount Washington.

I don't know if this statistic is true. But it made me feel better. It also convinced me to return to that boulder on Mount Webster, where I stopped and turned around, a half mile up from the eyeballs.

My opportunity came a few months later, with Labor Day Weekend. All summer I'd stewed about getting up

Mount Washington. I'd even dreamed about it. It became a white whale I just had to harpoon.

Living in our neighborhood is a guy named Kurt. Years ago, he and some friends had thru-hiked both the Appalachian Trail and Pacific Crest Trail. When my dog Sheba and I do our two-mile evening runs through the neighborhood, I sometimes see him in his driveway, and we have short conversations about backpacking. He knew that I'd hiked the White Mountains. When he later asked me about it, and I sheepishly told him that I'd tanked my hike, he nodded.

"Yeah, I remember those Whites," he said in his soft-spoken manner. "When I heard you were hiking them, I wanted to say something. Maybe I should have."

I did a lot of back stretching over the summer, especially an exercise called the "dead bug," where I push my lower back against the floor while raising one leg and reaching back with my opposite-side arm. Surprisingly, it helped. By the time Labor Day arrived, my spondylolisthesis had diminished significantly. I'd also returned to my standard weekly running mileage, so my stamina was much improved.

Most importantly, I set more realistic goals. Instead of trying to tackle Crawford Notch to Rattle River, a stretch of forty-seven miles that includes a supposedly brutal section of White Mountains called the Wildcats, I settled on a more modest section between Crawford and Pinkham Notch: twenty-six miles. Although short, this section still involved long stretches above treeline, and encompassed Mounts Eisenhower, Jefferson, Washington, and Madison.

Also important: Lynn was supportive. I think the fact that I'd backed down after my first attempt helped convince her that, after thirty years of marriage, I do, indeed, possess a little common sense.

I park my Honda Civic at the Crawford Notch, Ripley Falls parking lot at 8 a.m. on September 1. It's a nice, sunny day with no rain in the forecast. I'm looking forward to acquainting myself with the "turnaround boulder." *Hey, it's possible the eyeballs will be watching for me!* Little familiarities like these get me excited, and after only a half hour of preparation and toiletries, I'm ready to hike.

I find a smooth, solid walking stick in the woods near the lot and start pounding down the drive. I cross Saco River, then head upward into the wilds. I keep my eyes open for the painted, stone eyeballs. But it looks like someone swiped them over the summer.

Hey, I'm feeling good. Really strong. I'm ready to tackle the cliffs of Webster. This is so different from several months ago. I soon arrive at the familiar turnaround boulder. I slip off my pack and resume my pose from May 31. I recall how tired, deflated, and lonely I felt back then. Good physical health and an upbeat attitude make all the difference. I'm curious to see if this climb is as difficult as I anticipated, and if I made the right decision in turning back.

I slip on my pack and take one small step for a man.

Mount Webster isn't *too* difficult. It's a moderate climb, but the biggest challenge are some tricky rock faces. Higher and higher I go, skirting along the edge of the mountain. There are some steep moments where I force myself not to turn around due to my acrophobia, and I try to keep my pack as level as possible, so its weight doesn't pull me backwards into the void.

Willey House is visible way down below, a speck along US-302. In 1826, a massive rainstorm caused a boulder landslide there. Although the house remained intact, the thundering debris killed nine people, including the entire Willey family. Three children were never found.

Way in the distance, north of Willey House, is the massive, red and white Mount Washington Resort. Here, tourists can ride a train to the summit. *I'd rather summit this way.*

I soon reach the top of Mount Webster, where I stop for water and snacks. A young couple arrives only a few minutes after me. They have rings in their noses. I feel old again.

After some moderate hiking, I arrive at Mitzpah Springs Hut. It's a big, solid shelter, no different than Zealand Falls Hut, but it lacks the splendid setting of Zealand, with its expansive mountain valley, cascades, and beaver pond. I rest here, then summon the courage to broach some conversations.

I see the ring-nosed couple from Mount Webster. We have a friendly chat, and I discover they're from Oregon and are NOBO thru-hikers. They claim that the White Mountains are the prettiest section they'd yet seen, but (only after I press them) agree that the rocks are a bitch.

I also meet a young woman with the alias "Big Bird," so named because of her height, and a large yellow rain poncho she carries. She's from Brentwood, Tennessee. Big Bird is thru-hiking by herself.

"Aren't your parents worried?" I ask her.

"Well, Mom is. But both she and Dad are supportive. My dad actually just wants Mom to be content."

Sounding like a nosy sexist who can't believe a young woman is thru-hiking alone, I ask her if she has a boyfriend. But she's cool with it.

"I did, but we broke up just before my hike. So, the timing was perfect."

At Mitzpah Springs, I also meet a 46-year-old German man who left his job to fly over here and thru-hike. After he finishes the AT, he also wants to hike the PCT and CDT.

All of these thru-hikers plan to overnight at Lake of the Clouds Hut, which is *the* base camp rendezvous for hiking Mount Washington. I plan to pitch my tent south of there. And despite my leaving Mitzpah Springs Hut ahead of them, within a half hour they whizz past me like dragonflies on caffeine.

I don't plan to push myself this time. Problem is, I don't want to be caught on an exposed ridgeline. I'm also reluctant to meander too far off-trail, and all this rock and scrub make it difficult to locate a smooth, level tentsite. Another concern is water. My modus operandi in Georgia and Virginia was to overnight near a stream, or close enough to a water source so I can cook my food, and also have sufficient drinking water, but there are no streams above treeline.

But I left Mitzpah Springs Hut with a full 48-ounce bottle, so I should be ok until Lake of the Clouds tomorrow.

I summit Mount Pierce and am treated to a nice view of Washington in the distance. I next arrive at Mount Eisenhower Loop Trail. By this time, I'm almost above treeline again and, since it's getting late, I'm cocking my head right and left for a good campsite. But the few flat areas are either too rocky, or they're exposed to potential lightning strikes.

I curve around the loop trail, slightly disappointed that I won't be climbing Eisenhower to "bag another president." As I approach the north side of Ike, a young guy with curly, dark ringlets and horn-rimmed glasses comes up behind me. We exchange greetings. He tells me he's thru-hiking, but he eschews trail names and goes by his given name: Nathan. *Interesting.* He's also one of the few hikers who, like me, uses a wooden stick instead of a pair of aluminum and carbon trekking poles.

"I see you have a wooden stick, too" he says. "Nothing like the feel of a solid hunk 'o hickory in your hand."

I immediately like Nathan.

Nathan continues walking, his boot tips pointed outward, moving ponderously around the loop trail. He's not nearly as rushed as other thru-hikers I've seen. He has a natural smile and placid manner, as if to say "I'm just out enjoying a long stroll. No sense in taking life too seriously."

He may not approve, but I invent my own private trail name for Nathan: *Woodstock*.

"Where are you from?" I ask.

"Well…" he pauses. "My parents are in Nederland, Colorado."

Nederland is located high up in Rocky Mountain ski country, about 16 miles west of Boulder. It's a sort of mountain outpost of Boulder, itself a progressive town populated by New Age acolytes, health food junkies, rock climbers, and other outdoor sports enthusiasts.

"Yeah, I know Nederland," I say. "It's a cool town. That big lake. I lived in Boulder. A basement room in a house on 43rd Street. But it was way back in 1983, before you were around, probably."

"Yeah, it was," he drawls, sleepily. *Gee, Nathan, you didn't have to agree so quickly.*

Then he continues. "I lived on 45th Street for a while, uh, behind a friend's house, back when I was doing a lot of climbing."

"No kidding. You, uh, say *behind* a friend's house?"

"Yeah. She let me dirtbag in her backyard in my tent. I was trying to raise money to, like, fly to Norway to see my girlfriend. I lived in the tent a couple months, working at a climbing gear store and eating bologna sandwiches."

Although I just met him, this bit of information doesn't surprise me. Not only because I'd already pegged Nathan as being eccentric, but also because I fondly remember the rock climbers in Boulder, with their ropes, harnesses, carabiners, belaying devices, and knack for suspending time space to instead suspend in physical space. I had "career" beaten into me by my parents, teachers, and peers. But the climbers I met sang their own tune (or the tune that the climbing *community* sings, anyway). For someone like me, back then—a recent college graduate from a conservative family in the conservative Midwest—it was a refreshing eye-opener.

I ask Nathan how Norway was.

"I don't know, I never got there. A week before I was to fly over, I got a Dear John letter. Or Dear Jan or Johann letter, I guess. She'd gotten engaged to some, like, ski instructor she'd known from childhood. I'd already bought the plane ticket and everything. Oh well."

Nathan confesses this so glibly, all I can say is "What a bummer."

"Yeah. No big deal," he continues in his offhand way. "I probably wouldn't have gone anyway."

"Why not?"

"Well, I came down with viral pneumonia. Probably from sleeping in the tent. It had a hole in the roof."

We talk a bit more, then Nathan disappears into the fog that's beginning to accumulate around Eisenhower.

As I arrive at the junction of the loop trail and Eisenhower summit trail, I glance left and see a small field. It's right at the base of the peak. I also spy a few small conifers at the edge. I plod over some mushy earth and arrive at a semi-hidden marsh. I poke around a little and discover a small area tucked between some stunted pines. It has a slight slope, but I might be able to squeeze my tent in.

After flitting about for about five minutes, I decide this is the best spot available, so I unload my gear and pitch my tent. The wind is picking up, but the slope and pine trees help to stifle some of it. *This will be my home tonight.*

If this patch were a foot or two smaller, I wouldn't have been able to fit my tent. In fact, I leave one or two sections of canvas unstaked, and I'm only barely able to stretch out my rain protector. The pines here are small due to the altitude, so stringing up my rain protector is more laborious than usual, since the branches are so tender. But eventually I eke out a cramped little tent space, arrange my pack, stick, and cooking gear nearby, then crawl inside to rest until dinner.

Ah, it's been a good day. Beautiful views from Webster Cliffs, good distance traveled, good campsite, and no rain. I feel much more fit than I did last Memorial Day. Then I hear several children's voices. Peeking out, I see an Indian family that I'd passed about an hour ago. They're coming down from Mount Eisenhower. *They're running a little late. Where they gonna stay tonight? No huts nearby, and it's a long hike to the nearest parking lot.*

I fix some ramen noodles, then clean up some trash that a previous hiker or hikers left behind…including a pair of wet, eggplant-colored underpants. I lift the pants with a stick, carry them over to the Eisenhower trail, and lay them on a large rock, hoping a trail volunteer might see them. *I'm sure the owner doesn't want these back.*

The little marsh next to me shows no signs of life. It's merely a soggy vale at the base of the mountain, the ugly flip side of picturesque Ethan Pond.

The wind is whipping stronger, and I pull on another shirt and jacket. I feel snug and warm once I climb into my sleeping bag. Soon, darkness arrives. Though there's no hefty tree nearby where I can hang my bear bag, I can't imagine any bears this high up. Despite my isolation, it's a noisy night, with mountain dew splashing against the tent roof, and heavy winds whipping the canvas. I sleep fitfully.

The next morning, my tent and protector are still intact. I'm itching to summit Eisenhower, and it doesn't look like too long a climb, so after packing up, I shinny up the rocks. Summiting takes about fifteen minutes, and soon I'm enveloped in clouds on a very flat summit and facing a huge pyramidal cairn; I'm at the tiptop. With the cairn and shroud of clouds, I half expect a company of dancing druids to emerge.

This is a weird, otherworldly place. I think of images I've seen of Stonehenge, or Patagonia, or the Moon. Despite the many rocks, it's flat enough here that I could have easily overnighted. Sleeping here, alone, at night, would have been memorable.

149

I see my first hikers of the day on the descent from Eisenhower: another gent with a wooden stick, then a 70-something man, who asks me about Eisenhower summit. It remains cloudy as I continue up and over Mount Monroe, and I continually remove my glasses due to moisture accumulating on the lenses. Like Eisenhower, I have the spooky summit of Monroe to myself. There's a scary moment trying to descend Monroe, when I lose my bearings and have trouble locating the trail. I worry about injuring myself on all this jagged rock. So, rather than shortcutting over the peak, I backtrack to the loop trail. After a few thousand steps, I round Monroe, and tumble into appropriately named Lake of the Clouds Hut.

Since I'm at base camp for Mount Washington, the hut is buzzing with people. From what I've already learned, it's difficult to nab an overnight cot here. Preference is given to thru-hikers, but even these folks must reserve early. One woman I earlier met, who was unable to get an advance reservation, told me she slept in a storage room called The Dungeon. I later visit this place. It's a dismal, damp hovel on the outside of the hut, at the rear. I peek in. The room is so loaded with junk, wheelbarrows and sawhorses and chairs and, of course, rocks, that I can't imagine how she even unrolled her sleeping bag. But it's shelter, and up in this unpredictable nether world, shelter is extremely important.

White Mountain huts are famous for their hot, homemade soups. Right now, soup is foremost on my mind. I buy a bowl of apple lentil soup. *Nectar of the gods.* While slurping away, I overhear a German couple conversing. *This beautiful range has worldwide appeal.*

I also meet a young brunette woman from Minnesota. She calls herself "Waterfall" and says she's solo thru-hiking. As with Big Bird, I feel a big "Wow." I'm totally impressed with these intrepid women, but I don't think it's from any innate chauvinism. Maybe it's because I have a grown daughter that I still think of as "my little girl."

Holly's incredibly confident and self-assured, but I couldn't imagine her solo hiking the full Appalachian Trail. I'd be compelled to tag behind her, surreptitiously ducking behind trees, just to make certain she's ok.

Waterfall is very quiet, keeps her head averted. I wonder if she struggles with shyness, or loneliness. I tell her about Big Bird being only a half-day ahead. She merely says that she's heard of Big Bird.

If she's hiked all the way from Springer Mountain, she conquered her loneliness a long time ago. All those nights sleeping alone, in the dark, in the woods? I think of the society of thru-hikers. They continually cross paths with each other. They share stories, trail tips, biographical tidbits. Most of them take advantage of the shelters and huts. They take sabbaticals at motels and restaurants. And every year there are more AT thru-hikers.

On surface, solo hiking the Appalachian Trail for four or five months straight seems like an incredibly solitary enterprise. But it probably isn't. On the contrary, it forces a person to share and communicate. Solo hiking the AT would, in my opinion, force a shy person to deal with their shyness. Not having completed a thru-hike, I can't vouch for this, but it's my observation as a section hiker.

FALL 1974—SALTSBURG, PENNSYLVANIA

It's a pretty campus. Trees that look like skyscrapers. Then we see that man again, hunched over and shuffling along the sidewalk outside the red brick classroom building. A crumpled little man with horn-rimmed glasses, baggy brown corduroy pants, skinny tie, and faded tweed sport jacket with patches on the elbows. Puffing a pipe. He waves at us.

"These places always have a few eccentric characters," says Dad with a smile. "My school had 'em too. They struggle in the real world, but they find a home in private boarding schools."

"Oh, I don't think he's eccentric," says Mom. "He seemed like a very nice man. What was his name, Peter? Mr. Miller?"

"I think so," I respond glumly. Part of me wants my parents to leave. The other part wants them to stay, to delay the inevitable.

We arrive at my dorm room. Room 202, second floor in Clark Hall. Music is blasting. My parents walk in, and I follow. A boy is standing in the middle of the room in front of an ugly green dresser. The room chart in the dorm lobby said his name is "Rod." He's taller than me, with olive skin and greasy black hair. He's shirtless, and his chest flesh looks soft and flabby. His lower lip protrudes, like he has chewing tobacco stuffed under it. The record spins on his record player. He turns the volume down. My parents introduce us.

Rod looks down at me and shakes my hand. He doesn't smile.

***

Now my parents are gone. Time to skate solo. I don't feel as nervous as I thought I would. I've got my tennis playing and my books. Like Alfalfa's hair spike, they're my "personality." They're something to cling to and give me identity in this alien place.

I lay on my bed, curled up on my side, with my paperback, Thomas Tryon's "Harvest Home." Rod's ignoring me, broadcasting his music again. A few other guys wander in, and Rod and they talk about the music, which I know nothing about other than what I overhear: "Bell Bottom Blues" by Derek and the Dominoes. The guys are all bigger than me, and their voices have already changed.

Then the boy in the adjoining room comes in. He looks at me and my book. He walks toward me.

"I read his book 'The Other,'" he says. "It was a good book. How do you like this one?"

Ultimately, I decide Waterfall isn't lonely, and is probably as solid as the granite around us. If she's made it all this way from Springer Mountain, she's more than likely found a place within the AT thru-hiker subculture. And if she chose to stay outside this subculture—which is entirely possible and understandable—then the trail's helped her find her own companionship, either internal or external.

It would be nice to join Waterfall for the Mount Washington ascent, but she's a lot stronger than me, so I hold back and let her get a good lead.

Just north of the hut lies the small lake for which the hut is named, half hidden amongst the murky, grey-white cloud canopy. Dark and still, I imagine weird gill creatures with bulging eyeballs living deep under the water surface; Gollum-like evolutionary mistakes, nurtured by this cold, hostile, high-altitude weather.

Just after the lake, there's an extreme altitude spike to the top of Mount Washington. The trail is switchbacks, but the switchbacks are very steep and seem to go on forever. And it's all rock and boulder, rockslide all the way. The large Mount Washington Observatory, way up at the top, looms over the entire climb as if to say, "Come on, a little further, you can do it, don't give up, keep climbing, I'm waiting for you, I'll be here for you."

I stop to take frequent oxygen breaks. A lot of young day hikers scurry past me. The hiking is long and slow, but the tower pulls me forward, and eventually I see moving forms at the top.

Mount Washington weather is some of the most extreme and unpredictable in the world. I already mentioned the incredible wind velocity. Summer temperatures rarely get above 70 degrees Fahrenheit, and from December through March, they rise above freezing for an average of only fifteen days.

In addition to the AT and various side trails, the Mount Washington Cog Railway climbs the mountain from the west, and an auto road traverses the eastern slope. Hiking is the biggest activity, but runners, bicyclists, and hang gliders also come up here, and nearby Tuckerman Ravine hosts skiers. So there's usually lots of activity at the top. Today is no exception.

The peak is crawling with hikers and tourists, young, old, and in-between. I ask an anonymous tourist if he'll take my picture. He agrees, happily, and I pose next to a wooden sign signifying the high point.

"That's a real achievement, hiking all the way up here," the man says, noticing my backpack. "I had to come up by car!"

He's a lot younger than me, so his comment pumps my ego. I try to think of something to say that won't sound like feigned humility, but all I can summon is "Well, that's an achievement, too. You burned a lot of gas." He gives me a funny look.

I visit the historic Tip-Top House, a small hotel built in 1853. It's filled with various souvenirs, but there's a fee if you want to go beyond the front room, so I merely sign my name in the guestbook. Then I visit the train depot/visitor center. Inside is a crowded restaurant and adjoining post office. On the wall opposite the post office is a depressing list of all the people who have died in the Presidential Range, most from exposure or hypothermia, some by natural causes or avalanches. Around the corner, down a half-hidden stairway, is a hiker rest area. While the upstairs tourist area is clean and bright, the hiker refuge is just the opposite. A few dilapidated chairs and tables, some hooks to hang backpacks, and a dirty wash area. It's obvious what has lesser priority on the top of Mount Washington.

The people, warmth, and hot food up here rejuvenate me, but after a half hour, I start feeling oppressed by the swarming tourists, so I head outside, sit on a bench, chomp on a granola bar, then locate the AT once again.

But just before I resume my trek, I check my flip phone like a good tourist. Earlier, I'd taken advantage of the phone reception here to reassure Lynn and the kids I was ok. My son Nick, who lives in Denver, has already responded:

"Hope the hike is going well, Dad. I love you."

Feeling a catch in my throat, I fold my phone and get up from the bench. I put the swarming horde and mountaintop at my back, and trudge downward, across the Cog Railway tracks, and toward the Great Gulf Wilderness.

The Great Gulf is a vast glacial cirque of the Presidentials formed by glacial erosion. The AT skirts along the top of the Gulf. At this point I'm thinking of a campsite, and I briefly ponder going off-trail, risking a treacherous descent into the Gulf, and camping in the beautiful lush valley in the bottom…just like Melville in 1842 in Typee Valley. But my better sense prevails, and I continue toward Jewel Trail. This side trail, according to a New Hampshire man I met on the WhiteBlaze website, supposedly dips below treeline and has several good primitive campsites.

When I arrive at Jewel Trail, however, I only see flat, treeless rock. *Don't want to risk going too far off the AT. Better continue onward.*

This is one of the negatives of high-altitude hiking. As pure and scenic as it is to hike above treeline, it's also difficult to find an appropriate tentsite. Later, I come face to face with that reality.

Soon, the clouds disappear, and the temperature starts to rise. I round the Great Gulf and continue through a long, rocky section reminiscent of Utah or west Texas. Far ahead, I spy some brightly colored backpacks, and as with my marathoning, I create a game of trying to reel them in like fish, to boost my pace. Eventually I'm at the base of rocky Mount Jefferson. Unlike Lafayette, Eisenhower, or Washington, Jefferson rises to a single point. The AT follows a loop around this pinnacle, but a peak trail heads up and over, rejoining the AT on the other side.

Remaining on the AT is probably safer and quicker, but I'd really like to visit our third president, one of America's most learned, accomplished, interesting, and controversial. I've already visited his home at Monticello, his university in Charlottesville, Virginia, and his memorial in Washington, D.C. Now it's time to visit a natural feature that bears his name.

The tip of Mount Jefferson is directly in my line of sight, with no clouds or fog to obscure it. Although tired from summiting Mount Washington, I find the energy to scramble to the neck of Jefferson. I unload my pack and lean it against a boulder. Then I carefully wend my way up his head.

Not only does the peak of Jefferson taper to a single point, but the highest point of the point is a single rock, with a small cairn balanced atop. I take in all 360 degrees. *No one in the vicinity.* My breathing slows, and I rest atop the hard stone. A hawk glides over the valley to the north. Climbing Jefferson after a long day of hiking is as satisfying as summiting Washington. Possibly more so. Here, it's peaceful and unblemished. There are no traffic zones, metal signs, cafeteria lines. Only the sound of mountain breeze whisking through the rock crevices, and a hawk soaring in the distance. Here, it's easy to think, and breathe.

It was great to get that text message from Nick. Resting atop Jefferson, I picture him, the smallest kid on the baseball team, crouching at second base.

The ball is hit toward him. He crouches, lower, his glove at the ready. He can't miss scooping the ball. It dribbles straight toward him. But the ball shoots under his glove into the outfield. Ugh.

He doesn't look at the outfielder, nor the baserunner. He doesn't look at the coach. He looks toward me. I'm in the grass behind third base line. I'm disappointed. We

practiced scooping grounders all week. I hold up my hands
as if to say, "How could you miss that?"

He drops his little head in shame.

Parents carry some images with them the rest of their
lives, and I'm not sure I'll ever lose this one. But I'm
lucky. Unlike poor Guy Waterman, I haven't had to create
a memorial to a lost son. And Nick still tells me "I love
you."

I slowly descend from the small cairn atop Mount
Jefferson.

Stumbling in the Land of Moses

The descent from Mount Jefferson is short, but steep. *Most of the northbound hikers I've seen today are probably nearing the hut at Mount Madison.* Mount Madison is farther than I can make tonight, so I once again scan the terrain for a primitive camp spot. I arrive at a major trail intersection called Edmund Col.

Should I continue north on the AT, toward Madison Hut, through Thunderstorm Junction, hoping for a protected tentsite? Or hike on Israel Ridge Path to Perch Shelter, which is over a mile to the west? I haven't seen many good, primitive tentsites this entire White Mountains hike, and the name "Thunderstorm Junction" scares me. After hemming and hawing for a few minutes, I decide to hike Israel Ridge and overnight at Perch Shelter.

Muscle-bending challenges after eight hours of intense hiking is not a good idea, but I have no choice on Israel Ridge. I'd already summited Mounts Eisenhower, Monroe, Washington, and Jefferson, so my once-taut muscles are now as soft and shaky as Jell-O. Israel Ridge Path runs along the face of a long, seemingly endless talus ridge. It's

all rock, so there's no visible trail, and I have to rely on a
string of well-positioned cairns for trail identification. I'm
now using both arms for balance and bracing, and despite
my fatigue, I'm trying to maintain concentration, so I don't
stick my boots in a crack that might jerk my ankles the
wrong way.

After a half hour of hiking this nightmare path, I
experience the ugliest wipeout I've ever had.

Israel Ridge offers an outstanding view of farmlands and
meadows ahead of me, to the west. Closer, on my left, is a
deep trench in the mountains. It's reminiscent of the Great
Gulf Wilderness, back near Mount Washington, but it's
rockier and more imposing. *If a hiker became injured down
there, he might never pull himself out.*

I'm grateful to whomever took the time and effort to
erect these cairns, which are my only direction arrows.
Amongst the millions of rocks and occasional scrub along
this ridge, cairns provide the only signposts for a trail. They
look like miniature stone tributes to the gods. *Maybe
there's an old manuscript under one of these, a White
Mountain version of the scrolls at Qumran Caves, written
by some Abenaki Indian ancestral civilization.* I arrive at
one pyramidal stack of rocks, then immediately peer ahead
to locate the next, then carefully weave my way toward it
as best I can. Hopefully, I don't accidentally get
sidetracked on a connecting trail, since wooden signposts
are now few and far between.

Once again, fatigue teases my sense of reality. I expect
to tumble into Perch Shelter any minute, but at each cairn,
there's nothing other than another long stretch of pale rock.

Then, somewhere along the endless ridge, in my
exhaustion and frustration, I become impatient and increase
my walking speed. It's only incremental, but evidently just
enough to bypass some neurons in my brain. I misplace my

boot. My body pitches forward, my walking stick goes flying, and my arms barely manage to swing forward to brace my upper body. Not enough, apparently, because my head smacks against a small patch of bird's nest spruce at the edge of the rocks.

Momentarily stunned, I lie prostrate, my pack pressing me against the rock. For a few minutes, I'm perfectly still. Then I collect myself and roll over on my butt. *Holy crap. If that tiny patch of greenery hadn't been exactly where it was, it might've been days before anyone found me. 'Dead Hiker Found on Israel Ridge,' would be the headline Lynn would read. She has a lot of unfounded worries, but fracturing my skull on rock is a concern for which she's justified.*

I sustain a mild headache, only, but the accident makes me more cautious. I drag myself upright and trudge onward. Eventually, the cairns disappear. I reach treeline and plunge downward into thick, ragged forest along a narrow trail. I expect to see Perch Shelter at each new vista, but…as usual…the trail merely spills into more trail. The shadows increase, and I worry about not having enough light for supper.

After a seemingly endless descent, I arrive at a sign for Perch Shelter, managed by the Randolph Mountain Club. Another quarter-mile later, on a side trail, I arrive at a standard, open-air, log shelter with roof. It's like all those I've seen on the AT, except this shelter has two large, adjacent tent platforms. I'm the only person here. In fact, since Mount Jefferson several hours ago, I haven't seen one hiker.

I also feel slightly queasy and chilled, which bothers me. *Maybe my head trauma is worse than I think.*

I fix a bowl of hot noodles, hoping this might alleviate my chills. It does. As darkness descends, I follow another side path to a gentle creek spilling down the mountainside. I replenish my water bottle. It's a long trek along more rock. *Jeez, is everything ROCK around here?*

Returning to Perch Shelter in the dark, I arrange my gear and prepare to crawl into my sleeping bag, when I see a white light bouncing along the creek trail I just hiked. Coming into view is a young brunette woman. *I can't believe there's another human out here.*

The woman cheerfully introduces herself as Hannah, the "Perch Shelter caretaker."

"Hi, I'm Pete. Where the heck do you live?"

"I live in a cabin about a mile down that trail, across the stream" she says, pointing to the narrow, rocky side trail.

"And you hike over here every night?"

"Yeah. I just check on things, and make sure everyone's ok. It's not bad!"

I'm stunned. I can't reconcile someone living way out here. I'm assuming she stays here alone. To think she has to hike two miles every evening, over a treacherous, rocky footpath, in partial or total darkness? This knowledge once again drives home the realization that I'm aging, and that New Englanders are a different breed than Midwesterners.

Hannah tells me she's surprised no one else is in the shelter tonight. But the shelter seems so isolated, I'm not surprised at all. After all, I almost fractured my skull trying to get here. The only *reason* I'm here is because I felt compelled to summit Mount Jefferson, which delayed me and forced me to go off the main AT to find overnight lodging.

I give Hannah the ten-dollar lodging fee that Randolph Mountain Club charges its guests. Just before bouncing off in darkness, she tells me to let her know if I need anything else. *Thanks, Hannah...but unless my life is in jeopardy, I'm staying put until morning.*

The queasiness and chills I felt earlier eventually subside, but I have a dull headache that makes sleeping difficult. During the night I'm visited by only one mouse. After flicking on my flashlight once, he leaves me alone.

161

Next morning brings renewed energy. *I'm ready to take on the day.* While packing up, I hear laughter coming from the other side of the shelter. *Sounds like a man and a woman. Must've had some visitors arrive during the night.* Just before I finish stuffing my pack, two people appear around the corner of the shelter. It's a blonde woman, followed by a man with long, dark, curly hair. He turns slightly, and I see that it's Nathan, the easygoing guy I met the day before and nicknamed "Woodstock."

"Hey, we meet again," I exclaim.

He says something like "awesome," and the three of us have a short conversation. I tell them about my visit from Hannah. They ask if there are any fees. I then mention my scary tumble on Israel Ridge, anxious to share my drama while seeking a kindred spirit.

"I thought I was a goner," I gush. "If it hadn't been for that scrub evergreen, I'd still be up there."

"No, we'd have found you," Nathan replies, in his bon vivant way. "We came down that way in the dark. Man, those rocks were something else, weren't they?"

It's the first time since the ring-nosed Oregon couple that someone else has confirmed how unforgiving these White Mountains are. Hearing this confession lifts my spirits. For a long time, I'd been thinking I was a bigger whiney-pants than normal.

Nathan and his friend say they're headed to Osgood Tentsite, the same place I'm going. I never determine if Nathan just recently met this woman, or if they'd already known each other awhile. He seems mellow enough to charm any woman he desires.

As I begin the long, upward hike toward Israel Ridge, I glance back at Perch Shelter for a mental snapshot of this isolated refuge in the White Mountain woods. *Without Hannah and Nathan, this lodging would have been a lot less agreeable. One mouse in the middle of the night is cold company for a lonely old man who experienced a near-concussion.*

The hike back to the AT is long, but less grueling than yesterday. Once again, the well-placed cairns guide me to my destination of Edmund Col. I turn left toward Thunderstorm Junction. Immediately, I begin passing hikers moving southward, and recall that it's the first day of Labor Day Weekend. The next few miles bring hordes of holiday hikers. At Thunderstorm Junction, there's a plush little meadow that would've made a perfect camp spot. Had I continued a little further past Edmund Col, I could've avoided grueling Israel Ridge. But...I'd have also missed out on meeting Hannah, seeing Nathan again, and enjoying some spectacular views.

The hikers become thicker as I near the base of Mount Adams. Most of them hike in groups. Occasionally, I move to the side of the trail to let them pass. Sometimes they glance up and acknowledge me. Other times they continue to converse with their companions, keeping their eyes on the ground.

Everyone's different. Even at work, or at the gym, or in the park, some individuals never make eye contact. But at least out here on the trail, they're not clutching their digital gods like a baby clutches a bottle... usually.

Soon, I arrive at a large, open field. Off to the right are several worn footpaths leading to a rocky summit: Mount Adams. President John Adams always seems overshadowed by larger-than-life Washington and Jefferson, so I commit myself to climbing the summit in honor of our second president. Like Adams the man, the peak is small, but it's majestic. A number of other hikers also scramble to the top. There's no worn path, just a jumble of grey boulders to negotiate however one chooses. Unlike at Mount Jefferson, where I left my pack at the summit base, I haul my pack up Adams, which makes for a slow climb. But very soon, I'm at the top, surrounded by a mass of day hikers.

For the first time in a while, there are no clouds, and I'm treated to a panoramic view. The view isn't as stunning as

at South Twin Mountain a few days ago, but I also don't
have to deal with that day's heat or exhaustion. Since it's
still early in the day, I linger here longer than normal. The
Labor Day crowd makes for a buzzing social scene.

Back on the Appalachian Trail, at a large cairn signaling
the mountain's location, there was a bustling crowd of kids
and adults. I figured it was maybe a church or civic group.
Not long after summiting Adams, several of them make
their way to the top. Immediately, I notice something a
little different about them. The kids all have dark tans and
long hair. They wander by themselves, without adult
supervision, and chatter excitedly. One of them, long-
haired and lithe, looks neither boy nor girl.

Then a man bounces over the edge of a boulder,
standing with his hands on his hips, scanning the crowd on
the top. He's wiry and healthy-looking, with a sandy brown
ponytail that's streaked with grey, and he has a beaming
smile. I can't tell his age. He could be in his late thirties,
but with his greyish ponytail, he could instead be twenty
years older.

"What an *amazing view*!" he exclaims with extroverted
zest. "And all these *amazing* hikers!" I see him shoot me a
quick, white-toothed glance.

He scurries around the rocks, taking in all the views. I sit
on a rock in silence, observing two large dogs panting
nearby. But my ears are open. Before long, the ponytail guy
is carrying on a conversation with two young men. I
overhear him say "Plymouth" and "Blue Bell Bakery," or
something. They chat for about five minutes, interrupted by
the man's gasps of amazement at the views. At the end of
the conversation, I hear him extend an invitation to the two
men to visit the bakery.

This is one of those times when I feel isolated. Like I
don't belong. I get this way occasionally. I'm not a shy
person, in most situations. But in other situations, I have a
difficult time opening up. It's probably a combination of
the loner in me, plus some social anxiety I've dealt with

most of my life. These three people, after only five minutes, act like they're old friends. Yet I can know someone for five years and still feel like a stranger.

I observe this ponytail fellow like he's a celebrity. He looks good, and there's a magnetism about him. His wispy ponytail and extroverted manner remind me of certain free-spirited hippies I knew back in school. They always seemed comfortable with themselves, and never took things too seriously. While I've always been drawn to these types, envious of them, I'm also always a little intimidated. For lack of a better word, they exhibit a "karma" that I don't have, and probably never will.

Until I got to know him, and until we talked Richland County, Ohio and Browns football at Woods Hole Shelter during my Georgia AT hike, I also felt intimidated by chatty Chad.

Eventually, I zigzag my way down Mount Adams. The descent seems longer than the ascent. *Which boulder should I choose to step on? This one. No...this crested rock is a good fit for my boot.*

The two dogs and their owners quickly pass me by. So do the two young men. Ponytail guy is already at the cairn with his large group. I don't see the kids anywhere.

I reach flat ground and angle toward the AT. But I deliberately taper my angle so I can pass by the cairn. I'm still curious about ponytail and his group. *Maybe I can pick up some clues from their conversation.*

As I get closer, I shoot a few glances out of the corner of my eye, hoping that I won't appear nosey. But ponytail guy catches me looking.

"You've got a big pack there!" he shouts at me. "Where are you headed?"

I veer toward him. "Headed for Osgood Tentsite tonight," I answer shyly. "Then my car tomorrow, and back home to Ohio."

He asks me a few more questions, and before long, we're into a free-flowing conversation. We talk about the

White Mountains, Mount Washington, the scenery, the details of our respective hikes, and the town of Plymouth, Massachusetts. He and his group are doing a several-day hike. Then I see the kids. They drift in and out of the group. If their parents are here, I'm unable to determine who they are. The kids seem to belong to no one, and everyone.

Then I ask him his name.

"Shemet," he says with a smile.

"Sh…Shemet?" I ask.

"Yes, Shemet." Then he tells me it's an old Hebrew name that he adopted a while ago. Suddenly, a sandy-haired teenage girl approaches us.

"This is my daughter, Mehenomet." Mehenomet tilts her head and smiles broadly. Her open, unguarded, bubbly demeanor reminds me of a pig-tailed gal I met at a campsite before a Grateful Dead concert in 1990.

"Nice to, uh…meet both of you," I manage to blurt. I suddenly don't feel so intimidated.

Shemet tells me that all the members of his group live communally and have adopted Hebrew names (even though they're probably all Gentiles). He mentions something about an Act in the Old Testament. He then tells me he used to work as a park ranger. He hints about certain unsavory activities he engaged in when he was younger. ("Didn't we all!" I assure him). He and his wife divorced, and he eventually joined the group he's with today. But he doesn't give me its name, or purpose, or affiliation.

I ask Shemet why he's no longer a park ranger. It's a career which I thought about pursuing when I was younger, and which I've always considered meaningful and fulfilling.

"I had no meaning or fulfillment," he says. "I got tired of rattling on about birds and animals and lakes. *There's a bird, duh, here's a lake,*" he says mockingly. "*Boor*-ing! I didn't want to serve nature anymore. I wanted to serve *people!*" he says with enthusiasm, as if people and nature weren't inseparable, and park rangers didn't serve both wildlife *and* people.

His rock-headed revelation hits me like a right hook to the jaw. So much for that blissful "karma" I thought about on top of Mount Adams. His coolness quotient drops as precipitously as the mountain. I don't mind his offbeat religion as much as his offbeat words about nature. *Pearls before swine.*

But I guess I'd set myself up for this shock.

We continue to chat, but I slowly inch my way toward the trail. Then, a swarthy, dark-haired man approaches and introduces himself. It's another Old Testament-type name. He hands me a pamphlet and tells me to read it at my leisure. I say "Sure," thank him, wave goodbye to Shemet and Mehenomet, turn northward on the trail…and feel like a leash has been removed.

I slip the pamphlet into a pocket on my pack, promising myself to at least glance at it later. After I return home, I do. The title is "The Twelve Tribes." Just below the title is a watercolor of long-haired stick people, children and adults. They're holding hands and dancing in a circle. I read the cheery, upbeat words inside the pamphlet. Later, I visit the internet and read more about The Twelve Tribes.

As with the Honeymoon Hikers' commandment to "Walk with Jesus," I try to be open-minded about things. Religion can offer solace and meaning in an often-brutal world. And you can't make snap judgements from a pamphlet, and certainly not the internet.

But like so many other "clubs," large and small, that rely on dogma and a fixed set of rules, beliefs, and practices, what I learn about The Twelve Tribes further convinces me of Shemet's scrambled thinking.

Shakespeare undoubtedly had a pithy observation about all of this. In lieu of his words, I'll go with someone more contemporary, like singer John Prine:

"It's a big old goofy world."

Hot Soup and a Good Cigar

James Madison was America's fourth president. Like Jefferson, Madison was a "Founding Father," Virginian, Democratic-Republican, and served as Jefferson's vice-president (among many other things), so it's probably appropriate he has a mountain near his mentor, Jefferson. Madison's wife, Dolly, is one of America's most familiar First Ladies, famous for her lavish parties and genteel social graces. I'm hoping that Madison Hut will be similarly festive. Just thinking of more of that heavenly apple lentil soup gets my saliva trickling.

The trek between Adams and Madison is typically deceptive. A quarter mile feels like four miles. Although I'm feeling strong and moving swiftly, each new horizon brings disappointment. But there's a sparkling sun, and I have plenty of friendly hiking company, so there's no reason to complain.

As I round a bend in the ridge, a deep and magnificent tree-ringed valley appears. And in the valley bottom, wedged between some tall, cucumber-green pines, is a long building, with tiny red, blue, green, and yellow shapes moving around. I can't help but once again think of the book and movie *Lost Horizon*. I can already see the steaming pot, and taste the syrupy apple-ginger elixir.

The descent to Madison Hut is steep and stony, but not difficult. I reach flat ground, but must wind around several times before arriving at the hut. About six or seven Labor Day hikers are reclined on the patio outside. Some are airing their feet while looking at maps. Burgundy red, navy blue, and forest green backpacks are lined up against the building. I unload my bright blue pack and head inside. I pass one young hiker and cheerfully mention arriving at "Shangri-La," but merely get a blank look.

Ah, such a relief to have fresh, hot food, cool lemonade, and a washroom in which to clean up. I'm beginning to like these White Mountain huts. Although I'd prefer to rough it overnight in my pup tent and make time with trees and critters (and circumvent the hefty overnight fees), huts and shelters are great safety valves, and the huts up here are all clean and well-staffed. The young woman behind the counter smiles broadly as I trundle to an empty bench near the back. An older woman with a tan, leathery face and long, grey ponytail carries plates and bowls back and forth. *Why are there so many ponytails in the mountains?*

I lie Kip on the bench, then head to the washroom, where I splash on some water and soap and change into lighter clothing. Then I head to the counter.

"How about some of that great apple lentil soup you guys serve?" I ask the young lady.

"Oh, sorry, we're all out of apple lentil," she replies. "But we've got a little split pea left…it's really good!"

Split pea it is. And…oh…writing about it now has me drooling. Warm, thick, spicy, an ambrosia of steaming dark green and light brown that massages my taste buds and warms my tummy. I sip it slowly to savor the flavor, spooning up small pools from the edge of the bowl, then scooping larger dollops from the center. I ponder the ingredients while I drink: *dried peas, ham, onion, maybe a little carrot and celery, tinged with any of several spices like thyme, garlic, pepper, bay leaf, with maybe some chicken stock and potato. This soup has a mild smoky flavor...maybe they used smoked ham.* (I forget to ask for the recipe afterwards.)

I'm hard-pressed to decide which is better: apple lentil or split pea. Today, split pea is my favorite.

Hunched over the steaming bowl, sucking in the aroma of split pea and wood, the weight of my pack off my back, Kip stretched out on the wooden table in front of me, the cheerful voices of the hut volunteers, the soft thumping of boots on the wooden floor, the joy of having summited Mount Washington...all of it contributes to a deep feeling of satisfaction. You can measure monetary wealth. Just add up the dollars and material possessions. But it's the things we can't measure that we remember the most, like being inside a cozy mountain hut and enjoying a steaming bowl of mouth-watering soup.

While sipping, I gaze at my map. Just one more mountain, then it's all downhill. Osgood Tentsite looks about halfway between Mount Madison and Pinkham Notch, where I'll finish up and (hopefully) hitch a ride back to my car at Ripley Falls parking lot. Everything's looking good. My only worry is site availability at Osgood. With Labor Day Weekend, the AT is like an airport terminal. I can't dawdle too long here.

Back out on the patio, I find an open spot on a bench, remove my boots and socks, and air out my sore, clammy feet. It's early afternoon, and the air's getting hotter. There's a carnival of hikers here, speaking with a variety of accents: German, British, Boston ("Bah-sten"). Most are young, but a few appear close to my age. One couple in particular draws my attention. The man looks like he's in his late 60s. He approaches me and asks my name, where I'm from, how far I'm headed. He introduces himself as Max, from Easton, Pennsylvania. After he's done with me, he cheerfully approaches the other hikers. *Really nice guy. One of the most outgoing hikers I've yet met.*

His wife looks much younger, at least from the back. She's wearing tight, olive-green hiking slacks that show off her curves. She turns around to adjust something, and her face is pretty, too. She's wearing wire-rimmed glasses, giving her an intellectual look. I'll confess I've always had an affinity for good-looking women who wear eyeglasses. (Maybe it's a teacher fetish of mine...must've been Miss Barger in kindergarten.)

She has to be at least ten years younger than Max. I glance at her tight pants again. A cynical thought crosses my mind: *Is Max deliberately being so conversational to divert attention from his hot wife?* Then another cynical thought: *With a wife like that, no wonder he's so happy.* Then a more sober thought. *Maybe he's just friendly, Pete.*

My interest in the tight olive-green pants gets diverted when Nathan and his girlfriend appear on the trail, headed for the patio.

"Déjà vu all over again!" I yell over. Nathan smiles and lopes onto the patio. We update each other on the day's hiking. He says they're still aiming for Osgood Tentsite. But they're arriving for lunch awfully late, and I have my doubts they'll make it that far. Even if they do, they'll be lucky to find an unoccupied tentsite on this busy weekend. I'm tempted to say something, but Nathan seems so laid-back, I don't think it matters to him.

As they meander into the hut, I tip them off to the split pea soup. I mention that it's a lot tastier than cold bologna. Nathan smiles and lifts his "hunk 'o hickory" in acknowledgment.

I pull my gear together in preparation for attacking Mount Madison, which looms like the Matterhorn above the back wall of the hut. But just before hitting trail, I duck inside the hut to glance at the register, just out of curiosity... as one might flip through obituaries in the city paper to see if a familiar name will emerge. What happens

171

next is like something Rod Serling might have scripted.
Four pages into the register—where the hiker entries date
to several days prior—whose name do I see scribbled at the
bottom of one of the entries? *Rainbow Slug!* Yes, the very
same hiker who'd signed in just before me at Springer
Mountain three years earlier. She (or he) had written a brief
note complimenting the staff on the split pea soup. *Great
minds think alike, Rainbow.*

For several seconds, my legs get wobbly, and my brain
bobs like a cork on the ocean. A serendipitous meeting with
a phantom in the crinkled pages of two journals, three years
and over 1,200 miles apart. What are the odds of such a
thing occurring? Slim, indeed. But... there you have it.

*Rainbow Slug. How many trails have you hiked since
Springer? Where do you hail from, and to where are you
headed? What are your aspirations, your hopes and
dreams? What forces work inside you? I'll never know.*

We're all corks on the ocean. All anonymous aliases.

There are times when I have sudden urges to shoot off-
trail and go "primitive," to just explore. Like after crossing
the cog rail tracks near Mount Washington, and gazing
down at that big green valley of Great Gulf Wilderness. But
now is not one of them. I like the comfort of a good trail.
While I remain on it, I'll be safe. It'll carry me back to
civilization, to my car, then to my home and Lynn.

(I hike off-trail only once, out of necessity, and it
doesn't turn out well. I describe this experience later in the
book.)

Mount Madison pushes right up against the backside of
the hut. *Very* steep angle. I tilt my head and see dozens of
hikers poking amongst the boulders. There's no "welcome
mat" at the foot of Madison, no entry ramp, no soft
climbing to ease one into a steeper ascent later. It's
immediately straight uphill. Cairns and painted blazes

aren't needed here, one only needs to follow the hikers in front, picking whatever boulder seems appropriate that second. Max and his foxy wife soon appear alongside me. They wear smaller day packs, which means they're soon in *front* of me. But I'm ok with this. I focus on Max's wife, whose svelte figure helps pull me up the mountain face, until her soft form gets lost amongst the rocks and the other climbers. *Hopefully I'll see her...them...at the top.*

The south face of Mount Madison could be my steepest climb since Blood Mountain in Georgia. The climb is just a repetitive body-hoist over large boulders. I keep myself as close to horizontal as possible, fearful that my heavy pack will pull me backwards. And because I'm severely acrophobic, I never look down.

I reach the top in about a half hour or so, feeling very winded. *A short, steep climb.* The social club here reminds me of Mount Adams, and there are maybe a dozen hikers lolling about the rocks and crevasses, some with panting dogs alongside. Max is here and offers me a big smile and nod, as if to say "We made it! By the way, don't I have a hot-looking wife?" (She's curled up next to him reading a map, looking very attractive, and very intelligent.) I munch on some granola, resting just long enough to catch my breath. Then I start down the north face.

This side of Mount Madison is just as rocky as the south. *Is there any part of the White Mountains that isn't rocky?* Rather than a steep drop to a small valley, however, it's a long glide into the distance. I meet a few interesting hikers on the way down: a middle-aged French-Canadian couple who speak broken English; a father and his son, originally from Newport, Rhode Island, who say they hike the Presidentials regularly, but only so they can drink the soup; and several other small groups, all taking advantage of the holiday and enjoying short day hikes, mainly via the many side trails.

I can't forget that day down in Georgia when I went an entire day without seeing anyone, until Chester, at Dick's Gap. But my hikes thus far have all coincided with holidays, and it seems to be getting really crowded out here. I'm feeling more like a tourist than a backpacker. The Appalachian Trail is getting increasingly popular, spurred on by books, movies, and people's ever-burgeoning need for a little natural healing in these dark days of mass shootings, and the spiritually bankrupt world of sitcoms, dot coms, and emoticons. More and more, the city seems to be infiltrating the trail. *I think I'm ready for a different hiking experience.*

Horace Greeley famously wrote "Go West, young man, and grow up with the country." He didn't intend his words to apply to a backpacking trip undertaken by a 58-year-old man. He was referring to the now-contentious idea of Manifest Destiny. But, coming down from Mount Madison, I decide maybe it's time to "Go West, *old* man, and *explore* the country."

First, I need to take flight from the Whites.

The north side of Mount Madison continues down, then down, then down, and it's a long while before I reach treeline. Then it's a lengthy trek along a narrow rockpath through evergreen scrub. I pass one lone hiker, who appears to be in a hurry, and no wonder: sunlight is diminishing and there are no overnight spots where the poor guy's headed.

As the last rays of sunlight filter away, I come to an intersection. A sign indicates Osgood Tentsite is to the left. I enter this modest campground and count about a dozen flat tentsites, all of them occupied except one tiny area toward the rear, on the left, up a little hill. It's just big enough for my two-man tent. I'm fortunate to arrive when I do, because while pounding in my tent stakes, several other hiking groups appear, only to have to retreat toward the AT. I'm not sure if Nathan and his girlfriend ever arrive…they may have chosen to remain at Madison Hut. He was in no hurry, anyway.

Since this is my last night in the Whites, I reward myself with my favorite freeze-dried meal of chili-mac, followed by a thick, aromatic Romeo y Julieta cigar. A big group of college-aged kids, camped next door, sound like they're having a storytelling contest. They make a decent racket (but are polite enough to hit the sack after I click off my headlamp later).

It's been a good day. My legs returned me to the main trail from lonely, isolated Perch Shelter; my pack and I then corralled Mount Adams, where we met several confused lambs from Abraham's flock; then my legs, arms, and Max's wife pulled me to the top of Mount Madison, where Max's smile—and his wife's figure—helped soften the hard rock. Oh, and I can't forget Nathan. And Rainbow Slug.

I blow smoke rings for all of them.

After dousing the light, I reflect some more. I chose to hike the Whites because, not only do they present to the AT backpacker one of the most scenic portions of the entire Appalachian Trail, but they're also a challenge. Thru-hikers have told me that Pennsylvania is difficult due to the rocks, and southern Maine is tough due to the isolation and ruggedness. Although I haven't hiked in those places, I'm sure the White Mountains of New Hampshire are also up there. The jagged, angular boulders require careful footing and strong hamstrings and calves. The rock isn't as pretty as the pink granite in Acadia National Park, but it's more intimidating. The altitudes don't compare to those on the Pacific Crest Trail and Continental Divide Trail, but the Presidential Range nonetheless offers steep and strenuous vertical ascents. The volatile weather, too, especially on lofty peaks like Lafayette and Washington, has to be

175

respected. One needs to be well-prepared and in good shape to hike these hills. But the rewards are many.

I'm a little disappointed that I had to break my hike into two sections. But I know I could've gone from Franconia Notch to Pinkham Notch in one fell swoop, had not my spondylolisthesis not interrupted my running, which sapped my strength and stamina. And I'm glad I was perceptive enough to quit after reaching Crawford Notch.

On Labor Day morning, I get a good early start. I predict just a couple hours of hiking until I reach Pinkham Notch, where I'll either hitchhike or find a shuttle to my car at Crawford Notch. At the trail intersection, I fill my water bottle. I meet two men, one of whom looks about my age. I let them get a head start, telling them they'll end up passing me, anyway. But after about ten minutes, I whisk by while they're catching their breath.

This fills me with confidence, and my hiking stride becomes powerful.

At a river crossing, I encounter two thru-hikers who'd camped out by the bridge. They look like two forest trolls who've just awakened. *Probably refused admission at Osgood.* One, the older of the two, has a silver beard and is smoking a cigarette. Cigarette smokers are rarely seen on the AT. I'm tempted to have him pose for a photo as a rare souvenir, but don't want him to toss me over the bridge, so I decide against it.

I continue downward as the trees become taller, the trail becomes wider, and soil begins replacing rock. I cross Mount Washington Auto Road, where a shuttle van filled with Mount Washington tourists sits on the roadside. The driver is walking around outside the van. She sees me with my big blue pack and warns me about bears, telling me she saw bear prints about a quarter-mile down the trail.

The tourists are looking at me benignly from inside the van. Just like arriving at Walasi-Yi at Neel's Gap in Georgia, and despite the reality that I'm merely a lowly section hiker nursing a bad back, I feel like a celebrity, with my pack, bedraggled beard, and soiled bandana. *Someday, I'll be inside one of those vans, leaning on Lynn. Maybe perusing an AAA pamphlet, with dribble at the corner of my mouth, looking wistfully out the window at backpackers much younger and fitter. Hopefully, I have a few years left before it happens.*

But that's not my only thought. The tourist van reminds me of a scene in the book *Desert Solitaire: A Season in the Wilderness*, by Edward Abbey. (Abbey was a spiritual father to the environmental organizations Earth First! and Greenpeace. He was around long before the word "environmentalist" even existed. Blunt in his opinions, whose pen was both poetic and fierce, and who raged against government, the military-industrial complex, unrestrained technology, industrial tourism, and agri-business, Abbey recognized as far back as the 1950s that America was rapidly losing large chunks of pristine wilderness areas…and that *desert* wilderness isn't just barren wasteland, but it possesses its own unique vibrancy, mysticism, and spirituality).

In 1956 and 1957, Abbey found employment as a park ranger at Arches National Monument in remote and desolate southeast Utah. While working there, he lived alone in a trailer. His solitude allowed him to do a lot of observing and thinking. Occasionally, though, he met and conversed with a rangers and ranchers, and also some tourists.

One of the tourists was a businessman who accused him of being opposed to civilization, science, and humanity (familiar accusations levied at those, like Abbey and myself, who feel wilderness should exist on its own terms, and not on man's terms):

> We were not communicating very well. All night long we thrashed the matter out, burning up half a pinyon pine in the process…With his help I discovered I was not opposed to mankind, but only to man-centeredness, anthropocentricity, the opinion that the world exists solely for the sake of man; not to science, which means simply knowledge, but to science misapplied, to the worship of technique and technology; and not to civilization but to culture.[4]

After burning up those pine logs and parting with the man, Abbey says he disappeared from Arches sometime before the following evening. But the man left a forged signature in the tourist register. Abbey writes "it wouldn't have fooled anybody—*J. Prometheus Birdsong*. He won't be back."

Then Abbey closes his chapter with the comment "But don't get discouraged, comrades—Christ failed too."

I glance back at the Mount Washington tourist van, filled to capacity. I wonder if any tourists approximate those whom Abbey encountered in 1957, just before "bureaucrats" and "pencil-pushers" stopped up the Colorado River with Glen Canyon Dam, so that motorboats could buzz over what used to be ancient grottos, natural tunnels, emerald pools, and the pictographs and petroglyphs of mysterious, indigenous societies of long ago.

Regrettably, comrades, many are the J. Prometheus Birdsongs in this world.

I never see the bear prints the van driver warned me of, but I start to see young couples with small packs. Then

---

[4] Abbey, Edward, *Desert Solitaire: A Season in the Wilderness* (Touchstone, New York, 1990)

young families with *no* packs: parents with their children, courageously battling the effects of NDD (nature-deficit disorder), some taking selfies. Then I arrive at a cluster of red, wooden buildings, comprising a lodging facility, restaurant, gift shop, storage shed, and bathrooms. People are everywhere. Cars are parked on the side of NH-16 for probably a half-mile down the road. It's a palpable shock after being in the mountains for the last several days.

I locate the sign that reads "MEN," then go inside to urinate and examine my ugly mug in the mirror.

I don't know if hardcore distance hikers experience this, but I have some disconcerting emotional shifts when I return to civilization after being isolated (or semi-isolated) in the wilds, even for a short time. Here's the plot of my screenplay of *Return to the Zombie Apocalypse*:

The first thing I do is call Lynn. "Hi honey. I'm still alive. I really missed you. Can't wait to get home and see you. I know you missed me. Did Sheba?"

I arrive at the motel and drag myself to the front desk, with gnats stuck to the stubble on my face. In the lobby, heads turn, but I don't mind. The desk clerk hands me my room key, and I trudge down the hallway, salivating while anticipating dinner at the Italian restaurant she recommended. I enter the room. The cool air-conditioning refreshes me like lemon-lime ice. (*Chester, you're a nice guy, but I don't care what you think about motel air conditioning.*) Then I strip off my rags and enter the shower, turning the knob so the water stings without burning, then spend ten minutes rubbing soap over every inch. *Ahhh.*

Then find the red-and-green décor restaurant and stuff my gut with lasagna, garlic bread, Caesar salad, and Samuel Adams while being serenaded by Frank Sinatra.

Back to the motel, turning fewer heads in the lobby this time, into the cool room, flick on Turner Classic Movies, fling a couple pillows against the bedstead, then lose myself in an old flick (hopefully a film noir with a bad girl like Gloria Grahame).

The good vibes continue until morning, as I anticipate one more glutton-fest, this one an all-you-can-eat breakfast buffet.

Then things begin to change. Incrementally.

During breakfast, there's an out-of-shape couple sitting next to me wearing t-shirts reading "GATLINBURG DINOSAUR PARK" and "PIGEON FORGE FUDGE."

The motel deems it important to serenade me with cable news ("breaking," of course) delivered by the glass teat mounted above my breakfast table. Maybe it's the wildfires in California. Or the latest mass shooting that Congress won't address. It's often a U.S. presidential speech, inevitably concluding with the line "…and God bless the United States of America!" (I'd love to inform the president that, assuming there *is* a God…He, She, or It probably doesn't recognize geographic boundaries, and *certainly* doesn't bless the United States for its treatment of the original inhabitants.)

(Long ago, Herman Melville used the phrase "civilized hypocrisies and bland deceits.")

Driving to the interstate, I idle at several stoplights while viewing animal carcasses on the roadside and billboard messages that want to claw into my wallet. Often, I have to honk at the vehicle in front, because the driver, head bowed in reverence to her digital god, is busy texting her friend or checking her Facebook status.

If I can find a good blues or jazz station at the left end of the FM dial, I'm doing well.

As I drive further from the trail toward home, the green spaces thin out, until eventually it's all asphalt, fences, tract housing, outlet malls, and Chick-fil-A's. If it's election season, the suburbs abound with political yard signs. If it's spring, I need to roll up the windows to block the odor of selective herbicide.

Not long after arriving home, and smothering Lynn with hugs and kisses, and throwing the ball with Sheba, I'm ready to return to a place where "man is a visitor who does not remain."

Maybe the moral of my screenplay is that wilderness—for me, at least—is about reaching something, but also about getting *away* from something else.

Today, on NH-16 at Pinkham Notch, I'm fortunate. After only a half hour of my thumb in the air, a Subaru with two kayaks on top picks me up. This gets me to the town of Glen. From there, it's a 20-minute wait until a young guy in a pickup truck stops. His daughter is asleep in a baby seat in the back. He's a local who works a low-paying maintenance job at a nearby lodge. I try to press some money on him, but he politely refuses. Eventually, I talk him into it.

As I get out of the truck, I tell him to enjoy his little girl while he can, because the years fly by. He toots his horn as he pulls out of Ripley Parking Lot.

Turning my car key, I realize that this second backpack trip in the White Mountains is my first camping excursion in thirteen years in which I wasn't rained on. And other than my potentially catastrophic fall on Israel Ridge, when I smacked my head on spruce-covered rock, I have no physical complaints. My minor queasiness and headache quickly disappeared, and my spondylolisthesis never returned. And my new inner-frame backpack didn't aggravate the shoulder ailment I had in Shenandoah and Georgia.

My only irritation is a minor sunburn on my upper arms, which I got while extending my thumb for a ride out of Glen.

Then again, there's always something wrong with me. If nothing's wrong with me, then something's wrong.

The Continental Divide Trail— Centennial Range

But she's never seen the Northern Lights
Never seen a hawk on the wing
Never seen Spring hit the Great Divide
And never heard Ol' Camp Cookie sing

—Michael Burton, from the song "Night Rider's Lament"

Old Friends and Weathered Guitars

E arly in this book, when I began section hiking at Springer Mountain on the Appalachian Trail, I first mentioned my walking stick. I'd named it "Kip." I chose this name for my wooden talisman because it's also the name of a camping friend from childhood. He played an important part in my writing this book and was one of the motivators for me to begin section hiking. When I took my own advice and decided to leave the bustle of the AT and go West, I chose to hike the Continental Divide Trail (CDT), which extends 3,100 miles from Mexico to Canada. I decided to visit a segment that I'd learned Kip himself had traversed thirty years earlier. Because he's so vital to this book, particularly this trail segment, I'd like to talk about him.

In the spring of 2013, I visited my mom, who, after a long absence, had moved back to the town where I'd grown up. I'd left my hometown several decades earlier, having scurried away after college to travel the country, then relocate to the city and start a family. While visiting Mom,

I decided to do an early Sunday morning run through one of the neighborhoods where our family had lived in the 1960s. If you've ever visited a familiar place from long ago, especially a place where little has changed, you know what a strange and exhilarating experience it can be. Memories trickle in like dappled sunlight. The hill where my bike skidded on gravel and sent me tumbling to the pavement. The houses whose lawns I wrestled on and ran across, and that now may or may not contain familiar faces.

The park where my dad taught me how to ice skate.

As I approached our old house, I ran past a well-maintained single-story yellow house with black shutters and two front doors. This was where Kip had lived. Although Kip wasn't one of my regular playmates (he lived on a street parallel to mine, which is practically across the ocean when you're a kid), we were still pretty close. He was the only kid who was in all my classes from kindergarten through fourth grade. We were also in the same Cub Scout den, learning to tie various knots and encouraging each other as we collected merit badges. And I think we feasted on cake and ice cream together at a few shared birthday parties.

Physically, Kip was very striking. He had silky, coal-dark hair, and his skin was a deep shade of sienna brown. He had dark-brown, sparkling owl eyes, and a small, impish smile. Though he wasn't Indian, he could have easily passed for one. I remember him being slightly short and, unlike most of my friends, not too athletic (although I later learned he became an excellent snow skier). His small stature, unusual looks, and quiet demeanor made him a perfect target for teasing or bullying. But, while kids can be unbelievably cruel, I don't remember Kip ever being bullied. He had a nobility that even we kids could recognize.

I knew a little about what some of my other friends had become after they grew up. Mike and Whit became doctors and moved far away. Jim was a plumber, John a lawyer,

Bill an accountant, and Joe worked in a Coca-Cola plant.
But I never knew what happened to Kip. He was bright, so
I imagined him joining the so-called "professional ranks."
He had a unique name, and I figured it wouldn't be too
much trouble to locate his whereabouts via the internet. As
I jogged past his house that chilly, grey March morning—
with the tang of cold air on my skin, fresh oxygen in my
lungs, and a deep feeling of nostalgia—I made a mental
note to do this.

What I later found out surprised me. Kip hadn't become
a doctor, lawyer, or accountant. In fact—as the cliché
goes—he'd shunned the standard American Dream to
pursue his own dream. Sometime during the 1980s, he'd
moved to the mountains of Montana to become a
folksinger. And, as I later discovered after listening to
recordings of his songs, a very good one. Probably at the
same time I was checking guests into motel rooms, Kip was
skiing, hiking, writing and learning songs, and performing
his music in dimly lit bars and warm, cozy ski lodges. He'd
also made a lot of friends and become a local legend,
blowing harmonica and strumming a well-worn guitar...a
sort of mountain Woody Guthrie, singing heartfelt tunes
about the cafes, cowboys, white-tipped mountains, and
sprawling green valleys of Montana.

I regretted that I didn't get to know Kip as an adult. We
seemed to share a lot of the same ideals and interests. Like
Kip, music and nature are very important to me. Like him, I
have songs I want to live in, and wild places that I dream
of. Even beyond childhood, I know we'd have hit it off.

But unlike Kip, I never managed to fully break those
chains of conformity that dreamers almost unknowingly
become entangled in. I'd progressed only enough to touch
the hem of my aspirations. But Kip had the guts to thrust
both his hiking boots into the great unknown. However
brief, he'd adopted a lifestyle that was free and organic. He
believed in himself enough to pursue a less-traveled road of

his own choosing, one not crowded with other commuters hungry to "fit in."

I have two vivid memories of Kip. Strangely, they both coincide with pivotal moments in my life, when my character was still forming. The first occurred in kindergarten. Kip was Jewish, and I remember one day during show-and-tell he shared his faith with the class. He also brought in matzo crackers to pass around. Even though they were unsalted and unlike our regular diet of sugared cookies, we all liked them. More importantly, Kip's presentation was my first awareness that people can have differences that are beyond the physical. And that this is a good thing. It's a lesson I need to relearn time and again.

The other memory occurred when we were about nine and attended summer camp together. Our moms had signed us up as buddies and cabin bunkmates for two one-week stints. It was the first time either of us had been away from home for longer than a night. I was pathetically lonely and homesick, and I still remember crying into my pillow at night. But Kip made friends with another kid in our cabin. This kid, Eddie, was maybe a year older, from the rougher side of town, and he had a swagger. I didn't like Eddie, but he liked Kip, and the two of them teamed up. Of course, this made me even more lonely and homesick. But I distinctly remember Kip approaching me later in the week and saying "Pete, I don't think Eddie likes me anymore, he hasn't talked to me in a while." Maybe I'm romanticizing here. But I really believe this was his way of trying to make me feel better.

I didn't return after that first week of camp. I was just too homesick. In hindsight, I wish I *had* gone back, because my avoidance initiated a pattern that dogged me for a long while. But Kip, who was more courageous than me, did return. I've often wondered how he fared. My family moved out of the neighborhood soon after, so I didn't find out. I never saw Kip again, either. My guess is that those wooded hills, where we lived, hiked, and listened to stories around late-night campfires in the summer of 1967, helped inspire Kip's migration to big sky country.

Kip died at a young age, very suddenly, in 1991. At his memorial on the Gallatin River, in single-digit temperatures in the snow, hundreds of people showed up to pay their respects. In fact, he was so beloved, an environmental charity was established in his name, and there are people in southwestern Montana who to this day tell stories of how he touched their lives.

Only a year before his death, Kip strapped his battered guitar to his backpack and hiked the CDT along a ridgeline in the Centennial Mountains. This section of the CDT is unusual. It skirts two great states, Montana and Idaho. It also offers a spectacular view of the Teton Range near Yellowstone National Park. At the northwestern corner of Yellowstone, the trail meanders westward toward the sunset; the largest section of the Continental Divide to do this.

So, I got the urge for going. I was so looking forward to visiting that stretch of trail in the Northern Rockies where, so many years before, my childhood friend had hiked into the red-orange glow of the West.

Bozeman is in southwestern Montana in the shadow of the Northern Rockies. For many people, it's a jumping off point for Yellowstone National Park. The town was established in 1868 and named for John M. Bozeman, who blazed a trail through here to connect the emigrant Oregon Trail with a Montana gold-prospecting town called Virginia City. (Virginia City refused to become a ghost town like so many other old mining towns, though its population is now under 200 people.) Before Bozeman's trail opened up the area to white settlement, it was occupied for thousands of years by indigenous tribes, most recently the Crow Nation.

Evergreen Dreaming

Today, Bozeman is a thriving "college town," with a distinct outdoorsy Western aura. Main Street is littered with bars, cafes, brick alleyways, green store awnings, chained-up bicycles, used bookstores, apparel shops, fishing gear and outdoor adventure stores, and eye-catching rococo adverts pasted indiscriminately in the windows. Mature, green trees sprout from the sidewalks, and a few hanging flower baskets add to the warm naturalness. The smells of burger grease and wood-fired pizza wafts from cafe windows and doorways.

West of town is the manicured, soulless, and ever-sprawling retail zone, pushing up against old "BoZone" like a carcinoma.

After pushing my car from Casper, Wyoming, and making a side pilgrimage to Little Bighorn in sizzling heat (I was hoping to join Sitting Bull and Crazy Horse in a big Indian encampment that I'd heard rumors of), all I want now is a soft bar stool and a cold, frothy beer. But I need to buy bear spray for my hike the next day, so I cruise past the bars and old brick buildings downtown and continue west.

I get directions and find the strip mall with an REI (it stands for "Recreational Equipment, Inc."). REI is an outdoors version of Wal-Mart that sells every hiking and camping item imaginable. *Twenty bucks for a plastic trowel to scoop your poop?* I'll estimate that eighty percent of this gear is unnecessary. But, long ago, P.T. Barnum said a certain type of person is born every minute, and those people are still being born.

(Before any loyal REI customer or employee tracks me down at my home, let me say that I buy all my hiking and skiing equipment at REI. It's a great store, with high-quality merchandise, fantastic deals, and over-the-top customer service. The company is also a Green Power Leader (recognized by the EPA) and environmental steward (recognized by Leadership in Energy and Environmental Design, or LEED), among other things. I merely feel the store is guilty of product excess. But in the land of buttermilk and Tupelo honey, which celebrates its amassed junk with reality shows like *Storage Wars*, excess is everywhere.)

After ten minutes of vainly searching for bear spray, I find someone with a name tag who isn't helping anyone else. He's a short, skinny guy with glasses and one of those popular "lumberjack" beards. His beard is so large and bushy, and his body so slight, he looks like a little tumbleweed whisking around the aisles.

Bearded one shows me how to use the spray. Just snap back the plastic tab and squeeze the trigger, like a miniature fire extinguisher. It seems easy. But in a crucial moment, with 500 pounds of clawed fury in front of me, would I panic and spray myself instead? I shudder at this thought.

I decide not to buy a pooper scooper, figuring I can use a stick or rock to bury my shit. But I do grab an extra water flask. There's evidently a 17-mile stretch of the CDT with little or no water, so I want to be prepared. Between my BPA-free water bottle and the flask, I can now carry up to eighty-two ounces of water. *Hopefully that's enough for the dry stretches.*

I wave goodbye to bearded one and stroll out of REI with my necessities. I call Lynn to assure her I've safely arrived at my jump-off point, and that I'm now armed to defend myself from any aggressive grizzlies I might encounter.

For me, the grizzly bear is, along with the timber wolf, the most impressive mammal on the continent, a fearless and fearsome predator that surpasses even man on the food chain. Grizz once flourished throughout most of western America. Today, there are only small populations in Greater Yellowstone Ecosystem (GYE), Glacier National Park, and isolated pockets in the Northern Rockies. So, it's possible I could see one. But even these few, small populations aren't secure. In 1975, there were only an estimated 136 grizzlies in the GYE.[5] In response, the Endangered Species Act protected them by designating them as "threatened." Over the past forty years, the grizzly population has rebounded to approximately 690 animals.

But in 2017, the year of my CDT hike, the U.S. Fish and Wildlife Service delisted grizzlies from protection. This means that the states of Wyoming, Montana, and Idaho will now manage non-Yellowstone bear populations, not the federal government. This action could precipitate indiscriminate removal of what the states consider "nuisance" bears. It could also reintroduce sport hunting of grizz. Republican politicians in these three states have been pushing for this for years. With a reckless and environmentally insensitive president now in the White House, and a Republican majority in Congress, this could become reality.

Biologists and conservationists are increasingly concerned. They argue that, while Yellowstone grizz will still be managed by the National Park Service, Yellowstone is a very small terra island, and climate change will increasingly imperil the genetic diversity of wildlife there, including grizzly food sources. Numerous Native American tribes in the West, who consider the grizz to be sacred, also oppose delisting, saying they weren't even consulted.[6]

One positive bit of news, arriving six months after my hike in March 2018, was Interior Secretary Ryan Zinke's expression of support for grizz in the Northern Cascades. "I grew up on the flanks of Glacier National Park," Zinke said. "And I have dealt with grizzly bears all my life...I'm in support of the great bear, and in support of doing this right. This is not reintroduction of a rabbit."

---

[5] https://www.nps.gov/yell/learn/nature/bearesa.htm
[6] https://www.nytimes.com/2017/06/22/science/yellowstone-grizzly-bear-endangered-species-list.html

(A grizz recovery had been announced during the Obama administration, but halted—without explanation—after his successor took office.)

After Zinke's announcement—still only a verbal endorsement of grizz—Western cattlemen immediately rushed to respond, arriving at a strange conclusion that reintroduction would be "a blow for the entire North Cascades ecosystem," and characteristically demonizing supporters of grizzly reintroduction as being "radical environmental activists."[7]

After the Lakota's land was stolen, and the bison herds reduced to near-extinction, Chief Sitting Bull famously said, about the American republic and its government, "They claim this mother of ours, the earth, for their own use, and fence their neighbor away...If America had been twice the size it is, there still would not have been enough."[8]

As late as 2009, historian Edmund Sears Morgan put his own spin on Sitting Bull's words:

> (G)reed is simply one of the uglier names we give to the driving force of modern civilization. We usually prefer less pejorative names for it. Call it the profit motive, or free enterprise, or the work ethic, or the American way...[9]

We decimated the American bison. Then poisoned and shot the gray wolf until extinct in the lower forty-eight

---

[7] https://www.seattletimes.com/seattle-news/interior-secretary-ryan-zinke-throws-support-behind-grizzly-bear-recovery-in-north-cascades/

[8] https://en.wikiquote.org/wiki/Sitting_Bull

[9] https://www.smithsonianmag.com/travel/columbus-confusion-about-the-new-world-140132422/

states. Miniscule wolf populations now exist in the
Northern Rockies, thanks to reintroduction efforts by a few
sympathetic groups.

The grizzly bear, America's largest and most noble
carnivore, now hangs in the balance. Rid the land of the
grizz? So much easier then to drill, extract, build, develop,
exploit.

Call it the profit motive, or free enterprise, or the work
ethic...or the American way.

Whenever I go on a long car trip, like many people, I
bring music. At one time I brought cassette tapes. Now, it's
compact discs. One of the discs I bring on this trip is a
collection of live performances by Kip.

I don't know much about the history of these songs.
They were cobbled together by various Montana friends
after Kip died, then released independently on cassette. I
assume he performed them in local clubs to small groups of
people, because he gives spoken intros to a few of them.
Most are cover songs. Some are by artists I'm familiar
with...Tom Rush, Hank Williams Jr., Michael Martin
Murphy, and Bob Marley...but others I've never heard of.
Many songs have Montana as a theme, love notes to that
spectacular state, which Kip adopted as his second home
after fleeing Ohio.

When I first heard the cassette (listening comfortably in
a beanbag chair one cold winter night), my reaction was
"Holy shit. That's Kip's high-pitched voice." I realize this
statement sounds fishy, considering I hadn't spoken with
him in almost forty-six years. But it's true.

Recovering from the initial shock at again hearing his
voice, I settled in to absorb his muse. Initially, he sounded
like someone struggling to be something he wasn't. He
sounded like your typical suburban Ohio exile trying to cop
a folksy cowboy pose. I was impressed by his guitar

playing and his ability to sing and project himself. But not much else.

After a second listen, though, I noticed something. It was a plaintiveness in his voice. Particularly on the song "This Here Mandolin" (aka "Hobo's Mandolin"). It's a well-written song to begin with, a story song written by a little-known songwriter named Michael Peter Smith, and covered by folksinger Tom Rush on his 1975 album *Ladies Love Outlaws*. It's about a guy who inherits a mandolin from an old hobo who's approaching his last hour. Before the hobo bequeaths the mandolin, he gives the man some personal history about the instrument. He talks about the "old barns and watertanks" that make up its body, about the instrument's magical capacity to make a young girl open her window "like a warm bed on a rainy night." The mandolin has the "sound of the railroad" and can take "a hobo back home."

Rush's rendition of the tune is good. But Kip's stripped-down version is more personal. He adds some inspired minor-key, twelve-string guitar chords that—although I'm an adequate guitar player—I've yet to be able to duplicate. And he sings like he's the hobo himself, loath to part with his instrument, his protector and best friend. Or maybe he's the lucky man who inherited it. Whatever, there's an emotional honesty in his singing that's uncomfortably intense. Kip sings like he hopes his guitar will carry *him* back home.

Two other songs where Kip achieves this emotional depth are "Don't Count the Rainy Days" (Michael Martin Murphy) and "No Woman No Cry" (Bob Marley). Like "This Here Mandolin," they're sad songs. Marley's song is about government hypocrites that infiltrate Marley's group of friends, which he calls "the good people." He encourages his lady to hold on for brighter days. Murphy's song talks about "the dark before the dawn," and it, too, is about trying to hold on. But whereas Murphy's song is smooth, polished, and upbeat, Kip's is rough and pleading.

I'm not sure these songs are the best choices for embarking on a solo hike on an unfamiliar trail in the Northern Rockies, but they help connect me with Kip.

Another connection awaits me at The Haufbrau, where Kip once performed. From what I've read about this place, it's a cramped and raucous dive bar that specializes in live music, and it has a healthy disdain for propriety and cleanliness. It's been around since the Sixties. Most of the clientele are regulars: ex-hippies, bikers, construction workers, grey-whiskered bohemians wearing baseball caps, college professors, and occasional Montana State University students who want to look seedy and drink beer with people their parents' age.

(Years ago, my copy of *On the Road* tucked in my jacket, I was just like these students. *Many* years ago, I might add.)

I figure I've got time to guzzle a couple beers before heading south toward the town of West Yellowstone, where I'll be meeting my shuttle driver tomorrow at noon. So, I park my car near the corner of 7th Avenue and Main, and ask some folks outside a nearby bar for directions to The Haufbrau.

"It's that ugly building over there that looks like a bomb shelter," says one of them.

I stroll over to the bomb shelter, then wind my way through a crowd of smokers outside the main door (I think it's the main door...but I'm not sure). After I enter the L-shaped room, I'm taken aback by the scene. Although dinner time on Sunday evening, the juke joint's jumpin'. Several large, rectangular tables are plunked down in the middle of the main room, and every seat is occupied. Most of the bar stools are also occupied. I jostle between small groups of people and find a lone unoccupied stool near the end of the bar.

"WHAT'LL YOU HAVE!" yells the bartender over the din.

"WHAT'S ON SPECIAL!" I yell back.

He rattles off some names of local brews I don't recognize. I parrot back one of the names.

"GOOD CHOICE!" he screams.

I glance around. Peanut shells are scattered on the bar and floor. The ceiling, walls, and glass beer cases are covered with posters, stickers, and signs. A bicycle dangles from the ceiling above the bar like a pop-art chandelier. Wooden tabletops are affixed to the main ceiling, and every square inch of wood has carvings of people's names. *Trashy collegiate chic.*

There's a little stage in the corner. I barely make out what looks like a mural of a naked woman on the wall behind the stage. I focus on the stage stool while drinking my Bridger Brewing Antilogy Black IPA. I dim my eyes and envision Kip up there. I picture a skinny guy with aviator glasses and large baseball cap pulled down over fluffy black hair. There's a big brass harmonica strapped to his neck. His long fingers are stretched into unknown chords over the neck of his capo'ed guitar.

Over the noise, I struggle to recall the words and notes to "This Here Mandolin." It takes me a few moments, but eventually I hear the lonesome, high-country sound of Kip's voice:

Like a hex sign on a barn
This here mandolin keeps a hobo from harm

Maybe Kip's name is carved in the wood somewhere here. But it doesn't matter. Just to know that he played here is cool enough.

I drain my IPA, drop a couple bucks atop the peanut shells on the bar, then head outside. I snake through the smokers. It's still bright outside, and hot, too. I've heard that single-digit temps are normal in winter here. But in early August, it's still very hot. I've got winter clothes stuffed deep in my backpack for emergency, since one of the rangers told me there's still snow on top of the Centennials, but I find this hard to believe. *We'll see.*

197

I find my car on 7th Avenue. I remember seeing a road sign to West Yellowstone, so I glide down Main Street looking for the turnoff south. Near the center of town, I see a Subaru with a "KEEP IT WILD!" bumper sticker, the same sticker on the bumper of my Civic (next to my "I CLIMBED MT. WASHINGTON" sticker). "KEEP IT WILD!" is the unofficial saying of the Montana Wilderness Association, which is trying to preserve as much wild Montana territory as possible from industry and development. Though I live in Ohio, I'm a member of this group, among other environmental organizations.

I pull in front of the Subaru and, like an unapologetic pack animal, hope my fellow pack animal will see my sticker. Some folks, like Jackson in Virginia, prefer "DON'T TREAD ON ME." I'm a "KEEP IT WILD!" kinda guy.

After a few confused wrong turns, I find the turnoff and head east, then south on US-191 through the Gallatin Gateway toward West Yellowstone. The road runs parallel to the Gallatin River, crossing it several times. This historic river flows northwest from the northwestern corner of Yellowstone National Park, with its source at Gallatin Lake (elevation over 9,000 feet). It converges with the Jefferson River and Madison River at Three Forks, Montana, northwest of Bozeman, to form the powerful Missouri River. All three rivers were named by Lewis and Clark in 1805 during their journey with the Corps of Discovery to the Pacific Ocean. They named the Gallatin after Thomas Jefferson's treasury secretary, Albert Gallatin.

On July 28, 1805, Meriwether Lewis wrote in his journal that the Gallatin was seventy yards wide, shallower and more rapid than the other two, but that all three tributaries have "great valocity and throw out large bodies of water." He recorded that the beds of the rivers "are formed of smooth pebble and gravel, and their waters (were) perfectly transparent; in short they are three noble streams."

I'd already read excerpts from *The Journals of Lewis and Clark*, so I know about the significance of these rivers. The Corps of Discovery followed the westernmost Jefferson River. Lewis eventually arrived at a point where he could straddle the stream with both legs. The expedition then had to confront the Bitterroot Range of the Northern Rockies. The Gallatin River valley, on the other hand, remained unexplored for many years, and wasn't settled until 1863, after the U.S. government had, in a familiar tale, violated an 1855 treaty and stolen the land from the Blackfeet.[10] Today, the Gallatin River is a popular fly fishing destination. The movie *A River Runs Through It* was partially filmed here.

I reach the edge of the Bozeman commercial district and soon begin winding through dense forested foothills, following the course of the river, toward the Continental Divide. I see a small parking spot on my right, just before a bridge over the Gallatin. I slow down and turn in. There's one other car here. *Maybe someone is fishing nearby. It's starting to get dark.*

I step out of my car and walk across the lot toward the river. A narrow trail through low-lying brush leads me to the eastern bank of the Gallatin. Smooth, round stones and boulders litter the water's edge. I try to ignore the empty beer can sandwiched between two rocks. The river ripples gently. It is wide, although not as wide as the Little Miami River back near my home in Ohio. It's certainly more scenic, the water splashing over hundreds of rocks just under the surface, creating little sprays of white, singing a peaceful song of the mountains. Occasionally, a car swooshes over the bridge above me, disturbing the river's song. I gingerly step across the rocks until I find a pool of water, then I lean over and cup the water in both hands and splash it on my face. The cold liquid feels good against my hot skin.

---

[10] http://genealogytrails.com/mon/gallatin/earlyhistory.html

Evergreen Dreaming

With my camera, I preserve this view of the Gallatin, upstream and downstream. Then I return to my car. I pull out onto US-191, having not seen anyone. I've never been here before, but it feels like I have.

Evergreen Dreaming

As the sun continues to set behind the mountains west of me, I see a sign for Big Sky. Three things are now on my mind: a place to eat; an isolated yet safe location for the night, where I can park my car (my mobile tent); and Lone Mountain Ranch.

Lone Mountain Ranch is a family-oriented getaway tucked in a mountainside west of Big Sky. It has 27 log cabins, a rustic dining hall, saloon, horse stable, and hiking/skiing trails. In winter, ski tourists flock here for the Nordic skiing, and to enjoy evening sleigh rides, or to alpine ski at nearby Big Sky Resort. Fly fishermen come here in summers to fish for trout in the Gallatin, Madison, and other nearby streams. Hikers and kayakers also make reservations here.

Lone Mountain Ranch isn't a working ranch, but rather a "resort" ranch. Whereas working (aka dude) ranches have actual labor that goes on, such as herding cattle or sheep, resort ranches are like cruise ships: they specialize in *relaxation*. In other words, you don't have to get your hands dirty (unless you want to). Lone Mountain even offers yoga and massage to its guests.

I'm interested in Lone Mountain because Kip lived and worked here back in the 1980s. He sang country and western songs in the saloon. He probably rode the horses, too. Somewhere around here, he carved the letters "K I P" into a fencepost.

In his guitar case, Kip kept all sorts of knickknacks: scraps of songs, embossed guitar picks, old letters, cards, photos, buttons. His case and guitar were plastered with stickers and slogans. The entire rear of his rickety Datsun was a canvas for bumper stickers, and the hood advertised the call letters of his favorite radio station. The whole package—guitar, case, car, his clothing and his various hats—reminds me of those ancient caves with walls decorated with hieroglyphs and paintings. Kip's songs, stickers, and gewgaws seem intended to tell a story; a treatise on his life, and the people and principles he held close; a sort of autobiography.

At Lone Mountain Ranch, Kip got to know a man named Big Dan MacKenzie.

Big Dan MacKenzie was a renaissance man: a distance hiker, wilderness activist, folksinger, poet, and artist. MacKenzie packed more solo hiking into his fifty-seven years than perhaps anyone since John Muir, somewhere over 28,000 miles. Not only did he achieve backpacking's exalted "Triple Crown"—thru-hikes of the AT, PCT, and CDT—he hiked them alone. He also walked coast to coast, and did many other solo hikes in the mountains and deserts of the West.

MacKenzie had experienced things most of us only fantasize about, or view on a television or movie screen. He'd come face to face with a dozen grizzlies; spent days crossing parched desert lands while draining his water supply; slid down an icy mountain slope, only to be saved from going over the cliff when his guitar neck jammed into the ice; and witnessed the Northern Lights (Aurora Borealis) on the Great Divide.

But unlike most distance hikers, MacKenzie took his connection to the wilds a step further. Like Muir, he worked long and hard to convince politicians and the public of the aesthetic value of wilderness. He cultivated a biocentric approach to the natural world, believing that untampered flora and fauna needed to exist on their *own* terms, not man's. When he wasn't hiking, he was either regaling visitors to Lone Mountain Ranch with his songs and stories of the wilds (and leading sleigh rides in the winter), or entertaining school assemblies and civic groups with slides of his travels, accompanied by song. He firmly believed in protecting America's last wild places. A tall, bearded man with a growling singing voice, from all accounts MacKenzie was a gentle giant, and one who loved kids, with a heart and spirit the size of Denali. When it came to conservation, MacKenzie talked the talk and walked the walk. Literally.

Sometimes I wonder if the lanky hiker I saw on top of The Priest wasn't Big Dan.

Big Dan and Kip were good friends. They did a lot of singing and hiking together. I never met Big Dan, and only knew Kip from childhood. But as I approach Lone Mountain Ranch, I feel a tenuous kinship with them.

I turn right at a gas station, then chug on up a gentle rise, past the upscale, unincorporated community of Big Sky, then turn right on a crushed gravel road. I roll into a small parking lot that sits just above a large horse stable. Just above me is a large grassy clearing with a fire area and a few benches. Several attractive burnt-orange log cabins are on the far edge of the clearing. *It looks like the dining hall is up there to the right. Hopefully there's a meal which I can afford.*

Before I mosey up to the ranch chow hall like a half-baked Randolph Scott, I saunter over to the stable. Two horses are lingering by the split-rail fence. *Wonder if either of these were alive when Kip was here?* I pat the long neck of one of the horses as her tails switches contentedly. I breathe in the crisp mountain air, a pungent mixture of lodgepole pine, Douglas-fir, wood smoke, and horse manure.

Such heady, high-altitude odors always stir me to think of the old "what-might-have-been." I reminisce about the lanky hiker on The Priest. *I shoulda hiked the AT when I had the chance.* Also, the mountain town of Whitefish, Montana, which I fell in love with when crisscrossing the country in 1983. *I could have lived there. I could have chosen to be a poor but happy bachelor ski bum, giving guided tours in the backcountry, then drinking cheap beer with the loggers on Saturday night.*

Then again, maybe I should have studied harder in school.

As always happens when mulling over the choices I made and didn't make, I think how lonely I would have been without Lynn. I chose a conventional life with family and a torpid line of pragmatic jobs in the Midwest suburbs. *But I had some youthful kicks, and my wife and kids have given me love and smiles, over lots of years, and we all have good health.*

I eventually realize I have few regrets.

Glancing to the left, I see a petite young African-American woman walking slowly along the fence line toward the parking lot. She stops to stroke the neck of one of the horses, then continues toward me, as I continue to pat the other horse.

"I see you've met Daisy," she says.

"Yeah, we've had an introduction," I respond. "We both agree it's a great evening."

"It definitely is," she says, as she glides past me.

I watch her slowly trudge up the hill toward the Horn and Cantle Restaurant. *This is a real horsey place.* After a few minutes, I follow her.

By now, the sun has dipped behind the mountains, and the mountain forest shadows have blended into nighttime darkness. The Horn and Cantle is lit up like a Christmas tree. It's a large, rust-colored log dwelling with a large, gabled roof and expansive windows, immaculately clean, and with oversized wooden rocking chairs on the porch. A few groups of well-dressed adults are seated in an outdoor patio area on the porch. They're smiling contentedly while a middle-aged woman with long, sandy brown hair and a billowy dress quietly strums an electric guitar and trills a peaceful song.

Inside, about fifty thick wooden tables are arranged at angles to each other. Several cowboy-related prints grace the walls. A moose head is mounted on one of the walls, a bison head on another, and a stuffed cougar balances on a log beam above a giant stone fireplace. It's a glossy magazine cowboy setting, quite a contrast to The Haufbrau.

Although late, there are still quite a few people in the restaurant. I circle around the room, then find a seat at the bar in an adjoining room. Two young guys are pouring drinks behind the bar. On my left, sipping a margarita, is the woman I saw at the stables. We talk for a few minutes, and I learn that her name is Diamond, and she's from Charlotte, North Carolina. She's working here during the summer, and she discovered the ranch through a friend who's one of the chefs.

She asks if I had a nice visit with Daisy, then if I plan to order anything.

"I'd like to, but I'm waiting for the bartender," I respond with a tone of irritation, since neither of the two bartenders has even made eye contact.

Immediately, one of the bartenders comes over and asks what I'd like. *Must've overheard me.*

I order another IPA. I mull over the appetizers and entrees, then settle for the Caesar salad with white anchovies and cheese wafer, despite the bartender's suggestion that I order the fifty-dollar bison steak.

I tell Diamond about my upcoming hike. She's mildly interested, asking the by-now-usual questions "Are you hiking *alone?*" and "Aren't you afraid of *bears?*" But the bartender, Steven, overhears our conversation, and he lights up. Despite his earlier reticence, he turns out to be a friendly guy. He shares his love of outdoor activities, especially rock climbing and backpacking, and we discuss hiking logistics, various trails in Yellowstone, hitchhiking, grizzly behavior, pack weight, water filtration, and so on. I tell him I'd one day like to hike in Yellowstone Park, and he relates a hike that he and a friend did on the western side of the park. *Gotta remember this trail.* He also mentions that, just the other day, he drove past a grizz in Yellowstone. *Glad I invested in that bear spray.*

Steven asks me where I'm starting and ending my hike. When I say I'm ending at Monida then hitching back to West Yellowstone, he scribbles something on a piece of paper.

I finish my salad and cheese wafer, say goodbye to Diamond and Steven, then step outside feeling mildly buzzed from the IPA and the conversation with Steven. The sandy-haired woman with the guitar, whom I've learned is named Delilah, is still softly playing, singing what I recognize as a Jim Croce song. She looks about my age, maybe a little older. I debate whether I should request "This Here Mandolin." The song is so obscure, though, that I figure my request will just embarrass her. Plus, I need to hit the road and find a place to crash. So, I continue down the steps of the Horn and Cantle.

Very nice place. Clean and well-lighted. But I think I'm still more Haufbrau than Horn and Cantle.

The full moon offers just enough light for me to see the nature trail that meanders up the hill into the pines. I follow it. Behind me, in the grassy circle, a large campfire is crackling. Several kids tumble around in the grass while their parents relax near the fire. To the left is a quaint cabin with the name "Rainbow" above the front door. Other, similar cabins are nestled further back in the woods. I catch a whiff of smoke on the evening breeze and hear a horse neighing in the distance.

JULY 1967—HIDDEN HOLLOW CAMP

Mom and dad seemed real excited. Got my new, black, hooded sweatshirt to keep me warm at night. Also got my canvas Indian Guides knapsack. They took a photo of me in front of The Borg-Warner. I'm a little scared. But they said I'll be fine. These woods really smell. Not like the woods on Sherbrook Road. Wonder when we'll have our campfire and hear the ghost story. Horse Thief Jack. Hope I like the food. Hope I don't have to eat vegetables. The counselors are Mr. Chuck and Mr. Nelson. Mr. Nelson has goofy glasses. Mr. Chuck has dark skin and black hair. Like Kip. Wonder when he'll get here. I got the top bunk. I like the cabin name. "The Knapp." Think that's the name. The farthest cabin down the hill. The air smells funny. Don't know anyone here. Just Kip. Mom and dad walked down the road toward the car a few minutes ago. Where should I go now? There are games at the lodge. No, I'll go back to the cabin and wait. Lots of tree things here. Big, knobby roots. Hope I don't trip. The car ride here was long. I like that new song "Light My Fire." Now I'm alone. A week is a long time. I'll open the screen door and walk into the cabin. That's a loud slam. There's that thick wood smell. Mr. Nelson says hi. My bunk is on the right, in the

*back. I'll climb on the top bunk and lay on my
back. Look at that log ceiling. Mom and dad
are gone. My stomach feels funny. I'll wait for
Kip.*

I follow the nature trail up the slope, occasionally taking
deep inhales of the thick, luxuriant evergreen smells.
Eventually, the children's voices disappear, and all I hear is
soft wind through tree branches. Dark green pine needle
and rusty brown bark are everywhere. I pass a few more
cabins, then arrive at a large dwelling near the top of the
hill. It's an employee house instead of a guest cabin. Two
dogs tear around the corner of the building toward me,
barking loudly, but with tails wagging. I approach them,
kneel, and hold out my hand, but they back away. Then a
woman strolls down the drive toward me. She's pretty, with
cinnamon hair, maybe in her late twenties.

"Don't worry, they won't bite," she assures me.

"Yeah, they seem friendly. Maybe they sense I love
dogs."

"Could be!"

Too young to know Kip. Maybe she knows Big Dan.

"I'm visiting overnight, and I wonder if I could ask you
a question."

"Sure!"

"I'm trying to find a trail here that's named after Big
Dan MacKenzie. He used to work here, and he was good
friends with an old friend of mine."

"Oh," she says, acting a little surprised. "Did you know
Big Dan?"

"No, but I'm familiar with his music and writings. He
talks about my friend. He's sort of an inspiration for me."

"Wow. Yeah, I didn't know Big Dan, but I know of him.
He died a couple years before I arrived. His trail's up there,
near North Fork Cabin," she says, pointing up the
mountain.

"Ahh…thanks."

It's too dark, and I really don't want to climb any higher, with my CDT hike on the horizon.

"Yeah," I continue, now patting the dog's head, "I didn't know Big Dan either, but he seems pretty incredible."

"From what I hear, he certainly was."

We say goodbye, and I trudge down the hill toward my car.

It's a shame I can't visit Big Dan's trail. But it's only a minor path. Wonder where Kip carved his name. Anyway, I've got the Continental Divide to hike tomorrow. Kip was there, too. In fact, he's all around.

Climbing Toward Bigger Sky

After leaving Lone Mountain Ranch, I coast downhill into the chic resort community of Big Sky. Diamond had told me about a campground nearby, where I'd planned to pitch my tent. But fumbling in darkness is no fun, plus I'm still mildly buzzed from the IPA, so instead I coast into the first lodge in Big Sky, park at the edge of the lot, then squirm into my sleeping bag in the car trunk.

(Seriously, bunking in one's car isn't a bad way for a single person to travel. Find a safe spot, roll the window down a crack, lock the doors. Not as comfortable as a bed, certainly, but travel wipes come close to soap and washcloth, and sleep is no less fitful than in a motel room. The hundred bucks I conserve goes, instead, to things like gas, IPAs, and Caesar salads with white anchovies.)

Breakfast the next morning is orange juice and a granola bar, courtesy the corner convenience mart. Then it's a long, smooth downslope on US-191, following the gorgeous Gallatin River, through the tree-studded northwestern corner of Yellowstone National Park. I arrive at the West

Yellowstone Visitor Center with ample time to spare. Get my free parking pass, call Lynn, organize my backpack, scribble nervously in my journal, and relax near the ranger shack until the Yellowstone RoadRunner van shows up a few minutes after noon.

My shuttle driver, Wayne, is a friendly, no-nonsense guy. He reminds me of my Georgia AT chauffeur, Rance (Durgood and Golden Eagle were also pleasant fellows, although slightly quirky, especially Durgood…grunt, grunt). Wayne doesn't ask many questions about my hike, maybe because he daily transports numerous tourists into Yellowstone. I'm surprised when he tells me he's never shuttled anyone to Red Rock Pass, which is on the Idaho-Montana line only forty minutes from West Yellowstone. Around here, the big draw is undeniably Yellowstone National Park, and the big sightseers are tourist families.

Wayne has an enviable biography. He grew up in Yosemite, where his father was a park ranger. Over the years, he'd seen a lot of wilderness and wildlife, including elk, a few grizz, and one cougar. Like my other shuttle drivers, his vehicle is littered with maps. I can think of few better occupations: meeting diverse and interesting people, observing American wildlife up close, and scouring map lines of latitude and longitude in one of the most breathtaking places on the planet.

We curl around the northern rim of Henrys Lake, dotted with rental cabins and A-frame vacation homes. The lake is about eight square miles. In 1877, following the Battle of Camas Creek, the Nez Perce passed by Henrys Lake on their way to Yellowstone during a heroic flight toward Canada, chased by General Oliver Howard and the U.S. Army. In 1923, a dam was built that substantially increased the size of the lake. Today the lake is a popular trout fishing destination, including winter ice fishing. The lake and adjacent wetlands are also a magnet for numerous migratory birds, such as white pelicans, cormorants, great blue herons, bald eagles, hawks, cinnamon teals, and trumpeter swans.

As Wes's van dodges ruts and potholes along the gravel road, I get my first clear view of the eastern side of the Centennial Range, where I'll soon be hiking: a dense wall of wilderness that seems to extend forever northwest into the distance. I grip my knees tightly.

Although we don't seem to be going uphill, a large wooden sign on the left indicates we've arrived at Red Rock Pass. Wayne slows the van, glancing left and right with curiosity, as if he wants to remember every detail. He stops at the edge of the dirt, and we both climb out. It's a hot, dry day, the sun straight above and piercing down, and the only sound is a rhythmic ticking from the van engine.

Wayne opens the rear door, and I unload my pack. He then walks about thirty feet forward of the van, staring at a faint brown line running up the slope to the right. It's the eastern Idaho side of the CDT, leading to Squaw Pass. On the left, somewhere in the shadows of the tall evergreens, the CDT continues westward, over the Centennials.

That white trailer in the shade, on the left, looks out of place.

I'm staring at an ugly rusted white trailer. I expected isolation at Red Rock Pass. I was told the CDT outside of Yellowstone was infrequently hiked. But the trailer, tucked into sun-specked shadows of a grove of tall evergreens, indicates I have company. It rattles my preconceived and idealized view. My night dreams and daytime visions of Red Rock Pass didn't include an ugly rusted white trailer.

But such is life and death. H.L. Mencken said that "Men get into trouble by taking their dreams and hallucinations too seriously."

Wayne strolls back. He tells me to call him from Monida, in case I need a ride after I finish. I thank him and promise I will, unless I get in a hitch. I pull out our agreed upon fee, but he only charges me half, since he overestimated the driving time. *It's nice to encounter an honest businessman.* I pose in front of the Red Rock Pass sign while he uses my flip phone camera to snap a photo of me, clutching my pack straps, a nervous "Do-I-know-what-I'm-getting-into?" smile on my face. After he hands the phone back, I turn it off, since there's no reception up here anyway. I won't be turning it on until I call Lynn at the end of my hike. It's a pact I made with myself.

There's always a touch of trepidation when I start these section hikes. After all, the geography is a mystery, and maps tell only a small part of the story. Hiking alone on the CDT is especially daunting. Unlike the AT, there are no rectangular white blazes every few hundred yards for trail signposts. My pre-hike research revealed that many long sections of the CDT are unmarked, and the trail is sometimes hidden by weeds, wildflowers, and brush.

As I hoist my 35-pound pack, straighten my bandana, and step into the trees, I recall certain veteran hikers, on the web, describing how the CDT often ends at a rocky cul-de-sac, or branches off several directions in the middle of a meadow. Several of them freaked out when I said I wasn't bringing a GPS, only topographic maps and a compass. One person told me to update my will.

Safety in the wilds is important. That being said, I also think you can "over-safety" to the point of diminishing returns. People successfully relied on maps and compasses for hundreds of years before the advent of GPS. One of the appeals of backpacking is the sporting aspect, which includes basic orienteering skills. Knowing how to read a map and use a compass gives you a feeling of satisfaction. You can catch a lot of fish if you drain the water out of the pond, but how many fishermen want to do that? The enjoyment comes from being skilled using a rod, line, hook, bobber, and bait.

I think I've prepared well. I know basic map and compass skills, and I brushed up my knowledge with a class offered by REI. I joined an orienteering club in Cincinnati and did well in several competitions. I'm equipped with bear spray, whistle, first aid kit, adequate water, extra food and clothing. I also spent a lot of time studying my Jonathan Ley topo maps of the Centennial CDT, so I know the important logistics, like water locations, side trails, and tent sites. Other than hiking with a companion, I can't think of anything safer I could've done. But if I hike with a companion, my chances of meeting people like Diamond, Steven, Shemet, and Dylan are far less.

Some people view backpack trips as athletic activities only. Others enjoy being part of a trail fellowship or subculture. Those are all valid reasons for strapping on a backpack. But another motivator is to experience wilderness (however that term might be defined). I like going to places where, as Big Dan MacKenzie once said, "things work the way they're supposed to work," not how humans have designed them to work. If I'm tired, I stop and rest. If my water gets low, I ration it until I can replenish. Back at Crawford Notch in the White Mountains, I aborted my hike because I was too tired to continue. I did the same thing in North Carolina when I took the Kimsey Creek cutoff. If necessary, I'll do the same here.

Mencken's right about taking dreams and hallucinations too seriously. You *can* get into trouble. But it would be a shapeless life without any dreams.

There are two cleared areas along the wood line, but no distinct trail leading into either of them. I wander into the area on the left, where the RV is parked. Lotsa pines, but no trail. I glance at the RV. An old bike is attached to a rack in the front. The windows are dark. I figure maybe there's a family of day hikers out on the CDT today. But when I circle around the rear, the license plate is Utah. *Long way to drive for a day hike.*

After looping around the trailer, I see Wayne's van in the road, inching forward slowly. *Maybe he's making sure I find the CDT. Do I appear that insecure?*

I enter the clearing on the right, then see a wide trail with tire tracks, leading into the woods. I pass a couple fire rings on the left, and my confidence rises slightly when I see a small, arrowhead-shaped, blue-white-black, tin marker nailed to a tree: *Continental Divide Trail.* Then a white pickup truck rolls toward me, out of the forest. The driver rolls down his window. Two rangers are seated in front.

"Going hiking?" the driver asks me. He's very young, and the passenger looks even younger, and I wonder if they think a grey-fringed man hiking alone appears odd.

"Yes I am. Just starting out. I'm following an old friend's footsteps…even if it's only with my feet. Came all the way from Ohio."

"Wow, that's a long way. Have fun. Looks like you've got your bear spray," he says, nodding approvingly at the red canister on my belt.

"Yessir," I respond, now feeling like a student whose teacher just complimented him. "Could you tell me, is the trail fairly well-marked?" I'm still concerned, particularly after so many anecdotes and warnings from CDT veterans about the amazing, disappearing, phantom-like CDT.

"Yeah, in fact we just finished posting markers. You shouldn't have any trouble."

"Great, thanks for the reassurance. And thanks for all the work you do on the trails."

"Well, thank you for hiking it!"

I continue walking, as the ranger truck exits the woods. Ahead is a gated fence. I swing open the wood-and-wire door. Then I enter the great unknown…the most exhilarating part of any long hike.

I begin to climb. As the ranger promised, there are many virgin-wood blocks with "CDT" carved into them, nailed to the trees. Interspersed with these are official metal,

arrowhead-shaped, blue-white-black CDT markers. I'd love
to grab one of these eye-catching markers as a souvenir,
maybe to pin on the grey nylon that wallpapers my cubicle
at work. Some are so close together that one missing
marker could hardly matter. They're much more attractive
than rectangular splotches of white paint. But the rangers
were helpful and friendly, and swiping one would be theft
of government property, and a crime. So, I decide to
respect the U.S. government, which, of course, never
commits crimes.

My goal on this first half-day is to reach either Lillian
Lake, or slightly more distant Blair Lake, located on a side
trail. According to the notes in my Jim Wolf CDT trail
guide, Lillian Lake is "a lovely place." To get there, I need
to cross Hell Roaring Creek several times (all routes to
heaven lead through hell). I hike a large loop around the
north side of Nemesis Mountain, stopping occasionally to
drink in glorious views of Centennial Valley far beneath
me. I see one lone farmhouse in the center of this gigantic
green bowl, and I wonder who the people are that live in
such a picturesque setting. *A little touch of heaven down
there. But it must be extremely isolated, especially when the
snows are deep.*

As I round Nemesis, I descend steeply into a deep, rocky
chasm. A massive rock escarpment faces me, a large talus
wash, spilling into Douglas fir. High overhead swoops a
raptor. *Probably a golden eagle.* As I round a bend, I see
my first wild animal: a mangy red fox, staring at me from
the middle of the trail. He observes me for a few seconds,
then trots up the rocky slope and disappears

I soon arrive at Hell Roaring Creek. I've yet to visit hell,
but the white water does roar some, and my descent
coincides with a heat increase. I take some photos of this
abridged version of the Grand Canyon, then whack my way
through some briars and cross a wooden bridge to the
western side. I cross Hell Roaring Creek twice more, the
second crossing requiring me to remove boots and socks.

Ouch! Ow! Yikes! Damn, this is cold! I make it across, but
my ivory-white, bony little feet are mangled by the slippery
rocks underwater. *Next time, I'm keeping my boots on.*

I cross several large meadows with stunning views of
the surrounding mountains. The wildflowers are in full
blooming glory, a mix of lavender lupine, pink sticky
geranium, orange and yellow balsam root, and masses of
purple and white columbine. I stop periodically to gaze
across the slopes and valleys, hoping to see a spot of black
or silver in the distance. But it's unusually hot for this high
an altitude, and most of the bears and large carnivores are
probably hidden in the shade, waiting for sunset when they
can hunt. The only sign of grizz I see are some silver hairs
stuck to sap on the fir trees, where they've given
themselves backrubs. This is exotic stuff for a suburban
Easterner, and I pluck off a few hairs, hold them to my
eyes, and allow my imagination to run as wild as the
mountains around me.

Before I realize it, I'm at Lillian Lake. *"Lillian" was the
name of my great-aunt. What a lovely, feminine name.* A
wooden sign posted to a tree points left. Just fifty yards
ahead, and I'm looking down on an authentic, undisturbed
mountain tarn. The water covers about two or three acres. It
reminds me of beautiful Ethan Pond in New Hampshire's
White Mountains, except this lake is more remote. And
unlike Ethan Pond, there's no manmade shelter, no tent
platform, no rules or regulations posted, and the trail here is
far less frequented than the AT. (The CDT is sparsely
populated to begin with, but even less so here, since there's
an alternate cutoff trail route further west.) Like at Ethan
Pond, I'm the only soul for perhaps miles. I rest for a few
moments, gulp some water, and drink in the peaceful calm
of mountain solitude. My trail guide is right: Lillian Lake is
a lovely place.

Feeling refreshed on this hot day, I'm emboldened with
the thought that I'm making good progress. *Should arrive
at Blair Lake at just the right time. Maybe an hour or so of*

daylight to allow me to pitch camp, take a dip, and rustle some grub.

Up ahead, more signs of grizzly hair stuck to tree sap. Then I leave the shade of the forest and enter another large meadow brimming with wildflowers. The trail is still easily visible, and it meanders through a large valley. Both my trail guide and topo map indicate I'll soon be hitting a series of sharp switchbacks that wind up the mountain. But the valley is wide, and I take my time, soaking up views of the towering cliffs behind me. The cliff to the northeast is Nemesis Mountain, but I can't determine if that's Red Rock or Jefferson Mountain to the south. Jefferson is the highest peak in the Centennials. *Maybe that's Jefferson. Topo maps are helpful, but I'm having trouble determining distance. Hope this doesn't impact me later.*

As on the AT, I keep my neck bowed and my eyes on the trail, watching for sharp rocks and holes, but occasionally I look upward in hopes of spying a furry form in the distance, maybe even a rabbit-like American pika (*Ochotona princeps*), which lives in high-altitude rock but is rarely seen. Other than the scraggly fox at Hell Roaring Creek, however, I see no carnivores, just an occasional feathered aviator gracing the sky overhead.

I don't know what awaits me in Idaho, but the Montana CDT is well-maintained by both rangers and volunteers. Lots of trail signposts, and a few sturdy wooden bridges over watery areas. The path is also easy to see. Eventually, I reach the other end of the meadow and begin climbing gradually. Then I hit my first switchback. My guide identifies a dozen switchbacks, so I play a game with myself and begin counting. *I'll knock them off one by one, and the climb will go easier.*

The switchbacks are spaced close together, which usually implies a steep ascent. This, combined with burning sun and thin air, soon takes a toll. My panting becomes heavier. At each switchback turn, I hunch over with exhaustion. Soon, I lose count of the turns altogether. Then

I begin taking rest breaks *between* the turns. Forget any scenery or "furry forms," my eyes are concentrated on each boot step. *Blair Lake must be close. Will this climb ever end? Hiking into afternoon sun is a bitch. How will I summit Taylor Mountain? I'll rest again at that shady spot ahead. No...I'll rest now.*

Finally, I reach a plateau. Although I've been hiking less than a half day, I'm beat. *Almost as bad as South Twin Mountain in the Whites. Have I aged that much in the last few years?* I unload my pack and gulp some water, then check the guide and topo map. *Shouldn't be much farther ahead.*

I tramp through some lodgepole pine. Then I arrive at a modest fork. *Yes!* This is where the CDT splits. The leftward path is the principal CDT. The right one loops around Blair Lake, then rejoins the main CDT a few miles ahead. I turn right, headed for water and my overnight campsite.

Not far ahead, I come upon a large metal sign posted to a tree: "U.S. SHEEP EXPERIMENT STATION." I'd researched this while planning my hike, so I knew this didn't refer to lab experiments on sheep for disease cures. It actually has an agricultural purpose. The century-old United States Department of Agriculture conducts ovine (sheep) research related to reproduction, nutrition, genetics, meat and wool quality, and grazing management. Most of the sheep stations are in Idaho (they're the second largest employer in Clark County), but the Centennial Mountains, which sprawl across the boundary of Idaho and Montana, has 16,600 acres devoted to sheep grazing.

I'm not sure why the government chose the Continental Divide for sheep grazing. Maybe the sheep have abundant food sources way up here? Regardless, the U.S. Sheep Experiment Station came into controversy in 2013, when environmental groups sued. They claimed the research interfered with attempts to reestablish grizzly populations in the Greater Yellowstone Ecosystem. They cited instances of sheepherders being chased by grizzlies, and one collared grizz being shot in 2012, ostensibly by a herder. Several other lawsuits have followed, and the courts are still debating this issue.[11]

I'm all for Idahoans being employed, and it's good to have as much information as possible about the food (lamb) we eat and the clothes (wool) we wear—after all, I'm wearing a snug pair of wool socks on this hike—but I side with environmentalists and threatened grizzlies on this issue.

I don't see any sheep grazing nearby, nor any herders being chased by grizzlies. The side trail loops northwest through more pines, then I round a curve and glimpse a flat, blueish sheen peeking through the branches. *Blair Lake.* I emerge from the trees at the eastern tip of the lake and take in the scene in front of me. Another gorgeous mountain tarn, slightly bigger and more rounded than Lillian Lake, this one with about eight mallards drifting on the surface in the middle. The northern side of the lake, where the trail crosses, is buffeted by a small field along the lakeshore. The western edge has rolling, forested hills that lead upward. The southern edge is a slab of vertical, jagged rock that stands over the lake like a sentinel. The entire valley is studded with timber.

Breathing heavily, I spend a few moments appreciating the lake's serenity and beauty. I like that this water treasure is isolated from the main trail. The CDT isn't well-travelled to begin with, and here's a tarn located on a *side* route. *Wonder if, before reaching my endpoint of Monida, I can discreetly violate the Leave No Trace ethic and search for a small, isolated lake with no trail at all? My own private pond in the Centennials, untouched by man?* I allow myself the luxury of such thoughts.

11

https://www.bozemandailychronicle.com/news/environment/groups-sue-sheep-experiment-station-to-prevent-grazing-on-centennial/article_1f1cc226-461d-5902-aa00-ff4bb23cbb98.html

Stephen Stills has a song called "Move Around." It's one of my favorites of his, a sublime tune about searching only for the sake of searching. In fact, if there's one theme song for this book, this might be it. When we're born, what do we do? We move around, of course. A dirt pathway is not unlike the asphalt of *On the Road*, or the Mississippi River of *The Adventures of Huckleberry Finn*. It's a physical feature, and also a clarion call, a message to move, to go somewhere else. Better a life of movement with all its risks, than a life of stagnation with smothering safety.

In 1809, after returning to a deskbound job following his epic adventure with the Corps of Discovery, Meriwether Lewis took his own life. Historians have cited several reasons for this, but it's still a mystery. His patron and mentor, Thomas Jefferson, who knew Lewis's immediate relations in Virginia, cited clinical depression that ran in the family.

> During his Western exploration the constant exertion which that required of all the faculties of body and mind suspended these distressing affections; but after his establishment at St. Louis in sedentary occupations, they returned upon him with redoubled vigor, and began seriously to alarm his friends.[12]

Perhaps stagnation killed Lewis. Maybe "moving around" in the great unknown, with William Clark, the Corps, and all that magnificent wilderness, kept his demons at bay.

---

[12] Harper's Encyclopedia of United States History; From 458 A.D. to 1906, Lossing, John Benson (Harper & Brothers Publishers, New York, 1907), p. 368

I cross a runoff on the eastern tip and make a mental note to make this burbling brook my kitchen. After about eighty yards I arrive at a large fire ring with wood-plank benches and a host of flat, pine needle-strewn tent sites under the trees. A large wooden pole stretches horizontally between two pine trees, perfect for hanging damp clothing.

This well-maintained campsite isn't a total surprise. One of my Montana Wilderness Association newsletters had advertised a guided hike to Blair Lake, coincidentally scheduled for two weeks after my visit, so I expected a well-maintained camp spot. In fact, when I told Lynn about the MWA hike, we had a little discussion about it:

"Why can't you go with those other hikers, why do you always have to hike alone?" she pleaded.

"John Muir always hiked alone," I replied.

"Who? I've never even met him."

On the Crest

Sometimes the best part of an experience comes in the moments before the reality of the experience.

When you're a kid, at Christmas, you anticipate the opening of your gifts, and you're filled with excitement that short period between going to sleep on Christmas Eve night and tearing open your presents the following morning. You don't know what's in store, but you know it will be good, and your body tingles with the excitement of discovery.

I can imagine certain great explorers and exiles feeling the same, although on a grander scale. Lewis and Clark pushing into their oars as they swept toward the Pacific Ocean on the Columbia River. Then Clark's simple exclamation, written in his journal the day the Corps arrived at the ocean: "O! the joy."

The Pilgrims peering ahead from the bow of the *Mayflower*.

All of the great discoverers had to, also, wrestle with the trepidations and disappointments that come with plummeting the unknown. Englishman Robert Falcon

Scott, in 1912, realized the nightmare of discovering he'd
been beaten in the race to the South Pole, after coming
upon a Norwegian flag planted by Roald Amundsen. "All
the day dreams must go," he wrote in his diary. "Great
God! This is an awful place." Scott and his companions
froze to death on their way back to base camp.

My arrival at Blair Lake isn't on the same scale as being
part of the second team to arrive at the South Pole. For one,
the weather is a lot warmer. The other thing is that, I'm not
there yet. The crest is scheduled for tomorrow. I don't
know what's in store. I don't know what the terrain will
look like, or how broad a vista I will have. But that
question mark makes being at Blair Lake fraught with
magic. Being here, just a few hours shy of standing alone
on the Great Divide, is like the feeling I got when a kid on
Christmas Eve.

I've frequently camped along streams on these trail trips,
but Blair Lake is the first large body of water. That being
the case, it feels a little weird. Other than the mallards, I'm
the only life form here. The placid water is directly in front,
pushed up against the shielding mountain. I glance toward a
grove of pine at the western tip of the lake, wondering if
another campsite might be hidden in the shadows.
Occasionally, I look behind me toward the eastern end,
where I hiked down the trail, curious if any other hikers are
arriving. But I soon decide I'm completely alone. Like
castaway Alexander Selkirk on his tropical island in the
Pacific, I'm the governor here, and my loyal subjects are
the family of ducks.

I decide to mingle with my subjects. Stripping naked, I
stroll tentatively across the brushy field to the water's edge,
clutching my bar of organic soap. I gradually ease myself
into the cold water, sinking about six inches into mud that
feels like soft butter around my feet and ankles. *Gotta be*

quick here, or I'll freeze my ass off! I venture into the water about thigh-high, and splash it onto my upper body and face. *BRRRRR!* Then I step out of the water, feeling suction from the soft mud under my feet. It's probably the quickest bath I've ever had. I glance back and notice that my subjects, little brown dots floating quietly in the distance, are unfazed at the temerity of their leader.

Wow, what a postcard setting! It occurs to me that at one time, long ago, there may have been mountain men camping at this very location, particularly since it's so close to the pass. Maybe legendary Jim Bridger, or Jedediah Smith. Shoshone lived around here until 1868, when the U.S. Government herded them eastward to the Wind River Reservation. The Shoshone might've used Blair Lake as a water source. In the suburbs, one doesn't often think of these connections to frontier history and indigenous cultures, but it's very easy to do out here.

In fact, maybe that's another reason why I like wilderness. I've always enjoyed reading about history (something that Dad passed on to me), and I frequently fantasize about having a time machine to transport me backwards in time. It would be great to just push a button and land in the Lincoln County Jail, to see just how Billy the Kid made his miraculous escape in 1881. Push another button, and I'm sitting around a campfire on the Marias River, next to Meriwether Lewis. Pure wilderness allows me to indulge in these time fantasies. Although I may not look like, or think like, a nineteenth-century fur trapper or explorer, my surroundings are almost exactly the same as they were back then. Wilderness enables me to momentarily suspend the passage of time. It's an antidote to the inexorable aging process.

I've only hiked a half day, but I'm already beat. Those switchbacks, combined with the 85-degree temps, took a lot out of my creaky frame, and my legs feel like rubber. So, after my traditional dinner of noodles (once again, I'm saving my freeze-dried chili mac for later), I backtrack on

the trail to the runoff I'd crossed earlier and wash my
dishpan and replenish my flasks, then I hoist my bear bag
on a lone tree off the edge of the trail. It's still early, and
only now beginning to get dark, but I'm ready to curl up in
my tent womb. After some quick journal entries, I flick off
my headlamp and drowse to sleep.

Morning arrives. Thus far I've been hiking north of the
Divide. But today I will make a short ascent on the loop
trail, then rejoin the main CDT to stand on the spine of the
continent: the royal Continental Divide, where Montana
and Idaho meet, and where all waters to the east flow into
river systems leading to the Atlantic Ocean, and all waters
west flow to the Pacific Ocean.

In my younger days, I crossed the Divide four times. But
each time was from inside an automobile on the freeway.
And two crossings occurred at low elevations, when I
didn't even know I was crossing.

This will be my first time *standing* on the spine. I'll be
at 8,700 feet, with an extensive view of the Idaho valley.
The Caribou-Targhee will be southeast, and beyond that,
the Teton Range.

Of all the mountain ranges in the United States, the
Tetons may be the most magnificent. The range extends
only about forty miles and is located southeast of
Yellowstone National Park, towering over the Snake River
and Jackson Hole valley on the eastern side. The Shoshone
and Crow lived in the shadow of the Tetons for centuries.
The first white man to encounter the Tetons was John
Colter, a member of the Lewis and Clark expedition who
had struck out alone on the expedition's journey home. But
the range was named by French fur trappers, who called the
three main peaks *les trois tétons*, or "the three nipples,"
since the peaks resembled women's breasts.

Vive le Francais!

The Tetons are unique, and celebrated for this uniqueness, due to their dramatic elevation rise at the base of the range. On the eastern side, the mountains rise sharply from 5,000 to 7,000 feet, with no foothills to obscure the view. Also, the largest of the three peaks, Grand Teton, holds the central position, rising to a dizzying 13,775 feet. For me, though, the most awe-inspiring thing about the Tetons is the rock. Jagged, naked granite alpine pinnacles, frosted with snow, a terrifying spectacle of masculine immensity and power against pensive and feminine sky. I can only wonder at what John Colter thought when he first laid eyes on this range. Even after all he'd seen with the Corps of Discovery, he must have been humbled after seeing the Tetons.

But there's another reason I'm anticipating today's hike: I'll be arriving at the spot where Kip and Big Dan summited the Divide at this same time of year in 1990. They stopped momentarily to rest and soak up the tremendous view, before continuing westward over Taylor Mountain.

Later today, I'll be standing where my old friend gasped aloud at a misty valley and mountain-studded horizon that lay, unrolled, like a carpet, at his feet.

First, however, I need to find the trail out of Blair Lake. I follow the patchy path running along the lake. It takes me past my swimming spot from yesterday, arriving at the copse of trees at the western tip of the lake that I saw yesterday. There's a shady little camp area here, framed by an arbor made of stripped conifer logs. But the trail ends.

I wander aimlessly across a marshy field, heading directly west. *No signs of a trail here.* I return to my tentsite and follow a few additional dead ends.

Eventually, I determine that the loop trail is buried under marsh grass and wildflowers, so I put my orienteering training to good use. I set my compass directly northwest, figuring I'll eventually intersect the trail. If I don't intersect after a reasonable amount of time, I'll then readjust my compass to southwest, which will point me toward the main CDT.

The climb out of Blair Lake valley is rocky, but doable. *I like this. I'm putting my knowledge to use and deviating from the beaten path.* I hop over a couple downed Doug-fir trunks, scrambling this way and that, keeping my compass level and faithfully following the direction-of-travel arrow. Near the top of the slope, I see a pair of faded jeep tracks. They head due southwest. *Exactly where I want to go.* Flush with confidence, I follow the tracks.

Despite not seeing any CDT markers, the jeep tracks lead me out of the timber. The trees get thinner, and I'm soon at the perimeter of a large open meadow. The tracks are like a yellow brick road leading toward the wizard's castle at Oz. I'm breathing deeply, sucking in thin oxygen and feeling dizzy, from both the air and from excitement. The farther into the meadow I wander, the more exhilarated I feel, alone on this upside-down bowl and headed into the morning sunlight.

Then I glance rightward across several hundred yards of mounded meadow. In the distance is a fringe of dark green subalpine fir. Beyond the fir is an unknown drop-off, and beyond that a series of peaks. The highest peak is a bald, grey cone with several ribbons of white that look like melted cake icing dribbling down the sides. I pull out my topo map: *Taylor Mountain.*

I walk in a sort of dream state into the massive meadow, following scattered dirt patches, remnants of jeep tires from days long gone. *This must be near where Kip hit the Divide. He may have stepped here. Or over there.*

My topo map indicates that the loop trail crosses the Divide somewhere around here, then meets again with the Divide at 8,400 feet, then both loop trail and Continental Divide adjoin the main Continental Divide Trail. But I'm less interested in these details than by the scenery around me. Thus far I've focused on Taylor Mountain, about five or six miles west of me. But now I direct my attention southeast.

The Tetons.

I let the map slip from my hands. I pull my pack from my shoulders and place it on the ground. I stand motionless and inhale the clean, crisp mountain air. Ahead of me to the south is a wide valley dotted with dark evergreen and cloudy blue ridges. *Idaho.* Island Park Reservoir is at my feet.

To the southeast is Reas Peak, and beyond that the Caribou-Targhee National Forest. Far in the murky distance is the Teton Range and Grand Teton National Park. I'm overwhelmed by the views, and slip into a reverie.

Sharing a jar of cherry-blackberry wine with Dylan...I find another stick when I reach the road at Unicoi, this one even smoother and straighter. I name it "Kip 2"...Old barns...Watertanks...The park where Dad taught me how to ice skate...The old fellow allows me to prop my pack against his scarred and withered trunk...A few feathery clouds grace the turquoise sky...I think of Dad, who's been gone for...what...eleven years?

Nathaniel Hawthorne wrote "Time flies over us, but leaves its shadow behind."

The Valley Below

It's a short, easy jaunt down the faded jeep tracks to the main CDT. Then I drop elevation to 8,200 feet. I'm in the middle of the bottom of a wide swale. I reach a large weather-beaten sign where the faded jeep tracks converge with a wide dirt-gravel road. The sign instructs vehicles, including snowmobiles, to "STAY OUT," due to efforts at wildlife protection and erosion prevention. *I wonder if these jeep tracks headed up the mountain were laid before or after this sign went up.*

The sun burns ever-hotter.

It's only been a short while since folding my tent and filling up on water at Blair Lake, and I still have all 82 ounces in my pack. I'm going to need most if not all of it for the stretch ahead. It's nineteen miles to Aldous Lake, which, other than a couple unreliable springs, is my next water stop. Also, I have a tedious ascent up Taylor Mountain. That kind of strenuous exertion in 80-plus temps can quickly induce serious cotton mouth and cotton throat, and possible dehydration.

But the hiking now is easy. I'm on a soft dirt-and-gravel road on the Idaho side, headed toward dry Schneider Creek, where I plan to eat lunch. *Should be able to get up and over Taylor Mountain, and I'll pitch camp somewhere on the other side.* I have a gorgeous view of blue-tinted Island Park Reservoir far down in the valley on my left. On my right is a flower-covered knob, smaller than the large bowl from where I just descended. It's covered by numerous forbs in full bloom: red Indian paintbrush, larkspurs, aster, fleabane, goldenrod, white mariposa lilies. In the distance are the subalpine firs I earlier saw, and grey Taylor Mountain beyond those.

Later, I'll scold myself for not seeing the thin, upright post that's half-hidden by the flowers.

I glance leftward and barely make out a bright object about fifty yards off-trail in the middle of a field. My map indicates it's a spring. Although my water containers are full, I'm curious to see what this high-altitude spring looks like. So, I veer over there.

I arrive at a metal cistern about the size of circular bathtub. Squatting down without removing my pack, I gaze into it. There's water, alright. But it's at a very low level, and what little water there is has been taken over by weeds and brownish scum. *Yeccch.*

I angle back over to the gravel road. I pass a couple large boulders. Now I'm beginning to get hot. But there are no shade trees, other than some alpine evergreens far south of the road. Just before I slip off my pack for a water break, I hear a low rumble. I stop and listen, as the noise gets louder. As I round a bend in the road, I see a pickup truck creating a dirt cloud and headed up the hill toward me. *Nice to have company, but I was hoping to have this Divide to myself. C'est la vie.*

The truck slows as it nears me. It's a ranger vehicle, like what I saw yesterday. However, the ranger truck yesterday hailed from the Madison Ranger District in Montana. This vehicle is coming up from Idaho, probably the

Ashton/Island Park Ranger District. And in a couple days, I'll be hiking a trail segment under jurisdiction of the Dubois, Idaho rangers. Maintaining the CDT is a cooperative effort between multiple ranger districts, and volunteer organizations like MWA.

I can only hope that the Idaho stretch of trail is as well-maintained as in Montana. Since coming upon the no-motorized-vehicle sign, I haven't seen any CDT markers.

The pickup window rolls down and I see a middle-aged woman with a forest ranger uniform. We exchange small talk. I ask if the pine trees to the south are lodgepole. ("No, they're probably Douglas-fir, you'll have to decrease elevation a little for lodgepole.") Like the other rangers, she notices my bear spray canister and advises me to be on the lookout for grizz. I mention I'm from Ohio. She tells me about her son, who's blazing fresh CD trail over at Black Elk, or somewhere. It's a pleasant five-minute chat, but after we say goodbye, it dawns on me that I never told her where I'm hiking. *She probably guesses I'm going westward on the CDT.*

I continue down the road, gradually dropping elevation. The sun is now directly overhead, and beating down like a burning laser, and I swallow some water to quench my increasing thirst. Then I reach a small grove of trees at a bend in the road. Here, I unload, then open a foil packet of salmon and spread it on a bagel, chomping contentedly while resting in one of the only shady spots on the ridgeline. Except I've now dropped below the ridgeline. *Hmm.*

I finish my salty lunch, pack up, and continue walking. I squint in the bright sun. *Looks like the road splits off ahead.* When I arrive at the fork, I see a big loop on the left. *Not sure what that's for. It looks like it reconnects with the road further up. Man, it's hot.* Then the dirt road rises, and veers left, heading directly south. When I looked at the map a little bit ago, I noticed that the CDT headed southwest a little. But this feels more like due *south* than southwest.

I still haven't seen any CDT markers. But I attribute this to being on a road. Many hiking trails coincide with and share jeep roads. It happened to me on the AT, near Standing Indian Campground. And my trail guide has many instructions to "follow the jeep road…"

So…I keep going.

The dirt road leads to the top of the rise, then begins to slope downward. I'm now walking directly south, *and* losing major elevation. On the right is a large field of charred pines and wild purple hollyhocks. On the left, nailed to a lone lodgepole pine, is a metal sign that's twisted and curled so the print is obscured. But I can make out "Clark County." *This doesn't feel right.* I focus on the road dirt, hoping to see boot prints, which will indicate previous hikers. But I only see tire tracks.

Reluctantly, I slip my pack off my shoulders. I cradle it in my arms and stumble over to the tall pine with the metal sign, the only tree in the vicinity with shade. I swig some more water, then splash some on my hot, tingly face. I dig into my pack pocket and pull out both guide and map.

I study and study. Swat a few mosquitoes dancing on my salty flesh. Study some more. *God, why am I still on a road? I couldn't be on Keg Springs Road. I could swear there wasn't any CDT sign back where the road and trail met. If it's the road, I completely missed the trail turnoff.*

I swat a few more mosquitoes, then re-pack my papers, hoist my pack (which is getting increasingly heavy in this heat), and trudge down the road further, hoping for some confirmation of where I am. After going a hundred yards further downhill…nothing.

There are no trees down here. Just a dirt road on a mountainside that seems to be dropping into the Idaho valley. *At this rate, I'll end up on the banks of Island Park Reservoir.* Once again, I unload my pack and pull out my papers. Gazing more intently at my topo map than ever before, I ignore the squiggly elevation lines and focus on one vertical straight line. I see where Clark and Fremont Counties meet up.

I realize with horror what I've done.

Back near the metal cistern with the scummy water, not long after the no-motorized-vehicles sign, the CDT angled off to the right, over the knob of blooming wildflowers. Maybe there was no marker. Or maybe the tall sunflowers obscured it. Regardless, I didn't see it.

My shoulders droop and my heart plummets. I've hiked over two miles out of my way, most of it downhill, into Idaho. I remember poor Chester, at Dick's Creek Gap in Georgia, ping-ponging between the trees. *Chester's now trading banjo licks with that creature from "Deliverance." Or maybe his bones are scattered along the Chattooga River. What's in store for me?*

I swig some more water while smacking dive-bombing mosquitoes. Then, for maybe the third or fourth time in the last hour, I pack my papers and swing my bulky burden back onto my shoulders. *Thank God I don't have that outer-frame pack, or my left shoulder would be jelly by now.* Head dangling under the burning sun, I trudge uphill past the blackened pines.

A slice of humble pie once in a while is good. I start spitting out the Humble Pie song "30 Days in the Hole," in rhythm with my steps, which jacks me up a little.

When I reach the copse where I ate lunch, two hours have passed, although it seems longer. I'd hoped the ranger truck would return down the road. But no luck. Still with a mile to go, all uphill, to reach the cistern and supposed turnoff, I have an idea.

I'll set my compass northwest, adjusting for magnetic declination, and bushwhack across the mountain slope to intersect the CDT. My orienteering worked when I was back near Blair Lake...maybe it will work again.

I step off the road and smash through the weeds. My left hand holds my compass level, and I swing my walking stick like a sickle, clearing a shabby path for myself. I feel a twinge of guilt, since this maneuver violates a Leave No Trace tenet, but, then again, the success or failure of my hike may hang in the balance.

Unlike when I lost the trail at Blair Lake, this tundra is thick with nettles and briars. My bare legs slowly become streaked with blood. Worse, the ground is sloped, and I'm constantly fighting against the physics of the mountain. Keg Springs Road is now out of sight behind me. Then I hear a low rumble. I stop thrashing and listen intently. It's the ranger truck, returning down Keg Springs Road. *She'll give me a ride back up the hill!* I run back, screaming like a lunatic, hoping she'll hear. My legs pumping, my pack jostling, I yell and yell. But the rumble continues, then becomes fainter. I reach a high point, where the road is visible. But there's only a cloud of dust.

There are times, in moments of weakness, when a person is convinced the deck is stacked. I turn around and resume my lonely bushwhack.

Plowing through weed and thorns, circling around fallen tree trunks, descending further and further into dried up Schneider Creek canyon that seems to have a lasso on me, my skin starting to burn and my dry throat constricted with thirst…alone on the Continental Divide miles from civilization…my worry increases.

I then begin to feel a slight twinge just inside my left knee. It is the knee that is downslope. My backpack and body are probably taxing some ligaments that are not used to being taxed. But, for now, it's a minor impairment. I work my way across the slope, going deeper into the dry creek bed, crossing it several times. After about three quarters of a mile, I see no sign of the trail. But there are woods ahead. *Shade. I'll bet the trail runs through the woods. If nothing else, at least I'll get out of this hot sun.* I'm wearing a t-shirt with the sleeves ripped off, so my upper arms are now red and tender.

I point my direction-of-travel arrow toward the trees. Twenty minutes later, I'm enveloped by tall whitebark pine. The grove is hushed and dark, like a cathedral. I work my way around clumps of briar and old logs, pushing forward, maintaining my direction, but with no sign of the trail. Then I see something moving uphill, in the tree shadows, up ahead and to the right. *Hikers?*

I squint my eyes and try to focus through the steam covering the lenses of my glasses. Two brown shapes. Mule deer. I collapse backwards on a massive uprooted tree, feeling total disappointment.

JULY 1967—BELLVILLE, OHIO

"Peter, how did you like the camp?" Mom says excitedly.

"Oh, it's ok," I reply. I sink back into the seat of our station wagon. Silence. Mom turns her head toward me.

"Did you play a lot of games?"

I twirl the string of my black, hooded sweatshirt. I stare at my feet, at the navy-blue boat shoes that I got for my birthday. My birthday was a couple weeks ago. It seems like a long time.

"Yeah, a little. We mainly went swimming. I had to stay in the shallow pool."

I glance at Mom. She's staring ahead and smiling. Wonder what she's thinking? If Dad were here, he wouldn't ask so many questions.

"And did you meet any new friends?"

I look out the car window at the woods. Mom gets to the bottom of the big hill and turns the steering wheel. Now we're on Possum Run Road. I sit up and raise my head. In the sideview mirror, I see another car turn behind us.

"No, not really."

Our car moves faster. We drive past the ski area. Mom turns the car left on a big curve.

> *"And how did Kip like it?"*
> *The car goes right on another big curve. Now*
> *we're on German Church Road. The car goes faster.*
> *We're heading home.*
> *"Do you think he liked it?" Mom asks again. I*
> *twirl the string again.*
> *"Yeah, he liked it. I guess."*
> *Mom asks if I want to go back for the second*
> *week. I tell her "Not really." She simply says "OK."*
> *It feels like the weight of the world has been lifted*
> *from my fragile shoulders.*

I use this moment to collect my thoughts and refresh myself. I unhook my flask from my pack and finish off the remaining water. It's still not enough to quench my thirst after the hot struggle through the canyon, but I need to save the contents of my 48-ounce water bottle for Taylor Mountain and the dry stretch ahead. *Only forty-eight ounces remaining for a seventeen-mile trek.* I subtract one mile to account for the bushwhack cutoff, since I'm still hoping to intersect the trail. Then I figure in water that I'll use for my noodles. *I'll have to skip the noodles. Tonight's supper is trail mix.* Then I remember my hike on the Georgia AT, where I was drinking sixty-four ounces of water a day. *Much hotter up here.* Then I debate whether I should backtrack to the metal cistern and the scum water. *Maybe it wasn't as scummy as I thought. How far will that be? Another mile?*

The numbers and scenarios roll through my head as the mosquitoes begin dive-bombing again. All of it merely confuses me. I begin to doubt myself. *Maybe I passed the CDT back when I crossed Schneider Creek back there. Pete, you fucking idiot.*

This should probably remain unsaid. But I'll say it anyway. Reading topo maps in an armchair in front of the fire, or scooting around schoolyards, using a compass, with a suburban orienteering club is much different than being alone, off-trail, near 9,000 feet, with severe thirst and anxiety setting in. When physically and mentally stressed, decision-making is elusive. Horror stories abound of people who, whether prepared or unprepared, freak out when confronted with dire wilderness situations.

I recall Jack London's short story "To Build a Fire," where a man, in sub-zero Yukon Territory, ignores weather predictions and the warnings of a more seasoned explorer, vainly struggles to start a fire, then freezes to death only a short walk from safety. And there's the very real tragedy of Everett Ruess, a mystical poet and artist who spent months alone in the deserts of the Southwest back in the 1930s, but tempted the "old clown" of death once too often and disappeared forever.

But the story that's freshest in my mind is that of Geraldine Anita "Gerry" Largay. It's a drama that played out in the Maine woods just six weeks before my Georgia AT hike. Her sad story has been told many times and is well-known in the hiking community. But she's foremost in my mind at this moment, so here goes:

Largay, whose trail alias was Inchworm, was a seasoned backpacker, from Brentwood, Tennessee (The same town as Big Bird...not the Sesame Street character, but the thru-hiker I met in the White Mountains.) Although in her sixties, she'd hiked all the way from Harpers Ferry, West Virginia, much of it alone, and was only two hundred miles from the endpoint of Mount Katahdin in Maine. Her husband, George, drove his car as she hiked, and they frequently reunited at road crossings, parking lots, and trail towns. They also kept in touch via mobile phone. On July 21, Largay texted her husband that she was just south of a lean-to at Spaulding Mountain. They arranged to meet the next day where the AT crosses ME-27.

She never arrived.

Despite weeks of searching by the Maine Warden Service, trained search and rescue volunteers, search dogs, and a reward of $15,000 that George Largay posted for information leading to Gerry's whereabouts, she could not be found. The strange thing is, backpackers who had seen her only hours before her disappearance reported nothing out of the ordinary. She was upbeat, and her pack was fully stocked. There were no odd-looking individuals lurking around the trail. Did she make the mistake of leaving the trail to take a shortcut? If so, why didn't she call her husband? Why were searchers unable to find even clothing or supplies? Was there foul play?

It was as if she was swallowed up by the forest. It was the greatest mystery in AT history…for a time.

Then, on October 14, 2015, an environmental impact researcher found human remains inside a tent in a thicket of woods near an overgrown logging road. The site was a hundred yards inside a restricted area of forest owned by the U.S. Navy. And only a half mile from the AT.

Medical analysts eventually confirmed that the remains were that of Inchworm. Police say there was no evidence of crime. Her death was ruled as "inanition." This is a rarely used word that means "a state of being empty." Empty of food…or, perhaps, empty of will.

Later, authorities revealed that she'd kept a diary of her ordeal. It appears she'd gone off-trail to go to the bathroom. After doing her business, she somehow turned the wrong way, and got lost. Then she panicked, went further off-trail, then set up camp in dense forest…and slowly starved to death. Her former hiking partner claims she often became confused on the trail. She also had a prescription for anti-anxiety medicine that she may have run out of. She either didn't have a compass, or didn't know how to use one. Feverish text messages she sent were never received due to poor reception.[13]

It wasn't so much bad luck as ill preparation and bad decision-making.

---

[13] https://www.nytimes.com/2016/05/27/us/missing-hiker-geraldine-largay-appalachian-trail-maine.html?_r=0

Don't make a bad decision, Pete. If you're gonna succumb to the elements, at least do so where your body can be located, so Lynn can have a proper funeral.

But losing direction doesn't have to result in tragedy. Or even frustration. It can often lead to a better place.

Several times during my hikes, I've wondered what it might be like to step off the trail, plunge into the woods, and just "get lost." Inchworm notwithstanding, it's tough to get lost these days. With road atlases, trail maps, Mapquest, Google, and global positioning systems, we're on track a hundred percent of the time. Maybe we need these things just to cope with the frenetic pace of our lives.

But some of the most memorable times of my life have happened when nothing was pre-planned, when I could just lose myself or wander without an adult gripping my arm, or a device spitting out instructions or admonishments. The prettiest road I ever traveled on was in the spring of 1982. It was a detour off the Pacific Coast Highway, going from Carmel to Greenfield, California, and it was completely unplanned. I was so smitten with the rounded, blossoming fruit fields, avocado-green trees, and warm honey sunlight, I stopped the car, climbed a small hill, and lay on my back in the meadow for an hour, listening to the birds and occasional swoosh of bicycle rubber on the road below.

I remember in '83 getting lost in the ebony-green hills of western South Dakota, cruising in my banged-up Chevy Impala, wondering where the heck the highway might be, then pulling to the edge of the road in front of two Lakota girls to ask directions. They ran up excitedly and jumped into my car before realizing I was a stranger... and a white guy! I chauffeured them for ten miles while the Rolling Stones sang from my car speakers, I could almost feel their limbs trembling in my front seat. We were a clash of age, gender, race, culture, and economics. How often does something like that happen on Pine Ridge Reservation? I'm sure they remember our road trip. I know I do.

It's good to get lost sometimes.

As frustrating as my current situation is, things could be much worse. *If I survive, I'll smile while remembering this little side jaunt up Schneider Creek Canyon.*

I take a deep breath, battle one more mosquito blitzkrieg, and look toward where the mule deer were sniffing. Between the trees I see a flat, vertical, brown shape, like a cliff face. I'm not worried about grizz, or even snakes. But the last thing I want to do is get my leg wedged inside a miniature slot canyon. *Wonder if any other humans ever came to this spot. Maybe Kip and Big Dan. They came down from the opposite direction. But I'm no seasoned backpacker like MacKenzie. Kip had a good guide along. All I've got is naiveté.*

I strap on my pack, set my compass southeast, and backtrack.

The hike back to Keg Springs Road goes quicker. A dozen more rips in my flesh later, I'm plodding uphill on the dusty road—my personal trail of tears. My throat now feels like sandpaper. I'm sure my eyes are glazed. There's an old movie called *The Wild North*, with Stewart Granger and Wendell Corey. It's not an A movie, but it's fun if you like outdoor adventure flicks. It's about a French-Canadian fur trapper (Granger) accused of murder, and a Canadian Mountie (Corey) has to bring him in for trial. While struggling against wolves in sub-zero snow in northern Canada, Corey goes temporarily nuts. The tables are turned, and Granger has to rescue Corey, who at this point looks like a zombie.

I now feel as whipped and licked as Wendell Corey. Except, instead of being frozen, I'm sun-stroked.

Just when I'm ready to abort my hike by swigging from my water bottle then returning to Blair Lake, I hear another rumble. It's a jeep headed uphill toward me. *Salvation.*

I stand to the side as the jeep slows, then brakes next to me. It's an elderly man wearing a baseball cap. I tell him my predicament, and he says to wait for another jeep behind him. Soon, another jeep clatters up, this one larger, with an American flag hoisted over the back. I spill out my sad story to the elderly couple in the front, and they tell me to hop in.

Over the engine noise, we manage to talk a little. Their names are Richard and Dorothy Bogart, from Rexburg, Idaho vicinity. They and their friend in front are headed for the top of the Great Divide, just to spend a little time enjoying the views and breathing the clean mountain air. *This is the way to retire. Buy a jeep and enjoy day trips in the Northern Rockies.*

As we talk (rather, holler) over the jeep noise, I frequently lick my chapped lips. Dorothy must notice, because she hands me a bottle of spring water that's as close to being ice without being ice. Within three minutes, I've emptied it. *Hope to God I don't look as bad as Wendell Corey.*

I keep my eyes peeled for the metal cistern in the field at the top of the hill. Then I see it. "This is good!" I yell out. "Thanks so much!"

They wish me luck, then continue onward to the no-motorized-vehicles sign, where they and their friend hop out to stretch their limbs and enjoy the vistas. Meanwhile, I slog across the field to the cistern. I peek over the rim. Unfortunately, the weeds and watery muck look just as before and haven't, miraculously, turned into water. But a baby bird has arrived. He's flapping around in the brown scum, trying to get out. I reach in, gently cup him in my hands, then set him down in the field. He flaps his wings a short distance, then disappears into the vast thistle.

I gaze back into the cistern…a "piped spring," according to my trail guide. *Yecch.* Although I've just downed sixteen ounces of fresh, chilled spring water, my throat is already clenching for more liquid.

I return to the road. I've got my topo map out this time. *Should be right here.* I walk back and forth on the road without seeing anything. Then I step uphill into the meadow.

By God, there it is!

About twenty yards to the west, I see the top of a wooden post. Thrashing through wildflowers, I arrive there. The cute little arrowhead-shaped blue-white-black CDT sign is nailed to the top of the faded wooden post, a post which looks like it's been there since the Cuban Missile Crisis. The lower half of the post is obscured by mature flowers. I've just wasted three hours trying to find it.

I then return to my trail guide, which refers to a "converg(ence) with the Keg Spring Road (FR 34)." In my zeal, and in my high-altitude intoxication, I missed this small print on page 77 of the guide. My overriding thought, however, is: *Why isn't there a CDT sign at the edge of the road?*

I rest in the shade of some firs. I'm back on top of the crest. I know where the trail leads. But I need to address my frustrating situation.

I've lost time. However, I'm not shackled by a timetable. I can still easily arrive where the trail crosses Schneider Creek, then probably get to the base of Taylor Mountain, if not close to the treeline, before nightfall. My knee irritation is still only a twinge, and I'm not limping. At least, not yet. Yeah, I'm a bit sun-stroked. But it's nothing serious, and I have a long-sleeved shirt in the bottom of my pack that I can ferret out, to protect my skin, until Monida.

Ok, I'm fatigued. My old bones aren't what they used to be. My strength has diminished since the Whites, and substantially since the Georgia AT. But I'm in no rush to finish. A good night's sleep tonight, and I'll be fine for tomorrow.

My biggest concerns are water, and trail markers. I'm down to forty-eight ounces water, with a long stretch ahead that's probably dry, judging from that low-level muck in the cistern. *Dehydration in this heat and solitude would be life-threatening.*

And then there are the markers. Sure, they were fantastic in Montana. But what about Idaho? So far, the CDT markers here are spotty. And I'm still far from expert with a topo map and compass. Maybe I SHOULD have brought a GPS. Maybe that guy on WhiteBlaze was right about updating my will.

Once more, like a hissing breeze rolling across the ridge, Kip enters my thoughts. *I'll bet he'd have struck out ahead. Guitar strapped on his pack, elastic bandage wrapped around his knee. And maybe without Big Dan's navigation.*

I decide to continue into the red-orange glow of the West. But only if I have a trail to follow. *I need something or someone to follow. Or lean on.*

So, for the ninth or nineteenth time that day, I hobble to my feet, swing my pack over my shoulders, take Kip 6 in my hand, and move on. Thirty yards south of the fir trees, I find the CDT post. I start walking westward, through the wildflowers. There's no trail. It's completely obscured by verdant foliage. But I see another marker ahead. I arrive at another blue-white-black CDT sign. Ahead of me is more multi-colored meadow, descending over a knob, sliding into dense evergreens below. But there's no trail. Nor signposts.

Then I look northward and gasp. Far down below, miles and miles in the hazy distance, flat on the floor of Centennial Valley, I see a massive haze of azure. It's Upper Red Rock Lake. So large on the map, so small from up here. My vision can easily absorb its entire breadth. After all, I'm at nearly 9,000 feet.

Momentarily, I totally forget about the trail.

A breeze tickles my hot cheeks. It feels good, like one of Lynn's caresses. I listen for sound. But there's nothing. Just total quiet, up here, on top of the world. Although I'm alone, I'm not lonely. I've got my thoughts and memories. Lynn...Holly and Nick...Mom and Dad...my dog Sheba...

I recall my previous hikes and the many times my efforts were rewarded with vistas like this. I think of Ramrock Mountain, where I posed for a photograph with Dylan, and where we saw Ed whisk by with his trekking poles, beaming from ear to ear. I think of the ancient gnarled oak where I rested at the Georgia-North Carolina state line and reminisced about Dad. I remember crouching in the rocks atop Mount Adams, when Shemet with his golden smile and ponytail bobbed over the edge to gasp at the *amazing view*. I smile at recollecting the perplexed bear in Shenandoah who was anxious for me to vacate his premises. And the Honeymoon Hikers. And Jackson, just bumming around—maybe trying to get lost—and enjoying some natural harmony before returning for his last year in high school. Big Bird and Waterfall. Slow and easy Nathan, too cool for a trail alias, who swings a wooden stick just like me. *I wonder if, like me, Nathan gave his walking stick a name?*

I think of Kip. *Did I hike with him?* No, not really. But I think of him anyway.

Epilogue

I didn't reach Monida. Resting on that knob of
wildflowers and gazing out at Upper Red Rock Lake, I
weighed my options and risks. Fatigue, water depletion,
knee worries, and lack of orienteering confidence
convinced me to turn back.

Blair Lake was as I'd left it: blue, tranquil, guarded by
the mallard family, swarming with hungry mosquitoes, and
with no trace of my presence the night before. The only
change was a massive pile of grizzly scat about ten yards
from the fire ring. It was the largest blob of dung I'd ever
seen, half the size of my tent. But it didn't spook me. I
examined it closely and saw no sheepherder belt buckles.
Plus, I was so exhausted, I could only think of water and
rest. I lay flat on my back in my tent, completely still, for
probably an hour, soon after draining a gallon of water. It
now being the second night in a row camped at this darn
tarn, I thought how I'd truly earned my governorship, and
how the mallards were lucky to have a benevolent leader
such as I. Then I ate a little food, then fell asleep.

The following day, in the cool shade of some aspen just before arriving at *lovely* Lillian Lake, I met the only other backpacker of my aborted three-day trip. He was a young solo hiker named "Backtrack." I thought this was funny, since *I* was the backtracker. Backtrack had only recently left Canada, thru-hiking over 3,000 miles to Mexico. He was a bit smarter than me: he wore a long-sleeved shirt, long nylon pants, and a wide-brimmed hat for sun protection. And, for convenient access, he stored his maps in a thin plastic tube attached to his pack strap. I thought this was a great idea. Had I more frequently consulted my maps and guide, I might not have wandered so far off-trail.

I looked for the scraggly fox at Hell Roaring Creek but didn't see him. However, I did see a lot of blackberry bushes and enjoyed a tart mid-morning snack. Maybe the fox dines here, too.

Although the fox was absent, the rusted white trailer was still sitting in the shade when I arrived at Red Rock Pass. This time, I met the owner. He was a middle-aged man who'd driven up from Utah to see the 2017 total eclipse. We had a short conversation, but he remained behind the rear door, in darkness, never stepping outside in the sun. I thought this was odd, since there were still three weeks until the eclipse. Maybe he was satisfied that he'd grabbed a prime viewing spot for a rare event. I'm sure the eclipse was spectacular at Red Rock Pass, although I wonder if it surpassed my own spectacular views of Centennial Valley, Island Park Reservoir, and the Tetons, while standing on the Great Divide.

Red Rock Pass had a large Doug-fir guarding the entrance to the Centennial CDT, on the south side of the road. In a little oval of shade, I sat and rested against its hoary trunk. Near here, Kip and Big Dan started their Centennial trek in 1990. I thought about them one last time. I then remembered that, through this pass, Chief Joseph guided his band of exhausted and starving Nez Perce while fleeing the U.S. Cavalry. It was a last desperate flight to freedom. For four months, 2,900 men, women, and children held off a hostile armed force of 2,000 soldiers. They came within forty miles of sanctuary in Canada. They couldn't quite make it.

Kip sang about this heroic flight in one of his songs. I wondered if this Doug-fir, which Kip and I both visited at different times, was growing way back in 1877. I'll bet a case of Bridger Brewing Antilogy Black IPA that it was.

While these inner clock thoughts ticked inside my head, I heard a low rumble. To the west, emerging from a hazy cloud of mid-summer heat and gravel dust, a flatbed logging truck, loaded down with tree trunks, chugged into view. The driver must've regularly picked up stranded backpackers, because he jammed on his brakes, jumped out, waved me over, and cleared room for me on the passenger side. He told me his name was Kelvin. During the ride, I tried to ask Kelvin where the timber company cut its wood. But, between the engine roar and Kelvin's frequent giggling, all I could get was that he hauled Doug-fir and lodgepole pine to Ennis, Montana. If he knew where the wood came from, he didn't care. He then tried to coax me into eating some of his leftover fried chicken and gave me a college-level course on flatbed truck axles, gears, hydraulics, winches, and gradients.

Kelvin was a jolly fellow, and he dropped me off at ID-87, after which I pounded sizzling pavement for five miles, then thumbed a ride on US-20 into West Yellowstone. My little red Civic was still in the parking lot of the visitor center, unscathed.

After turning the car key, I scanned the left end of the FM band until I found the first clear station. Just as had occurred near Springer Mountain, four years earlier, when I first met Dylan on my first section hike, I experienced one of those rare moments when the stars seemed aligned. The first song was "Radio Montana" by singer Casey Neill. I couldn't think of a more appropriate tune to conclude my ramble:

Evergreen Dreaming

He walked from burning mountain
To where sweet grass chokes the plains
Where sudden showers hammer down
Upon the soft terrain...
Radio Montana
Life is full of ghosts

I had a hard time finding lodging that night. Park tourists, and motorcyclists headed for the rally in Sturgis, South Dakota, had reserved all the motel rooms. My bloodshot eyes and the dried gnats on my greasy skin probably didn't help my efforts. I tried Bozeman, Livingston, and several other towns, unsuccessfully. I didn't nab an available room until Billings, Montana, 231 miles from West Yellowstone.

Lying on my back in that motel room at 1 a.m., it was hard to imagine that, only sixteen hours earlier, I was sleeping on hard ground next to a mountain tarn, alone, at 8,100 feet, my head just a few yards from a mound of grizzly shit.

Someday I'll return.

SELECT BIBLIOGRAPHY

The following books either directly or indirectly influenced *Evergreen Dreaming*:

Abbey, Edward, *Desert Solitaire: A Season in the Wilderness*

Ambrose, Stephen, *Undaunted Courage: Meriwether Lewis, Thomas Jefferson, and the Opening of the American West*

Berry, Wendell, *The Unsettling of America: Culture and Agriculture*

Bryson, Bill, *A Walk in the Woods: Rediscovering America on the Appalachian Trail*

Carson, Rachel, *Silent Spring*

DeVoto, Bernard (editor), *The Journals of Lewis and Clark*

George, Jean Craighead, *My Side of the Mountain*

Leopold, Aldo, *A Sand County Almanac, With Essays on Conservation from Round River*

McKibben, Bill, *The End of Nature*

Muir, John, *The Wilderness World of John Muir: A Selection of His Collected Works*

North, Sterling, *Rascal*

Stoltz, Walkin' Jim, *Walking with the Wild Wind: Reflections on a Montana Journey*

Thoreau, Henry David, *Walden; or, Life in the Woods*

Walker, Bill, *Skywalker: Highs and Lows on the Pacific Crest Trail*

Waterman, Guy and Linda, *Backwoods Ethics: A Guide to Low-Impact Camping and Hiking*

Made in the USA
Lexington, KY
11 September 2018